Channels of Prophecy ⎯⎯⎯⎯⎯⎯⎯⎯⎯⎯⎯⎯

Channels of Prophecy

The Social Dynamics of Prophetic Activity

THOMAS W. OVERHOLT

Wipf and Stock Publishers
EUGENE, OREGON

Wipf and Stock Publishers
199 West 8th Avenue, Suite 3
Eugene, Oregon 97401

Channels of Prophecy
The Social Dynamics of Prophetic Activity
By Overholt, Thomas W.
Copyright©1989 Augsburg Fortress
ISBN: 1-59244-303-6
Publication date 8/12/2003
Previously published by Augsburg Fortress, 1989

For Sally, my wife

Contents

Preface

One day in 1965, while driving from Yankton College to the University of South Dakota to give a talk on Old Testament theology, I encountered—via a "chapter-a-day" program on public radio—the traditional Sioux holy man Black Elk. Later, I read *Black Elk Speaks* and was fascinated with its account of the Ghost Dance of 1890, some features of which seemed so much like Old Testament prophecy. I began to think that my understanding of biblical prophecy might be enhanced by studying prophets in other cultures. Thus began the project that led to this book.

Initially, I concentrated my attention on the Ghost Dance. Basic similarities between the activities of its founder, a Paiute named Wovoka, and those of biblical prophets were easy to recognize, but the differences between late nineteenth-century native Americans and ancient Israelites were equally obvious. My first task was to devise a way to compare such apparently dissimilar figures. The solution I hit upon led me to place special emphasis on the social dynamics of the relationship between prophet and audience. As intermediaries, prophets are channels of communication between the worlds of gods and humans, and I assign particular importance to that part of the dialogue that occurs between prophet and people.

Over the years, I broadened my research to include a wide variety of prophetic figures and spelled out some of the implications of this approach to the prophetic process. Writing this book has provided me with an occasion to expand upon these views of prophecy and to state them in a systematic way. Preliminary studies have appeared in scholarly journals—*Ethnohistory, CBQ, JSOT, Semeia*—and their presence can be recognized in some chapter titles and section headings, as well as in blocks of text. That material, however, has been edited, revised, and organized with new material into a more comprehensive picture of the nature of prophecy.

I am pleased to acknowledge some of those who have contributed in various ways to this project. Sometime early on I became aware that my particular interests in prophecy were shared by Burke Long and Robert Wilson, and over the years I have benefited greatly from my associations with them. If something is to be praised in this book, please give them part of the credit. Gene M. Tucker also read and commented on the first draft of this manuscript, and I am grateful for his helpful critique. My colleagues in the Department of Philosophy deserve thanks for their creativity in finding ways to support faculty research projects, including my own, and for being a generally jolly bunch. An amiable atmosphere in which little psychic energy must be devoted to departmental "politics" helps to compensate for heavy teaching loads. In addition, several of them read and commented on sections of the manuscript. I appreciate that, and I want especially to thank Donald Fadner, whose thoughtful critique of drafts of the final chapter proved to be particularly helpful. Carolee Cote, our department secretary, has again been marvelously efficient and helpful. Finally, I offer special thanks to John A. Hollar, Editorial Director of Fortress Press books, for his encouragement and for incisive comments that made the work of revision both a challenge and a pleasure.

I dedicate this book to my wife, Sally, who has been supportive in many ways. At least a few of the good times we have shared over the past decades had discernible ties to this project!

THOMAS W. OVERHOLT
University of Wisconsin–Stevens Point
January 1989

Abbreviations

AA	American Anthropologist
ARBAE	Annual Report of the Bureau of American Ethnology
BA	Biblical Archaeologist
BBAE	Bulletin, Bureau of American Ethnology
BZ	Biblische Zeitschrift
CBQ	Catholic Biblical Quarterly
CSSH	Comparative Studies in Society and History
HR	History of Religions
HTR	Harvard Theological Review
IDB	G. A. Buttrick, ed., Interpreter's Dictionary of the Bible, 4 vols. (New York: Abingdon Press, 1962).
IDBSup	K. Crim, ed., Supplementary volume to IDB (Nashville: Abingdon Press, 1976).
Int	Interpretation
JAFL	Journal of American Folklore
JB	Jerusalem Bible
JBL	Journal of Biblical Literature
JNES	Journal of Near Eastern Studies
JRAI	Journal of the Royal Anthropological Institute
JSOT	Journal for the Study of the Old Testament
NEB	New English Bible
OTS	Oudtestamentische Studiën
RSV	Revised Standard Version
SBL	Society of Biblical Literature
SWJA	Southwestern Journal of Anthropology
VT	Vetus Testamentum

VTSup   Vetus Testamentum, Supplements
ZAW   *Zeitschrift für die alttestamentliche Wissenschaft*
ZTK   *Zeitschrift für Theologie und Kirche*

1

A Prophet
By Any Other Name

INTRODUCTION

This book is about prophets, a subject with which most people would claim some familiarity. Indeed, in current usage *prophet* carries some relatively well-known connotations. On the one hand, it calls to mind certain religious personages: Amos, Isaiah, Jeremiah, and other prophets of the Hebrew scriptures (known by Christians as the Old Testament); Jesus (see Mark 8:28); and Muhammad. On the other hand, we habitually refer to persons who predict the course of future events—from relatively trivial matters such as the score of a game to things as complex as international economic trends—as *prophets,* and call *prophetic* those statements or warnings that turn out to have been correct. The common denominator of these two connotations is the element of prediction, usually with some emphasis on its accuracy. Also as part of the term seems to be a sense that the person who prophesies has some source of information or insight unavailable to the majority of the audience. The predictions are, in other words, not simply a matter of luck.

We are concerned with prophecy as a religious phenomenon, but that limitation does not of itself solve the problem of who should be included in the category *prophet.* Consider the following examples:

1. In about the year 742 B.C.E. Isaiah ben Amoz, an inhabitant of the tiny kingdom of Judah, had a vision of his god, Yahweh. As this experience is reported to us in chapter 6 of the Book of Isaiah, he saw Yahweh garbed in royal robes, sitting upon a throne in his temple in the capital city of Jerusalem. The sight was awesome—the foundations of the building shook, the air was filled with smoke, and God himself was

1

surrounded by winged creatures who sang his praises—and Isaiah was filled with a sense of his own unworthiness. After an appropriate ceremony of purification, Isaiah was commissioned to carry a message from Yahweh to the people at large. This he did over the next forty years, and we find him embroiled in disputes concerning social problems internal to Judah, as well as critical issues of foreign policy.

2. Wovoka was a Paiute from western Nevada who flourished in the late nineteenth century C.E. at a time when his tribe and many others in the western United States had been subjugated by the whites and forced to live on reservations. On January 1, 1889, during a total eclipse of the sun, Wovoka fell into a trance and was taken into another world. There he saw God, as well as many native Americans who had already died, all of them healthy, happy, and leading the life that had prevailed before the arrival of the whites. He also beheld vast herds of the game animals that during his lifetime had become increasingly scarce. He was then sent back to earth to report to his people what he had seen, to announce that God intended to eliminate the whites from the land and reestablish the old native American cultures, and to instruct the people in a ceremonial dance that would hasten the coming of this great event. He did so, and over the next few years many tribes of the American west sent delegates to Nevada to see and hear Wovoka. An increasing number of disciples helped spread his message over a wide geographical area.[1]

3. Consider also the traditional Chippewa (or Ojibwa) of the woodlands of the western Great Lakes. On certain occasions, when, for example, someone was ill, an important item had been lost, or people were concerned about the well-being of absent members of the community, a "shaking tent" ceremony might be arranged. A ring of sturdy poles would be securely planted in the ground and covered with birch bark, blankets, or a canvas. After dark, a conjurer skilled in this form of communication would enter the cylindrical lodge, or "tent," and call the spirits. As the spirits began to arrive, the tent would shake, and their distinctive voices would be heard and recognized by the audience gathered outside. Eventually, the spirits would reveal the desired information—the cause of the illness and the proper methods for effecting a

1. For a selection of texts relating to Wovoka and the Ghost Dance, see T. W. Overholt, *Prophecy in Cross-Cultural Perspective: A Sourcebook for Biblical Researchers* (Atlanta: Scholars Press, 1986) 122–42.

cure, the location of lost or stolen objects, or the whereabouts of the absent people and the date of their return. According to reports, the information obtained through the spirits was often amazingly accurate.[2]

4. In 1923 the Danish ethnographer Knud Rasmussen traveled the entire Arctic coast of Canada by dogsled and spent time in numerous Innuit villages along the way. In one case he arrived just as a savage storm was descending upon the settlement. The blizzard lasted for three days and had winds so fierce that Rasmussen and three others had to walk huddled together in order to remain standing. They took an hour to cover the distance of half a kilometer between their shelter and a dwelling where a performance was to take place for the purpose of bringing an end to the storm. As the ceremony gained momentum, the chief performer, a shaman, went into ecstasy:

> At that moment there is a gurgling sound, and a helping spirit enters his body. A force has taken possession of him and he is no longer master of himself or his words. He dances, jumps, throws himself over among the clusters of the audience and cries to his dead father, who has become an evil spirit.

The ecstatic performance, in which the audience became more and more emotionally involved, took the form of a struggle to the death with the spirit that was causing the storm. At the end, the audience was confident that the effort had been successful. On the morning of the next day the weather cleared.[3]

5. The time is the mid-1960s, and the people the Shona of Rhodesia (now Zimbabwe). Messengers come from local villages to the shrine at Matonjeni with questions to be put to Mwari, the Shona high-god. After suitable preparations, they are taken to the mouth of a cave, where their questions are transmitted to Mwari by a cult official, who first translates them into an archaic dialect of the language. Mwari, speaking in the same dialect through a spirit medium stationed out of sight within the cave, answers.[4]

---

2. Ibid., 59–76.
3. Ibid., 208–13.
4. Ibid., 230–41. For an interpretation of such ecstatic behavior among the Innuit, see D. Merkur, *Becoming Half Hidden: Shamanism and Initiation among the Inuit* (Stockholm: Almqvist and Wiksell International, 1985).

The scholarly literature about the figures just described has tended to designate them by various names. Isaiah and Wovoka have been called *prophets*, the practitioners of the shaking tent *conjurers*, the Innuit performer *shaman*, and Mwari's spokesperson *spirit medium*. What makes practitioners of these distinct yet overlapping roles comparable is that their chief function is to communicate messages or information from the world of the spirits to the world of humans. If we were to follow a recent author in defining *prophecy* as "the proclamation of divine messages in a state of inspiration,"[5] we would have little trouble speaking of any of these figures as prophets. We could even avoid the terminological confusion by a more general and neutral designation of all such figures as *intermediaries*.[6]

Conversely, even such brief descriptions make clear the important differences among these figures, both in the specific patterns of their behavior and in the content of what they say to their audiences. These differences should be no surprise. Many cultures have believed in gods whose desires needed to be taken into account in the conduct of human affairs and have recognized special individuals as expert in communicating with the gods. The actions and words of such persons are largely shaped by the cultures to which they belong. The puzzle that therefore confronts us is how to describe more precisely the similarity that, despite their differences, such figures from other times and cultures bear to the biblical prophets.

In attempting to solve this puzzle, I adopt the strategy of "bracketing" the content of what these experts at divine-human communication say in order to focus more clearly on the social dynamics of prophetic action, which entails the interaction of intermediaries not only with the deities who commission them but also with their audiences. Of course, we never completely lose sight of the content of the message, which is important in making judgments about prophetic authenticity. It is just not the key category for comparison.

Comparing intermediaries of such diverse backgrounds is *not* to claim that they are in all important ways identical. The intent is *not* to

5. H. Ringgren, "Prophecy in the Ancient Near East," in *Israel's Prophetic Tradition*, ed. R. Coggins, A. Phillips, and M. Knibb (Cambridge: Cambridge University Press, 1982), 1.
6. See R. R. Wilson, *Prophecy and Society in Ancient Israel* (Philadelphia: Fortress Press, 1980), 27–28.

argue, for example, that biblical prophets are "just like" shamans.[7] The puzzle is a real one, however, and the strategy of focusing on social dynamics has several advantages: It allows us to describe and discuss the nature of the similarity. It also offers us insights into the relationship between the biblical prophets and their audiences, a matter in which the biblical books themselves have only limited interest. Moreover, it may clarify a problem of potentially more immediate concern: Has prophecy in the Judeo-Christian tradition in fact "ended"? How are we to deal with "prophetic" claims encountered today?

To choose one aspect of prophecy for comparison is not to deny the importance of others. Nor is it to argue that those who have taken other perspectives are wrong. That studies of biblical prophecy have been keenly interested in the prophets' messages is neither surprising nor lamentable. Such works have greatly enriched our understanding and will continue to be influential. In this respect, the criticisms sometimes heard of "comparative" (or "sociological" or "social scientific") studies of biblical prophecy seem beside the point. The theology of the prophets will not be lost; libraries are filled with such expositions.[8] Meanwhile, something can be gained from another approach.

APPROACHES TO PROPHECY

Scholars in several fields—biblical studies, history of religions, anthropology, and sociology—study prophets, but they tend to have different interests and to study different individuals. Students of the Bible, of course, are inclined to focus on prophets as a means by which God communicates with humans and therefore to pay particular attention to the content of the prophet's message. Social scientists are more interested in describing the sociocultural results of a population's re-

7. See Overholt, *Prophecy in Cross-Cultural Perspective*, 4–7.
8. As the reader is no doubt aware, the scholarly literature on even biblical prophecy is vast, and there is no possibility of summarizing it adequately in the context of a study like this one. I agree with David Petersen that it is more useful to "think critically" about the tendencies this body of literature displays than to attempt to be encyclopedic; "Introduction: Ways of Thinking about Israel's Prophets," in *Prophecy in Israel*, ed. D. L. Petersen (Philadelphia: Fortress Press, 1987), 2. For a general survey of research on the prophets, see G. M. Tucker, "Prophecy and the Prophetic Literature," in *The Hebrew Bible and Its Modern Interpreters*, ed. D. A. Knight and G. M. Tucker (Chico, Calif.: Scholars Press, 1985), 325–68.

sponse to a particular prophet's activity and, at a more general level, in classifying prophetic movements into types.[9]

Biblical Prophecy

Naturally enough, many studies of the ancient Israelite prophets have been preoccupied with what they said because that is the bulk of what the collectors of the prophetic books have preserved for us. This orientation no doubt also reflects the scholarly and religious interests of particular individuals. What the prophets said may provide some useful information about the social, economic, and political history of Israel and Judah or about the development of their religion. However, the prophetic books clearly provide statements of conviction about the characteristics of the biblical God and the nature of this God's relationship to the community of human believers. Because revelation from God is taken to be the source of a prophet's message, and because the prophets addressed themselves to both the promises and the obligations of the relationship between God and Israel, their proclamations have proven to be fertile ground for theological reflections about God's character and activity.

Furthermore, this concern for what the prophets said has been enormously productive. It has been a major motivating force behind form and redaction criticism and other critical methods of studying Israelite prophetic literature, insofar as these have sought to identify the actual words of the prophets or to chart the relationship of these words to the life of the community and its ongoing needs.[10] It has led, among other things, to descriptions of the function of the prophet, which has been likened to that of a royal messenger.[11] Considerable debate has

9. For example, R. Linton proposed a fourfold typology of nativistic movements (revivalistic-magical, revivalistic-rational, perpetuative-magical, and perpetuative-rational) in "Nativistic Movements," *AA* 45 (1943):230–40. Alternative classifications are presented by S. Clemhout, "Typology of Nativistic Movements," *Man* 64 (1964):14–15; M. W. Smith, "Towards a Classification of Cult Movements," *Man* 59 (1959):8–12; B. R. Wilson, "Millennialism in Comparative Perspective," *CSSH* 6 (1963):93–114; idem, *Magic and the Millennium* (London: Heinemann, 1973). See W. La Barre, "Materials for a History of Studies of Crisis Cults: A Bibliographic Essay," *Current Anthropology* 12 (1971):3–44.

10. See D. L. Petersen, ed., *Prophecy in Israel,* 3–5.

11. See J. F. Ross, "The Prophet as Yahweh's Messenger," in *Israel's Prophetic Heritage,* ed. B. W. Anderson and W. Harrelson (New York: Harper, 1962), 98–107; J. S. Holladay, Jr., "Assyrian Statecraft and the Prophets of Israel," *HTR* 63 (1970):29–51. Both these studies have been reprinted in D. L. Petersen, ed., *Prophecy in Israel.*

taken place over how God communicated with the prophets[12] and what part they themselves played in shaping the message they finally delivered.[13]

From the point of view of this study, however, the dominance of this interest in the prophetic message has resulted in a certain imbalance in our picture of the biblical prophets, as illustrated by some examples from the literature on Old Testament prophecy. Because I have already spoken about the usefulness of cross-cultural comparisons for understanding prophecy as a social process, we can begin with Johannes Lindblom's *Prophecy in Ancient Israel*. Lindblom assumes prophecy to be a universal human phenomenon. During the course of a first chapter devoted to prophets outside Israel, he establishes what he considers to be the three defining characteristics of prophecy: the prophet was a person who was conscious of having received a special call from his god, who had revelatory experiences, and who proclaimed to the people the message received through revelation. Notice the consequences of this definition for Lindblom's interpretation. By selecting precisely these characteristics and discussing them at length, he has essentially described the prophetic act as a one-way transmission of information: God speaks to the prophet, who in turn relays the message to God's people. In keeping with this description, the emphasis is on the content of the message, in which, according to Lindblom, the main difference between the primitive and classical prophets in Israel is to be found.[14] He devotes the last third of his study to an exposition of the words of the classical prophets under the rubric "the religion of the prophets."

Although form criticism has traditionally been interested in suggesting specific sociological contexts for the words of the prophets, it has on the whole only slightly modified this conception of prophetic communication. For instance, Claus Westermann argues that the prophets' utterances were essentially those of messengers and that the formal sequence of their speeches—"reason" followed by "announcement of judgment"—implies an active participation of the prophets in

12. See Wilson, *Prophecy and Society*, 5–8.
13. For example, G. von Rad, *The Message of the Prophets* (New York: Harper and Row, 1967), 9–29, 50–76, 100–101.
14. J. Lindblom, *Prophecy in Ancient Israel* (Oxford: Basil Blackwell, 1962), 216–19.

shaping the content of their message. This emphasis on the "alert" consciousness of the prophet leads him to play down the role of ecstasy in revelation on the basis that "it is impossible for a message to be received in a state of ecstasy."[15] Westermann thus attributes to the prophets some personal responsibility for formulating the messages they delivered, but significant interaction between prophet and audience is left entirely out of account, and that between God and the prophet nearly so. The prophet helped shape the content of his message on the basis of the revelation he received and the details of the current situation as he saw them. To accomplish this task, he had to be "alert," but any real dialogue between him and either his audience or God was apparently unnecessary.

R. B. Y. Scott's approach to prophecy is a particularly good example of what I have been describing. According to Scott, the "function" of Yahweh's prophets was "to declare his will; they spoke at the bidding of God rather than at the instigation of men." As the "champions of the religious ethic of Yahwism," they were unique figures, a "supreme element" differentiating Israelite religion from its neighbors and giving it "survival value."[16] Thus, in this interpretation the divine word embodied in the prophets' messages to their audiences is the focus of attention, and the last half of Scott's work is devoted to explicating its various aspects. These messages were relevant to the situations in which they were originally spoken and remain relevant today.[17]

About this revelation of the divine word, taken to be so basic to prophetic activity, Scott says, "Theirs was a positive and urgent message that was neither derived from tradition (though the tradition was part of it), nor produced by reflection upon an existing body of religious

15. C. Westermann, *Basic Forms of Prophetic Speech* (Philadelphia: Westminster Press, 1967), 62–63, 86–87, 102–3. *Ecstasy* refers to some sort of spirit possession and the characteristic behavior associated with it. For a different view, see R. R. Wilson, "Prophecy and Ecstasy: A Reexamination," *JBL* 98 (1979):321–37.

16. R. B. Y. Scott, *The Relevance of the Prophets* (New York: Macmillan, 1968), 56, 40, 55. First published in 1944 and revised in 1968, this scholarly (but nontechnical) book presents a standard and influential interpretation of prophecy in the Old Testament.

17. In terms of the dynamics of prophetic activity, an interesting consequence of this idea is that the continuing relevancy of the prophetic message does not depend upon transmission by or interaction with actual prophets. Rather, the Old Testament prophets "are the contemporaries of every generation because the truth they declare is permanently valid," ibid., 15; cf. 14–17, 216–38.

belief. They spoke at an immediate divine command."[18] That revelation from the deity and its transmission to an audience are critically important elements in the prophetic process goes without saying. The problem is that Scott seems to insist upon the one-way character of prophetic communication—the prophet "channels" Yahweh's words directly; the message he proclaims is influenced neither by his own "reflection" nor by any external factors, like audience reactions. However, this position is difficult to maintain consistently, and on the very next page we find Scott attributing Micaiah's "knowledge of Yahweh's purpose" to his "apprehension by prophetic insight" of his visionary experience of standing in the divine council (1 Kings 22).[19] Elsewhere, he says that being a prophet does not necessarily lead to an obliteration of "the human and personal factor" and holds that, as a result of his call, the prophet "was not a puppet, but a conscious instrument."[20] Indeed, the prophet "interprets the present experience of his auditors in the light of wider experience, that of his own call and communion with Yahweh and that of his people's religious history."[21] The contradiction inherent in these statements about Israelite prophetic activity suggests the need for a more precise understanding of the social dynamics of the prophet's role as intermediary between humans and God.

These examples illustrate that the great emphasis students of the Bible have placed on the content of a prophet's message has tended to limit our understanding of the phenomenon of prophecy. It has done this in part by fostering the notion that the prophets of the Hebrew Bible are unique figures in the history of religions. Although they may sometimes be compared with functionaries in other cultures, the emphasis is more often on differences than on similarities. In addition, it has tended to view prophetic communication as essentially a one-way process: God reveals the divine will to the prophets, who in turn convey it to the people. As a result, explanations of the social dynamics of prophecy have been limited in scope.

18. Ibid., 91. This is a recurring theme. Thus, "The prophet has no . . . secret lore and mantic skill. He can speak only when God gives him a word, and then he cannot choose but speak," 9. Cf. 13, 63, 90.
19. Ibid., 92.
20. Ibid., 97, 162.
21. Ibid., 113.

This imbalance can be seen in the way the context of prophetic activity tends to be discussed. That a prophet's message was addressed to a particular social and historical situation is routinely acknowledged. Still, historical events and social circumstances seem to be thought of as providing information and motivation mainly for God alone, who presumably saw the situation and rendered judgment on it. This assumption minimizes the role of prophets and their audiences in evaluating the flow of current events and in shaping the prophetic utterances that responded formally to them. Again, everyone recognizes that the prophets' messages were meant to evoke a response from their audiences, but not much attention is paid to the dilemma the hearers faced in deciding how to respond to what the prophet said, or to the possibility that the responses of the audience might in turn affect the prophets' behavior. The prophets faced a dilemma of their own in their need both to be true to the revelation they received and to conform to their society's understanding of what constituted acceptable prophetic behavior.[22]

Discussions of the problem of false prophecy in the Hebrew Bible are a case in point. The confrontation between prophets (e.g., Jeremiah 27–28) posed a dilemma for the hearers, who had to decide how they would respond to conflicting pronouncements. However, biblical evidence has not made possible the formulation of a set of concrete rules that could be applied in a straightforward way by anyone desiring to distinguish a true from a false prophet! As a result, interpretations of prophetic conflict have tended to have a theological cast.[23]

From another perspective, these conflict situations clearly indicate that the people had a vital role in the dynamics of prophetic communication. James Crenshaw, for one, has recognized this point, and his study of prophetic conflict stresses the active intellectual involvement of the prophets in shaping their messages, as well as the tensions and conflicts prophets experienced within themselves and between themselves and their audiences.[24] Still, the sociological dimension

22. R. R. Wilson, *Sociological Approaches to the Old Testament* (Philadelphia: Fortress Press, 1984), 72–74.

23. For example, T. W. Overholt, *The Threat of Falsehood: A Study in the Theology of the Book of Jeremiah* (London: SCM Press, 1970). See R. R. Wilson, *Sociological Approaches*, 69–70; G. M. Tucker, "Prophecy and the Prophetic Literature," 354–55; D. L. Petersen, ed., *Prophecy in Israel*, 9–10.

24. J. Crenshaw, *Prophetic Conflict* (Berlin: Walter de Gruyter, 1971).

of the conflict situation has for the most part not been studied systematically.[25]

To this point I have been suggesting that the dominant emphasis on the message of the Old Testament prophets has diverted attention from aspects of the social process characteristic of the way they and, as I believe, all prophets exercise their peculiar task. The general point at issue here can be put more broadly: In the study of prophets, both biblical and nonbiblical, the tendency has been to discuss prophecy less for its own sake than as an element in some larger process. In the Hebrew Bible the process to be elucidated (on the basis of the prophets' message) is usually the ongoing relationship between Yahweh and his people, encompassing the general development of Israelite culture and religion. Thus, we have discussions of "prophecy and covenant"[26] and of the relationship of prophecy to certain specific aspects of Israelite culture, like its sociopolitical structure.[27] This inclination to be more interested in the theological content of the proclamation than in the social dynamics of prophecy is particularly evident in some of the well-known "theologies" of the Old Testament.[28]

Extrabiblical Prophecy

In extra-Israelite phenomena, the situation is similar. The focus is not so much on prophecy itself as on the broader sociocultural movements of which the prophets are a part, a concern that Anthony F. C. Wallace made clear when he defined a "revitalization movement" as "a deliberate, organized, conscious effort by members of a society to construct a more satisfying culture."[29]

Among the many attempts to classify these movements in terms of their beliefs and goals and to define their causes,[30] the anthropologist

25. See Wilson, *Sociological Approaches*, 67–80.
26. R. E. Clements, *Prophecy and Covenant* (London: SCM Press, 1965).
27. For example, H. Donner, "Die soziale Botschaft der Propheten in Lichte der Gesellschaftsordnung in Israel," *Oriens Antiquus* 2 (1963):229–45; K. Koch, "Die Entstehung der sozialen Kritik bei den Propheten," in *Probleme biblischer Theologie*, ed., H. W. Wolff (Munich: Kaiser Verlag, 1971), 236–57; J. L. Mays, "Justice: Perspectives from the Prophetic Tradition," in *Prophecy in Israel*, ed. D. L. Petersen (Philadelphia: Fortress Press, 1987), 145–58.
28. For example, W. Eichrodt, *Theology of the Old Testament*, vol. 1 (Philadelphia: Westminster Press, 1961); L. Koehler, *Old Testament Theology* (London: Lutterworth Press, 1957); G. von Rad, *Old Testament Theology*, vol. 2 (New York: Harper and Row, 1965).
29. A. F. C. Wallace, "Revitalization Movements," *AA* 58 (1956):265.
30. In addition to the works cited in n. 9, see G. Guariglia, "Prophetismus und

Kenelm Burridge deserves special comment. Burridge sets out in detail a sociological interpretation of "millenarian activities" based on data from a variety of cultures. In the process he has much to say about prophets.[31] But millenarian *movements* remain the focal point of attention, and in the end prophets are seen in terms of the contribution they make to them.[32]

Scholars have not only had differing agendas but also studied different figures. Here we need to consider a second tendency in the study of prophecy: Data from "primitive" and "higher" cultures are usually dealt with separately. Studies of the Old Testament prophets, for example, normally make reference to extra-Israelite figures only to the extent that they bear directly on the development of Israelite prophecy. Much of the continuing discussion of the Mari prophets has centered on the question of the extent to which they were parallel in nature and function to those in Israel.[33] Conversely, some studies of prophecy are confined to its appearance within "lower cultures" or among "colonial peoples."[34]

Heilserwartungsbewegungen in niedern Kulturen," *Numen* 5 (1958):180–98; W. Koppers, "Prophetismus und Messianismus als völkerkundliches und universalgeschichtliches Problem," *Saeculum* 10 (1959):38–47; A. J. F. Köbben, "Prophetic Movements as an Expression of Social Protest," *International Archives of Ethnography* 44 (1960):117–64; V. Lanternari, "Messianism: Its Historical Origin and Morphology," *HR* 2 (1962–63):52–72; idem, *The Religions of the Oppressed* (New York: New American Library, 1963); idem, "Nativistic and Socio-Religious Movements: A Reconsideration," *CSSH* 16 (1974):483–503; and Y. Talmon, "Pursuit of the Millennium: The Relation Between Religious and Social Change," *Archives Européennes de Sociologie* 3 (1962):125–48.

31. K. Burridge, *New Heaven New Earth* (New York: Schocken Books, 1969), 11–14, 31–32, 111, 153–63.

32. Thus his conclusion: "For the action to become coherent a prophet is necessary. He focuses attention on the meaning of the millennium and brings order to the inchoate activities," ibid., 172. J. L. Mays, "Justice," 155; G. M. Tucker, "The Role of the Prophets and the Role of the Church," in *Prophecy in Israel*, 166–67; and H. W. Wolff, "Prophecy from the Eighth Through the Fifth Century," *Int* 32 (1978):25–27 are among those who argue that the biblical prophets did not propose a new set of laws or system of morality, an activity high on the list of what, according to Burridge, millenarian prophets do. The correct inference to be drawn from this contrast is not that we are dealing with two radically different *kinds* of intermediaries, but that the specific circumstances in which prophets operate shape the way they perform their roles in society.

33. The palace archives (dating from around 1800 B.C.E.) of the city-state Mari, located on the Euphrates River, contained documents describing several distinct types of prophetic figures. For a discussion and bibliography, cf. R. R. Wilson, *Prophecy and Society*, 98–110.

34. K. Schlosser, "Prophetismus in niederen Kulturen," *Zeitschrift für Ethnologie* 75 (1950):60–72; J. Fabian, "Führer und Führung in den prophetisch-messianischen Bewegungen der (ehemaligen) Kolonialvölker," *Anthropos* 58 (1963):773–809; V. Lan-

That these two tendencies exist should come as no surprise, for the cross-cultural comparison of prophets has obvious stumbling blocks. The basic problem is the real differences that exist between societies at the levels of material culture, historical situation, and world view. These differences give rise to the diverse content of the prophecies themselves, which in all cases is culturally conditioned. Even when several prophets seem to share a common theme, say, a hope for the eventual appearance or return of some valued person or thing, the specific objects of hope (e.g., the political restoration of a nation, the return of the buffalo, the ancestors bringing cargo) are likely not to appear directly comparable. In addition, the ethnocentricity of the investigator may hinder comparison by predisposing him or her to evaluate more highly what is more familiar and intelligible.

These tendencies are difficult to overcome.[35] Lindblom considers prophecy to be a universal human phenomenon, but his comparisons of Israelite and non-Israelite prophets are largely restricted to discussions of ecstasy and the prophets' reception of the divine word. Burridge implies that prophets, at least those associated with movements whose goal is "redemption,"[36] share a common function, but he never specifically discusses the biblical prophets or Muhammad in this context.

In fact, attempts to bridge the gap between cultures and solve the puzzle of prophecy go back at least as far as the very beginnings of professional anthropology in America. James Mooney, an indefatigable field-worker who wrote the classic study of the Ghost Dance, was not satisfied simply to describe the origin and development of this one prophetic movement but wanted to set it in the context of a number of others that he took to be similar in character. To this end he devoted the first eight chapters of his study[37] to descriptions of prophetic activity among various native American groups, beginning with the Pueblo

---

ternari, *Religions of the Oppressed*. Clearly the Judeo-Christian religious tradition has had an influence on prophetic movements in many native cultures (cf. Schlosser, "Prophetismus"; Koppers, "Prophetismus"; Burridge, *New Heaven New Earth*, 22–29, 69–73, 83–86). However, the influence of missionaries is not necessary for such movements to occur (cf. Burridge, *New Heaven New Earth*, 35–36). Because of mission influence, Burridge refers to Christianity often, but he never directly compares biblical prophets with the prophets of millenarian movements.

35. A brief study by D. Emmet, however, largely does so: "Prophets and Their Societies," *JRAI* 86 (1956):13–23.

36. K. Burridge, *New Heaven New Earth*, 4–9.

37. James Mooney, "The Ghost-Dance Religion and the Sioux Outbreak of 1890," *ARBAE* 14 (Washington, D.C.: Government Printing Office, 1896):658–763.

Revolt of 1680 and culminating with John Slocum and the Indian Shakers of Puget Sound in the late nineteenth century. In a later chapter he turned to "parallels in other systems" and discussed examples of prophetic activity from the biblical period, Islam, and Christian sects and movements from the Middle Ages to the nineteenth century. Mooney did not, however, formulate a clear set of categories for his comparisons. Instead, his discussion seems to have been guided by two general ideas. The first is the notion that messianic doctrines, wherever they are found, "are essentially the same and have their origin in a hope and longing common to all humanity."[38] The second is that certain traits—inspiration via dreams, dancing, ecstasy, and trance—are taken to "have formed a part of every great religious development of which we have knowledge from the beginning of history."[39] Although Mooney's study is broad in scope, in the final analysis it is more a listing of movements and figures than a systematic comparison, and it throws little theoretical light on the nature of the prophetic process. What is needed is a more systematic cross-cultural approach.

PROPHECY IN CROSS-CULTURAL PERSPECTIVE

Of course, studies of prophecy have been done from a cross-cultural perspective. Two recent and prominent works by Robert Wilson and David Petersen show something of what is involved in such an approach: both are characterized by a conscious use of methods and materials derived from the social sciences and an emphasis on prophetic behavior. Prophetic speech remains important, although the focus is not on content for its own sake but on speech as patterned behavior that provides insight into the roles these prophets performed and their interactions with various segments of their audiences.[40]

38. Ibid., 657.
39. Ibid., 928; see 719, 947.
40. Wilson, *Prophecy and Society;* D. L. Petersen, *The Roles of Israel's Prophets* (Sheffield: JSOT Supplement Series, 1981). Cf. also R. C. Cully and T. W. Overholt, eds., *Anthropological Perspectives on Old Testament Prophecy* (*Semeia* 21, 1981); and Overholt, *Prophecy in Cross-Cultural Perspective.* The approach is beginning to have some effect. J. Blenkinsopp includes a section on "the social location of the prophet" in his introduction and sometimes employs terms like *peripheral groups* and *support groups* in his interpretation in *A History of Prophecy in Israel* (Philadelphia: Westminster Press, 1983), 38–46, 74, 92, 99, 214. The chapter on the phenomenon of prophecy in J. F. A. Sawyer, *Prophecy and the Prophets of the Old Testament* (New York: Oxford University Press, 1987) has a decided social scientific cast.

My intention in this book is to set out as clearly and coherently as possible one strategy for studying prophecy cross-culturally and some of the implications that follow from such an approach. In my view a key requirement is a basis for comparison that focuses on intermediaries themselves but remains relatively free from the culturally conditioned content of what they said. With this in mind I propose a model of how the prophetic process works in chapter 2. My main concern is neither the normative aspects of prophecy nor the revitalization process as a whole, but rather *the social dynamics of the prophetic act itself.* For our purposes, the prophetic process is depicted as a set of interactions among a minimum of three distinct actors or groups: the supernatural, the prophet, and the audience to whom the prophet's message is addressed. These interactions take place within a concrete historical-cultural situation that is reflected both in the prophet's message and in the auditors' evaluation of it. The claim I wish to make is that although the specific content of their respective messages is culturally conditioned and therefore quite dissimilar, the prophetic activity of a wide variety of intermediaries conforms to the same general pattern.

2

The Social Dynamics
of Prophetic Activity

No one would deny that prophecy is a social phenomenon. Prophets speak for some deity, which necessarily implies that they speak to a particular group of persons. Indeed, we may define *religious intermediation* as a process of communication between the human and the divine spheres in which messages in both directions are "channeled" through one or more individuals who are recognized by others in the society as qualified to perform this function.[1]

THE COMMUNICATION ACT

Acts of communication are by their very nature complex. Every such act—even the simplest form of interpersonal communication where "one person (A) transmits information to another person (B) about something (x)"—involves "a transmission of information."[2] Even such a simple act involves a system of relationships in which both A and B are simultaneously oriented to each other and to x. Theodore Newcomb calls this *co-orientation* (or, *simultaneous orientation*), and claims that, insofar as the orientations of people toward other people are not "made in an environmental vacuum" and those toward things and events "are not made in a social vacuum," it is "essential to human life."[3]

---

1. M. J. Buss characterizes the prophetic role "as the receiving and transmitting of communications not available to ordinary conscious sensitivity" and suggests that "such communications are valued ... [because] they serve the making of decisions and the handling of problems" in "The Social Psychology of Prophecy," in *Prophecy*, ed. J. A. Emerton (New York: Walter de Gruyter, 1980), 6.
2. T. M. Newcomb, "An Approach to the Study of Communicative Acts," in *Communication and Culture*, ed. A. G. Smith (New York: Holt, Rinehart and Winston, 1966), 66.
3. Ibid., 68.

17

Another way of putting the matter is that feedback is an integral part of communication, and, as a consequence, A, the transmitter, does not completely determine the content of the communication. Alfred Smith, for instance, says that "the signal A sends to B is largely determined by the signal B sends back to A." The reaction of A to what B says or does, to what A anticipates B will say or do, or even to what A says are all instances of feedback. "Feedback serves to control and correct the signals fed forward. It serves to realign all the signals within a network to one another. It makes A and B truly interacting members of a communication system."[4]

The importance of feedback may be illustrated in yet another way. The words and other actions of an intermediary express a certain perception of the world in general and the specific details of the current situation. Like all perceptions, these are the result of two activities. The first of these may be called *cognitive filtering*, or seeing what is there. As a matter of fact, in most situations we are not likely to "see" with total accuracy and objectivity. Rather, we respond selectively to the stimuli the situation presents, and this selective response is in itself a socially based process: "the plausibility of our views on reality depends on the social support which these views receive from significant others within our milieu." The second activity that underlies perception is *cognitive mapping*, or seeing what something "means."[5] In order not to be overwhelmed by the flood of sensory impressions that confronts us in a situation, we endeavor to provide a frame of reference within which what is "seen" can be placed. Things have meaning for us only within such a frame of reference. Thus, meanings are assigned and are not intrinsic to the things seen themselves. They arise, rather, in the process of interaction between people.[6]

This is not to say that A and B always agree about x. Newcomb speaks of "the psychological strain toward symmetry" but recognizes

4. Smith, ed., *Communication and Culture*, 322. Smith's and Newcomb's remarks focus on interpersonal communication. The feedback process becomes more complicated as one moves into the arena of mass communications; see B. H. Westley and M. S. MacLean, "A Conceptual Model for Communications Research," in *Communication and Culture*, ed. A. G. Smith, 80–87.
    5. T. F. Carney, *The Shape of the Past: Models and Antiquity* (Lawrence, Kans.: Coronado Press, 1975), 3.
    6. H. Blumer, *Symbolic Interactionism: Perspective and Method* (Englewood Cliffs, N.J.: Prentice-Hall, 1969), 2–6. See also W. H. Ittelson and H. Cantril, *Perception: A Transactional Approach* (Garden City, N.Y.: Doubleday, 1954).

that factors like the nature of A's association with B may work against it.[7] Presumably, a person's perception of a thing or event, based on knowledge or conviction, could stand in the face of persistent negative feedback. Such steadfastness would not be easy in the face of strong opposition.

The last point should be emphasized. As we have seen, every act of communication contains both transmission of information and feedback. In fact, feedback is the only way A can get any indication of success.[8] The content of many communications is more or less directly testable on the basis of observation (e.g., "it is raining") or past experience (e.g., "there was no mail today because of the holiday"). Where this testability is not the case, however, the need is greater to rely on "social confirmation as the test of what is true and valid." As a result, A may feel under pressure to accommodate a communication to B's expectations.[9] Religious intermediaries, whose activities typically offer some interpretation of the current social-historical situation, would never be entirely free from such pressure.

Communication is by its very nature dynamic and interactional. Speakers may be able to control the words they utter, but they are hardly able to exercise the same degree of control over how the audience perceives them. Indeed, even the first type of control is not as complete as it appears, because specific elements of the physical setting, social situation, or audience reaction may influence the speakers' words or strategy.

OLD TESTAMENT PROPHETS

The richness and depth of this interaction is difficult to recognize in the prophetic books of the Hebrew Bible. Consider, for example, the evidence available in the Book of Amos for describing prophecy as a social process. The main participants in the process are relatively clear (God, Amos, and the people who made up Amos's audience), although the latter remain almost entirely anonymous. We can also arrive at a

7. Newcomb, "Study of Communicative Acts," 74–75.
8. For a description of experiments that demonstrate A's need for feedback in order to know that B "is getting the proper information," see H. J. Leavitt and R. A. H. Mueller, "Some Effects of Feedback on Communication," in *Communication and Culture*, ed. A. G. Smith, 352.
9. Newcomb, "Study of Communicative Acts," 68.

general outline of the situation in which the prophet worked. International tensions,[10] not the least of which are the frequent references to warfare[11] and the exile of captives,[12] are indicated, as are social injustice[13] and conflicts with high officials.[14] However, biographical information about the prophet is limited.

Our information on the interrelationships between the main participants is sketchy. We are told of direct contact between God and the prophet in the form of visions (7:1–9; 8:1–3; 9:1–4). Of the five visions described, the first four incorporate a dialogue between God and the prophet, and the first two (7:1–3, 4–6) portray the prophet's protest as effective in changing God's originally intended course of action. Some sort of direct contact with God is presupposed in Amos's account of his commissioning to the prophetic office (7:14–15), and 3:3–8 constitutes a more general statement concerning the regularity of such encounters between God and his prophetic agents.

Concerning the nature of the interaction between Amos and the various persons with whom he came into contact during the course of his activity as a prophet, we are left mostly in the dark. Only one of his auditors, Amaziah the priest of Bethel, is mentioned by name (7:10–17). The generally hostile tone of that encounter is also mirrored in 2:12. As for the rest, we get only a scattering of category designations, like "cows of Bashan" (4:1) and "those who are at ease in Zion" (6:1). Amos's message to the people is emphasized, but in the present form of the book it confronts us in small, disconnected units.

In Amos, then, we have some hints of the richness of Old Testament prophecy as a social process, but ultimately many of the details are hidden from our view by a veil of theology. The amount of information available to us in the Book of Amos about individual components of the prophetic process is greatly disparate. We learn more about the prophet's proclamation than anything else; whoever was responsible for collecting and writing down the material in the book was mostly interested in preserving Amos's message. Indeed, the prophetic books of the Old Testament are mostly "message." This message is essentially

10. Amos 1:3—2:3; 6:14.
11. Amos 1:4–5, 6–15; 2:2–3, 11–12; 3:6, 11, 14–15; 4:2–3; 5:2–3, 9; 6:8, 14; 7:9, 17; 9:9–10.
12. Amos 1:6, [9], 15; 5:27; 6:7; 7:11, 17; 9:4.
13. Amos 2:6–8; 4:1–3; 5:10–15; 6:4–7; 8:4–7.
14. Amos 7:10–17.

theological in tone: it interprets sociohistorical situations in terms of religious convictions. This theology forms a veil that hides from our vision important aspects of the social situation and of the dynamics of the prophets' reaction to it.

Our problem, then, is trying to penetrate the editors' and the subsequent religious community's interests in order to catch a glimpse of the social interaction that we must assume was integral to the prophet's performance of the role. Here the many accounts of non-biblical intermediaries may be of use to us. Mindful of the difficulties in making comparisons between prophetlike figures (see chapter 1), we will bracket the content of the prophets' messages in order to compare intermediaries better in terms of how they function within society.

A MODEL OF
THE PROPHETIC PROCESS

In order to do this, I intend to employ a model with which a variety of prophetlike figures can be compared. By *model* I mean simply an "outline framework, in general terms, of the characteristics of a class of things or phenomena." Such a framework sets out in visual form the major components of the class and shows how these components relate to each other.[15] Such a framework provides a structure for a systematic search for and arrangement of data in biblical and other accounts of intermediaries and allows them to be compared in terms of social structures and processes. As a result, specific historically and culturally conditioned aspects of the prophet's activity (of great importance in interpreting individual cases but distracting with respect to cross-cultural comparisons) can be temporarily kept in the background.

Thomas Carney's way of stating the case is to say that models help us confront the problem of our "partial awareness" of a phenomenon by specifying those aspects to be examined and those to be left out. If models are constructed carefully and fit the data well, then they have the power to tell us what we may expect to find as we move from case to case, although they do not require that we actually find every element in each case. Where data about a specific prophet are scanty, the model sometimes enables us "to patch over a gap in our data with a probable

15. Carney, *The Shape of the Past*, 8.

hypothesis which will enable us to proceed with our analysis."[16] As Jonathan Z. Smith's examination of the Jonestown mass suicide clearly shows, resorting to a model for purposes of comparison is sometimes the only way to gain understanding of a particularly puzzling phenomenon.[17]

Of course, models have their drawbacks. They impose what Carney calls an "iron law of perspective," encouraging us to look for just certain things and to ignore others. Even so, Carney suggests they have two advantages over "ordinary" single-minded concentration like that of a bird-watcher: they compel us "to look in a methodical way" and also "to be conscious of the fact that we have a viewpoint and are considering our problem only from that viewpoint." Model building is also inherently subjective, although models are not by any means untestable. As Carney points out, a model is "a speculative instrument" that is only "as good as the results it produces." Provided we can avoid its becoming an obsession, the "data themselves will tell us whether the model is a good one."[18]

Bruce Malina, a New Testament scholar, lists the minimum features of "a good social science model for biblical interpretation."[19] One item on this list captures what I consider to be the major advantage in working with a cross-cultural model of the prophetic process: it requires us to operate at a level of abstraction sufficient to allow similarities to surface for comparison. The illustrations in the next chapter demonstrate that the advantage is a real one.

Figure 1 represents in diagrammatic form the model of this prophetic process. The two essential features of this model are a set of three actors—a supernatural entity, a prophet, and an audience—and a pattern of interrelationships among them involving revelation (r), proclamation (p), feedback (f), and supernatural confirmation (s). When applied, for example, to prophetic materials from the Old Testament, the generic term *supernatural* would be replaced by *Yahweh*, and specific prophets and groups would be named as appropriate.

16. Ibid., 12–17.
17. J. Z. Smith, "The Devil in Mr. Jones," *Imagining Religion* (Chicago: University of Chicago Press, 1982), 102–20.
18. Carney, *The Shape of the Past*, 35–37.
19. B. J. Malina, "The Social Sciences and Biblical Interpretation," *Int* 36 (1982):241.

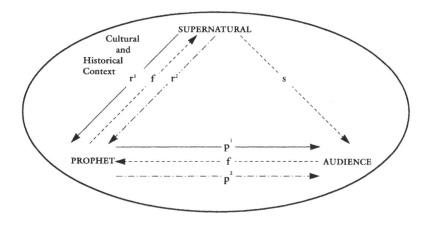

Figure 1

The focus on interrelationships that is evident here calls for some enlargement of traditional notions concerning a prophet's authority. Because prophets, generally speaking, function as messengers of a god, viewing their revelatory experiences as the primary source of their authority seems justifiable. In all instances of which I am aware, a person who is actually functioning as a prophet is assumed to have been the recipient of some such communication. These essentially private experiences form the theological justification for prophetic activity. Inevitably, they are also culturally conditioned, because both the perception and later articulation of these experiences are affected by the prophets' social and historical context. Moreover, a more public aspect of prophetic authority displays itself in various reactions to their message by the people to whom it is addressed. Because the act of prophecy must necessarily take place in a social context, these reactions are both inevitable and critically important. Prophets seek to move their audiences to action, and audiences may be said to attribute authority to prophets insofar as they acknowledge and are prepared to act upon the "truth" of their message. In their response, audiences in effect judge the acceptability of prophets by deciding whether or not their message is sufficiently grounded in their cultural and religious traditions and is relevant to the current sociopolitical situation. In this interaction, the specific content of the message—its theology—is of great importance. As Peter Worsley has put it, "Charisma is thus a function of recognition: the prophet without honor cannot be a charismatic prophet" (see chapter 4).[20]

Although audiences are mostly composed of members of the prophets' own cultural communities, we can expect that these persons are not all of one mind in their evaluation of the prophetic message. Whether individuals accept, reject, or are indifferent to it, however, they react to prophets in some fashion, and this feedback and the prophets' response to it define the dynamic interrelationship between actors that is central to the model. Similarly, prophets assess their own message against their perception of the events going on around them and the feedback they receive from their audiences. Because they believe that the message they deliver is not strictly their own but is revealed by the god, we also need to assume the possibility of feedback from prophets to the god and an eventual new revelation either confirming or altering the original message.

Thus, the model suggests the specific components that we would expect to find in any given example of prophetlike activity.

1. *Revelation.* Prophets generally claim to have had some sort of direct contact with a deity. Sometimes, for instance in cases involving ecstatic behavior, this contact can be confirmed by others.[21]

2. *A proclamation based on the revelation.* Although this component may contain innovative features, the prophet's performance is familiar

20. P. Worsley, *The Trumpet Shall Sound: A Study of "Cargo" Cults in Melanesia* (New York: Schocken Books, 1968), xii.

21. Much has been written on the nature of revelatory experiences. With respect to the biblical prophets, the discussion has often centered on the term *ecstasy* (e.g., J. Lindblom, *Prophecy in Ancient Israel* (Philadelphia: Fortress Press, 1962); cf. R. R. Wilson, "Prophecy and Ecstasy: A Reexamination," *JBL* 98 (1979):321–37; idem, *Prophecy and Society in Ancient Israel* (Philadelphia: Fortress Press, 1980), 5–8. More recently, the tendency has been to speak of "possession" (Wilson, "Prophecy and Ecstasy"; idem, *Prophecy and Society*, 32–41, 63–66, 144–46); for an opposing view, see S. Parker, "Possession Trance and Prophecy in Pre-Exilic Israel," *VT* 28 (1978):271–85. Discussions of possession frequently cite the cross-cultural studies of Bourguignon and her collaborators; e.g., E. Bourguignon, "The Self, the Behavioral Environment, and the Theory of Spirit Possession," in *Context and Meaning in Cultural Anthropology*, ed. M. E. Spiro (New York: Free Press, 1965), 39–60; idem, "Spirit Possession Belief and Social Structure," in *The Realm of the Extra-Human: Ideas and Actions*, ed. A. Bharati (The Hague: Mouton, 1976), 17–26. In a very interesting study, D. Merkur has interpreted Innuit shamanistic trances in terms of self-hypnotic phenomena in *Becoming Half Hidden: Shamanism and Initiation Among the Inuit* (Stockholm: Almqvist and Wiksell International, 1985).

enough to be recognized by the audience as prophetic behavior. The prophetic message must be conceived broadly enough to include both words and nonverbal behavior. The latter demonstrates contact with the god and is part of an action aimed at rectifying the current situation. Generally, the message is timely; present needs, not long-term fulfillment of predictions, are the issue.

3. *Audience reaction*. Feedback from the audience addressed by the prophet may be positive, negative, or simply indifferent. In any case it is likely to exert an influence on the prophet's subsequent performances.

4. *The prophet's feedback to the source of revelation*. Feedback is integral to revelation, conceived of as an act of communication.

5. *Additional revelations*. Intermediaries tend to be active over a period of time and to believe that they are in contact with deity on a continuing basis.

6. *Additional proclamations*. During the course of their careers, intermediaries are called upon to address a variety of situations.

7. *Supernatural confirmations*. Accounts of prophetic activity sometimes describe certain experiences that independently tend to confirm the god-given task of the prophet and strengthen people's convictions about the prophet's authenticity. Miracles would fall into this category.

8. *Disciples*. Sometimes prophets have one or more followers who serve as intermediaries between them and some segment of their audience. In such cases we have a fourth actor in the prophetic process, and a modification of the model is required (see Figure 2 on page 45).

The first three of these elements are often the most obvious, those that allow us to identify instances of prophecy. The others are usually present in some form, although our ability to discover them depends largely on the amount of data available for any given instance of prophecy. The whole process, of course, takes place within a specific cultural and historical context.

3

Illustrations of the Prophetic Process

Our model (described in chapter 2) identifies those characteristics of prophecy that are most important for understanding it as a social process and suggests how these elements are interrelated. At the intuitive level this construction may seem to be generally accurate, but one reason for using models is to take analysis beyond the level of simple intuition. The illustrations in this chapter show that the data from specific instances of prophecy do fit the proposed model. In the process the model's utility for comparing prophecy cross-culturally should become apparent.

THE GHOST DANCE OF 1890

The last third of the nineteenth century was for the native Americans of the Great Plains and western mountains of the United States a time of acute cultural crisis characterized by increasing white domination that threatened traditional ways of life. Repeating a pattern that had already occurred in other parts of the country, armed conflict between native Americans and whites led to land cessions and the confinement of tribal groups to reservations, the size of which was in many instances further reduced by subsequent cessions. Virtually overnight the once free-roaming hunters were required to become farmers. Their cultural, economic, and political situation was desperate.

One response to this situation was a millennial movement known as the Ghost Dance of 1890, which had its origin in the visionary experiences of Wovoka, a Paiute from western Nevada often referred to as the Indian messiah. Wovoka taught that the time was coming when the whites would be supernaturally destroyed and dead native Americans would return to the earth. In that day the buffalo, now nearly extinct, and other game animals would be restored to their original numbers, and the old way of life would flourish again on a reconstituted earth where sickness and old age would be no more. In preparation for this great event and to hasten its arrival, the native Americans were instructed to perform the Ghost Dance ceremonial at regular intervals. The Ghost Dance involved large numbers of people moving slowly around a central tree. One characteristic feature was a trance many of the dancers experienced in which they visited the spirit world, conversed with dead relatives, and often caught glimpses of villages of native Americans living in the old way.

During 1889 and 1890, news of this vision of future events spread rapidly among the native Americans of the Rocky Mountains and the plains. Delegates from many tribes traveled to Nevada, often by railroad, especially to hear Wovoka. Their return often occasioned a great deal of excitement, and the new religion spread rapidly. Among the Sioux of South Dakota, the doctrine and practice took on a note of overt hostility toward whites that inaugurated an unfortunate chain of events culminating in the massacre of Chief Big Foot's band at Wounded Knee on December 29, 1890.

Because considerable information about the Ghost Dance of 1890 is available, we have an opportunity to see how well the model of the prophetic process can comprehend the details of such a religious movement. This first case study focuses attention specifically on the individual components of the prophetic process outlined in chapter 2.[1]

Wovoka's revelation (element 1). The prophetic founder of what has come to be known as the Ghost Dance of 1890 was a Paiute, Wovoka, who lived all his life in the Mason Valley of western Nevada about forty miles northwest of the Walker Lake reservation. Because of his association as a seasonal worker with the family of a nearby white rancher, David Wilson, he was also widely known by the name John

1. The basic source for information about the Ghost Dance of 1890 is J. Mooney, "The Ghost-Dance Religion and the Sioux Outbreak of 1890," *ARBAE* 14 (Washington, D.C.: Government Printing Office, 1896); a selection of texts from Mooney and other sources is in T. W. Overholt, *Prophecy in Cross-Cultural Perspective* (Atlanta: Scholars Press, 1986), 122–42. This section contains material from my study "The Ghost Dance of 1890 and the Nature of the Prophetic Process," *Ethnohistory* 21 (1974):37–63.

(Jack) Wilson. Wovoka seems to have had his first revelation in about 1887, after which he began to teach the dance to his people. His most important vision, however, came on January 1, 1889, in conjunction with a total eclipse of the sun. On this occasion he felt himself to be taken up into the spirit world, where he met the supernatural and was given a message to convey to his people.[2] It is clear both from Wovoka's own account and from the reactions of others to him that this vision was perceived as the primary basis for his prophetic activity.

Wovoka's message (element 2). While it is certain that Wovoka's message was derived from his visions, it is difficult to state with assurance its original contents. Among the several reasons for this uncertainty is that, first of all, virtually every report we have of Wovoka's teaching is second- or third-hand, mediated to us through delegates from the various tribes who visited him and who brought back his teachings to their own people. As we will see, the particular perceptions and needs of these men and their tribes seem often to have resulted in embellishments and even substantive changes in the doctrine. Second, widespread interest in the Ghost Dance among native Americans of the mountains and plains began to develop in the spring and summer of 1889, and within two years of that date several events would have been strong motivators toward a doctrinal shift. On the one hand, the summer and autumn of 1890 saw increasing hostility between whites and Sioux ghost dancers that culminated in the massacre at Wounded Knee on December 29. On the other hand, the spring of 1891 proved disappointingly uneventful for adherents of the dance, among whom this was the commonly accepted date for the arrival of the millennium. Third, the earliest direct evidence we have for Wovoka's teaching, his interview with the ethnologist James Mooney, comes from a considerably later time than these important events (January, 1892). In attempting to reconstruct Wovoka's original message, therefore, we have to consider the nature of the source and its transmission, as well as whether it dates before or after the end of 1890.

Mooney was not particularly concerned about this problem of the doctrine's modification through time. His own account gives prominent place to an interview he had with Wovoka in January of 1892, and

2. Mooney, "Ghost-Dance Religion," 771–74.

he accepts as "the genuine official statement of the Ghost dance doctrine as given by the messiah himself to his disciples" a written account,
contemporaneous with the events it reports, of the instruction received
by a delegation of Southern Cheyenne and Arapaho who visited the
prophet in August 1891.[3]

Accounts of Wovoka's teaching from the period before December
1890 are all indirect. Perhaps the earliest is contained in a report to the
War Department submitted by Captain J. M. Lee in autumn 1890, in
which he records a conversation with a Paiute named Captain Dick,
who told him of the message of Wovoka as it had been described to him
by another Indian toward the end of 1888.[4] In addition we have several
reports from delegations of Sioux, Northern Cheyenne, and Northern
Arapaho who visited Wovoka during 1889 and 1890, as well as information about the doctrine as it was taught among the Pai of Arizona,
who first took up the dance in May of 1889.[5] Although perhaps not
accurate in all respects, these secondhand accounts are useful in con-
structing a consensus statement concerning the basic core of Wovoka's
teaching.

According to Captain Dick, Wovoka taught that the time was
coming soon when dead native Americans would return to this earth.
The youth of these returning dead would be restored, and their advent
would be accompanied by a restoration of the important game animals
and a supernatural destruction of all whites by a flood. In order to
facilitate this event, the native Americans were instructed to perform a
certain dance regularly, and those who disbelieved and did not take up
the dance were threatened with supernatural punishment. This description may be taken as a minimal statement of Wovoka's teachings, and
agreement is widespread regarding most of its elements. From all the
early accounts, as well as from the songs that grew out of personal
visions of the dancers and were used in the dances themselves, the early
return of the dead was clearly the basic hope of the participants, and the
act of dancing was viewed as necessary to expedite this event. The
notion that the youth of those restored would be renewed is frequent,
and that life would henceforth be free of disease and suffering is

3. Ibid., 780–81. He calls this document the "Messiah letter."
4. Ibid., 784.
5. See H. F. Dobyns and R. C. Euler, *The Ghost Dance of 1889 Among the Pai
Indians of Northwestern Arizona* (Prescott, Ariz.: Prescott College Press, 1967).

commonly added. The restoration of the game animals is either mentioned specifically or is included by implication within the more general framework of the new creation that would follow the millennium and make possible the reestablishment of the old ways of life.

The situation is not quite so clear regarding the destruction of the whites and punishment of Indian doubters. The Southern Cheyenne-Arapaho "messiah letter" of August 1891 mentions neither of these elements, and in his interview with Mooney Wovoka stressed the fact that he had instructed the people to "live in peace with the whites." Mooney further states: "when questioned directly, he said he believed it was better for the Indians to follow the white man's road and to adopt the habits of civilization."[6] Porcupine, a Northern Cheyenne delegate in 1889–90, hints that Wovoka taught the equality of native Americans and whites,[7] and the Pai do not seem to have emphasized the destruction of the whites. Both of these reports mention the punishment of unbelievers, however. The Sioux reports, on the contrary, stress the supernatural destruction of the whites, and Short Bull and Kicking Bear, as well as Sitting Bull the Arapaho, all attribute this teaching to Wovoka and all were members of the same delegation to the prophet as was Porcupine. Although among the Sioux Wovoka's more passive attitude became openly hostile, we could reasonably assume that, given the emphasis on the renewal of the world and restoration of the old way of life, the elimination of the whites formed an important part of the original doctrine.

In addition to this basic core of teachings, the Southern Cheyenne-Arapaho messiah letter and the Mooney interview add two other elements: Wovoka's claim that he could control the weather, creating rain or snow at will, and certain ethical admonitions. The list of these guidelines is not identical in the two sources. The messiah letter instructs the native Americans not to hurt anyone, not to fight, to "do right always," to cooperate with the whites, and not to lie. In his interview with Mooney, Wovoka omitted the first and third of these and added a sixth, not to steal.[8] Porcupine and the Sioux delegates allude to ethical admonitions. Porcupine mentions two from the list above (do not fight; cooperation with the whites is implied in his report that

6. Mooney, "Ghost-Dance Religion," 772.
7. Ibid., 794, 796.
8. Ibid., 781, 771.

Wovoka had taught that "all the whites and Indians are brothers"[9]), but the Sioux ignore this list altogether and mention three that are new: the native Americans should take up farming, send their children to school, and follow Wovoka's example.[10] The Pai apparently knew of Wovoka's claims to be able to control the weather,[11] but this element was ignored by the early Sioux and Northern Cheyenne and Arapaho delegates.

One other doctrinal element remains to be noted. The messiah letter reports Wovoka as saying with reference to himself and his mission: "Do not tell the white people about this. Jesus is now upon the earth. He appears like a cloud. The dead are all alive again."[12] On the basis of his interview, however, Mooney reports: "He makes no claim to be the Christ, the Son of God, as has been so often asserted in print. He does claim to be a prophet who has received a divine revelation."[13] This element is not reported among the Pai but is strong in the messages of the Sioux, Northern Cheyenne, and Arapaho delegates. Porcupine continually refers to Wovoka as "the Christ," and the notion is mentioned that the Messiah had formerly come to the whites, who killed him, and that he was now coming to the native Americans. Several delegates mention seeing the scars of the crucifixion on Wovoka's hands and feet.

Clearly, then, Wovoka proclaimed a millenarian expectation of a renewed creation in which the whites would be eliminated and the dead native Americans resurrected to enjoy an idyllic existence patterned on life as it had been in precontact days. This millennium could be facilitated by the people's faithful performance of the dance the prophet taught them. However, we have also seen indications that this doctrine was not static. Of particular importance are the apparent softening of the notion that the whites were to be destroyed through some supernatural cataclysm, an increasing elaboration by Wovoka of the ethical content of his message, and his disclaimer to Mooney about the opinion that he was Jesus. We will return to these matters shortly.

Because any prophet's message is addressed to a group of people living in a specific historical-cultural situation, its credibility is judged in

9. Ibid., 794, 796.
10. Ibid., 797.
11. Dobyns and Euler, *Ghost Dance of 1889 Among the Pai*, 34–35.
12. Mooney, "Ghost-Dance Religion," 781.
13. Ibid., 773.

terms of how adequate it appears to be for coping with the specific problems presented by that situation. One criterion by which this adequacy is likely to be evaluated is continuity with the broad cultural tradition of the people.[14] In one of the early published reports on the dance, Alice C. Fletcher approached this problem of continuity in a general way by listing four specific antecedents in traditional Indian cultures that prepared the way for the acceptance of Wovoka's message: various features of the dance itself were common to other ceremonies, belief in the reality of dreams or visions, belief that both men and animals live on after death, and belief in a deliverer who is known as the "Son of God" and is lighter in color than most native Americans.[15] She does not, however, discuss the supporting evidence for the last of these antecedents.

In addition, Wovoka's message stands in direct continuity with an earlier religious movement known as the Ghost Dance of 1870, which originated among the Paiutes and spread west and north. The founder of this movement was one Wodziwob, who was active in the vicinity of Pyramid Lake in western Nevada. According to reports cited by Mooney, the content of Wodziwob's message was virtually identical with the core of Wovoka's message as outlined previously.[16] The movement spread into California and Oregon, died out within a few years, and was succeeded first by the Earth Lodge cult and then by the Big Head cult. Yet throughout this diffusion and development and despite the fact that new elements were occasionally added by specific tribes, the doctrine remained fairly constant, the elements most frequently found being the return of the dead, the expectation of a world catastro-

14. L. P. Mair has noted that the manner in which the millennium is conceived in a new religious movement is not "open to the free play of the prophet's fantasy. The ideal world must be what most people desire, and the explanation must be in line with current explanations of misfortune and disappointments"; "Independent Religious Movements in Three Continents," *CSSH* 1 (1959):124. For a detailed discussion of the proposition that "any innovation is made up of preexisting components," see H. G. Barnett, *Innovation: The Basis of Cultural Change* (New York: McGraw-Hill, 1953), especially 181–224, 243–66. On the role of prophets in millenarian movements, see K. Burridge, *New Heaven New Earth* (New York: Schocken Books, 1969).
15. A. C. Fletcher, "The Indian Messiah," *JAFL* 4 (1891):57–60.
16. Mooney, "Ghost-Dance Religion," 701–4. Mooney credits Wovoka's father, Tavibo, with being the prophetic founder of the earlier Ghost Dance movement (764), and P. Bailey, *Wovoka the Indian Messiah* (Los Angeles: Westernlore Press, 1957), 21, adopts this view from him. On the basis of her field information, C. Du Bois points out the error of this claim and demonstrates that Wodziwob was the actual founder in "The 1870 Ghost Dance," *University of California Anthropological Records* 3:1 (1939):3ff.

phe, the destruction of native American skeptics, and the elimination of the whites.[17]

Furthermore, the Ghost Dance of 1870 may ultimately have had its origin in the Prophet Dance of the Pacific Northwest. The Southern Okanagon Prophet Dance complex from around 1800 contains nearly exact parallels to the main points of the Ghost Dance doctrine, including visions of the destruction of the world, prophetic visionary journeys to the spirit world, and a doomsday when the living would rejoin the dead, as well as dances concerned with the salvation of mankind.[18] During the nineteenth century these doctrinal elements became widespread throughout the northwest and the Great Basin, not only in the Prophet Dance proper but also in a compound of that dance with Christianity that arose in the 1830s and in the Smohalla cult of 1860 to 1880. Leslie Spier suggested that the doctrine reached the Nevada Paiutes by way of either the Modoc or, more probably, the Oregon Paiutes.[19] Subsequent to Spier's work, Wayne Suttles documented a similar precontact phenomenon among the Coast Salish.[20]

Whether the Prophet Dance was a traditional element of the Columbia River cultures or a response to the crisis of contact with white culture is uncertain.[21] Regardless of how this issue is resolved, however, clearly Wovoka's message stands in direct continuity with a series of specific religious movements among western Indians going back approximately a century.

Another criterion by which the adequacy of Wovoka's message would have been judged involves the degree to which it took cognizance of the people's current social and historical situation. For both

17. See A. L. Kroeber, "A Ghost Dance in California," *JAFL* 17 (1904):32–35; L. Spier, "The Ghost Dance of 1870 Among the Klamath of Oregon," *University of Washington Publications in Anthropology* 2 (1927):39–56; A. H. Gayton, "The Ghost Dance of 1870 in South-Central California," *University of California Publications in American Archaeology and Ethnology* 28 (1930):57–82; C. Du Bois, "The 1870 Ghost Dance"; P. Nash, "The Place of Religious Revivalism in the Formation of the Intercultural Community on Klamath Reservation," in *Social Anthropology of the North American Tribes*, ed. F. Eggan (Chicago: University of Chicago Press, 1955), 377–442.

18. L. Spier, *The Prophet Dance of the Northwest and Its Derivatives: The Source of the Ghost Dance* (Menasha, Wis.: George Banta Publishing Co., 1935), 7ff.

19. Ibid., 24.

20. W. Suttles, "The Plateau Prophet Dance among the Coast Salish," *SWJA* 13 (1957):352–396.

21. See D. F. Aberle, "The Prophet Dance and Reactions to White Contact," *SWJA* 15 (1959):74–83; D. E. Walker, "New Light on the Prophet Dance Controversy," *Ethnohistory* 13 (1969):245–55.

the Paiutes and the tribes to which the dance spread, this period was a time of acute cultural stress characterized by white domination and the breakup of the old way of life. This tale of extreme suffering and confusion has often been told and need not be summarized here[22] beyond recalling that the cultural, economic, and political situation of these tribes was desperate, and the message preached by Wovoka correlated perfectly with it: The whites had ruined the world by subjugating the native American peoples and destroying the bases of their traditional life. Now the time had come for a supernatural power to do what the Indians themselves could not: eliminate these invaders and renew the world they had so fatally scarred.

Wovoka's audience would no doubt have judged his message in terms of its apparent adequacy as a response to the problems afflicting them. In retrospect, we may be tempted to write off Wovoka's millenarianism as a foredoomed and "irrational" response to the crisis of white domination and to point to the fact that the whites were not destroyed and that the herds and the dead did not return as justification for our view. However, we should be willing to entertain the notion that for the people who heard this message and who did not have the benefit of hindsight the situation was in fact just the reverse. To them the white men they saw consumed with greed for the shiny gold metal "that makes men mad," the endless broken agreements, and the overwhelming destructive power of the soldiers must have seemed "irrational," and calling on the supernatural for aid in throwing off this grave menace must have been, in terms of their culture, an essentially "rational" act.[23] Many tribes never took up the dance,[24] and even in those tribes that participated most enthusiastically many did not join

22. See, for example, P. Bailey, *Wovoka the Indian Messiah*; R. M. Utley, *The Last Days of the Sioux Nation* (New Haven: Yale University Press, 1963); H. F. Dobyns and R. C. Euler, *Ghost Dance of 1889 Among the Pai.*

23. The question of the "rationality" of religious movements can be approached from several directions. Viewed historically and in terms of the knowledge available to a culture, such movements can often be seen to display a definite rationality. This tack is taken by P. Worsley in his critique of Weber's notions of rationality and charisma, *The Trumpet Shall Sound* (New York: Schocken Books, 1968), 266–72. So also I. C. Jarvie, who repeatedly insists upon the necessity of viewing the cults as rational within a given people's "horizon of expectations" in "Theories of Cargo Cults: A Critical Analysis," *Oceania* 34 (1963):12–13, 22–23, and often. The point is that our common standards of rationality and hindsight are not always the most useful tools for understanding such religious movements as the Ghost Dance.

24. See Mooney, "Ghost-Dance Religion," 926–27.

the dancers. For thousands of native Americans, however, the message seemed to cope adequately with the situation and offer a hope in which they could have confidence.

One last problem remains to be mentioned: possible Christian influences on Wovoka's message. Speaking of the prophet's early life, Mooney noted that through his association with the David Wilson family he "gained some knowledge of English, together with a confused idea of the white man's theology."[25] Paul Bailey elaborates on this point and stresses Wovoka's fascination with stories about the great wonders Jesus worked and his supposed knowledge of the teachings of the Mormons about Indians.[26] One early reporter of the dance went so far as to say, "There is little doubt but that this belief is a perversion of the Christian religion as taught by missionaries, and in its present form suits the wishes and hopes of the Indians. . . . Many of the Indians have joined the Mormon faith, and it is believed that the teachings of the Mormons have encouraged these prophecies, in order to increase their influence with the Indians."[27]

Between Christianity and the Ghost Dance religion there are, of course, certain similarities of both broad ideas (messiah) and specific traits (Jesus, scars of the crucifixion, the previous unsuccessful appearance of the Messiah to the whites, and the Mormon notions of a protective garment and a native American messiah). These similarities do not seem sufficient, however, to justify the opinion that the dance was simply a perverted offshoot of Christianity. Ignoring superficial traits and looking instead at the antecedents of the movement and the shape of the expectation it proclaimed, the dance appears thoroughly traditional in its basic values, beliefs, and hopes. A more balanced view is that of Alexander Lesser, who suggests that despite the incorporation of some Christian elements the "sanction" for the hope the doctrine brought ". . . was native to the Indian mind. It was based on the vision, on the direct supernatural experience. In the vision a message came

25. Ibid., 765.

26. Bailey, *Wovoka the Indian Messiah*, 31ff., 76, 99–101, 121–23.

27. M. P. Maus, "The New Indian Messiah," *Harper's Weekly* 34 (1890):944. Others also blamed the Mormons for instigating the dance. See, for example, the papers of Catherine S. Weldon, a correspondent of Sitting Bull and a member of the Indian Defense Association; S. Vestal, *New Sources of Indian History, 1850–1891* (Norman: University of Oklahoma Press, 1934), 102, 115.

from the deceased, telling the living what to do, telling the living what would happen."[28]

Feedback from the people (element 3). The role performed by prophets is a public one. Inevitably they evoke some response from their audiences, and this response may affect subsequent activities. For example, the prophet may be encouraged to continue speaking as before or may be pressured to modify the message. In the case of Wovoka, this feedback is seen most directly in the fact that numerous delegations were dispatched to Nevada to receive his instruction, and his teachings were accepted and spread rapidly among tribes of the mountains and plains. Special agent E. B. Reynolds's report of late September 1890 indicates that the Rosebud Sioux were selling their possessions and buying arms and ammunition.[29] This disposal of needed goods, apparently contrary to the long-term interests of the people, indicates the strength of their conviction of the nearness of the millennium. Similarly, the Arapaho Sitting Bull advised the Southern Cheyenne and Arapaho to go ahead with the sale of their reservation lands because they could use the money "and in a short time the messiah would come and restore the land to them."[30]

Not everyone believed, of course, or the doctrine would not have needed to include threats against native Americans who did not join the dancers. We have numerous references to doubts that were harbored about the truth of what the returning delegates reported.[31] Others adopted a wait-and-see policy. Little Wound, a Sioux chief, is reported to have told his people: "If it is a good thing we should have it. If it is not a good thing it will fall to the earth of itself. Therefore learn the signs and the dances, that if the Messiah comes in the spring he will not pass us by."[32] Nevertheless, the increasing popularity of Wovoka and his

28. A. Lesser, "Cultural Significance of the Ghost Dance," *AA* 35 (1933):109. The interrelationship of native American and Christian beliefs is complex. One obvious thing is that rather commonly individual native Americans subscribe to both. Black Elk is an example; see T. W. Overholt, "Short Bull, Black Elk, Sword, and the 'Meaning' of the Ghost Dance," *Religion* 8 (1978):176–81. See also W. K. Powers, *Oglala Religion* (Lincoln: University of Nebraska Press, 1975), 112–16; and chapter 1 of this book, n. 34.
    29. Utley, *Last Days of the Sioux*, 95.
    30. Mooney, "Ghost-Dance Religion," 899.
    31. See ibid., 796, 800, 804, 806, 809–11.
    32. V. T. McGillycuddy, *The Significance of the Indian Ghost Dance Religion* (New York: Progressive Education Association, 1942), 261.

message during 1889 and 1890 must be interpreted as strong positive feedback to the prophet.

Of course, the situation did not remain static. The violence among the Sioux in late 1890 and the failure of the millennium to arrive during the spring of 1891 were strong negative factors calling for some reevaluation of the message. Those who accepted the dance were not in absolute uniformity as to when the millennium was to be expected. The most common date seems to have been the spring of 1891,[33] although the autumn of 1891 and the spring of the following year were sometimes mentioned.[34] In 1891 the Pai apparently expected the event "sometime within the next three or four years."[35] As specific dates passed, the response of some was to shift the hope to the indefinite future or to another world or to abandon the dance altogether.[36] One skeptical Kiowa delegate even reported in 1891 that the prophet himself had repudiated his message and counseled his people "to quit the whole business."[37] Another reaction, seemingly that of the prophet himself, was to change the focus of the teaching by making moral preachment central to it. This alteration of the millennial emphasis allowed the movement to survive and Wovoka to continue to function as leader, albeit of a greatly reduced number of disciples.[38]

33. Mooney, "Ghost-Dance Religion," 784, 796–97, 806, 903; J. McLaughlin, *My Friend the Indian* (Boston: Houghton Mifflin, 1910), 185.

34. Mooney, "Ghost-Dance Religion," 781, 807.

35. Dobyns and Euler, *Ghost Dance of 1889 Among the Pai*, 20.

36. Mooney, "Ghost-Dance Religion," 778, 804, 808, 901.

37. Ibid., 913.

38. The millennial orientation did not at once die out completely, however. In 1895 the agent at Tongue River, Montana, reported that Porcupine had been thoroughly convinced of the error of his belief and was now "assistant farmer at the agency" and promising to "make a white man of himself"; G. W. H. Stouch, "Report of Tongue River Agency," in *Annual Report of the Bureau of Indian Affairs* (Washington, D.C.: Government Printing Office, 1895), 198. But in 1900 he led a brief revival of the dancing (again talking of the imminent return of the dead, destruction of the whites, and bullet-proof garments), for which he was imprisoned. After about five months, the commandant of Ft. Keogh reported him "thoroughly disciplined," and he was released, but the agent's remark about him is worth noting: "This man Porcupine is a smooth talker and a cunning Indian"; W. A. Jones, "The Revival of the Messiah Craze in Montana," in *Annual Report of the Bureau of Indian Affairs* (Washington, D.C.: Government Printing Office, 1901), 164. As late as 1896 some Kiowa were still dancing in expectation of the return of the dead and the buffalo; I. Crawford, *Kiowa: The History of a Blanket Indian Mission* (New York: Fleming H. Revell, 1915), 28.

An interesting recent reinterpretation of the dance along similar lines is provided by the Sioux medicine man John Lame Deer, who recites an old ghost song:

> They are butchering cows there
> They are killing cows,
> So make your arrow straight,
> Make an arrow, make an arrow.

His explanation of this song is as follows:

> They didn't mean real butchering or real arrows. The song meant: If you want to go to the new earth you have to make an arrow, and it has to be straight. And that arrow, that's yourself, and you have to be straight, be on the good side. For this reason bows and arrows were made for the dance and hung up on a pole in the center of the dance ground.[39]

A somewhat different development occurred on the southern plains, where the peyote cult and the Ghost Dance commingled with an apparent overlapping of at least some of the ritual personnel. Frank White, the originator of the dance among the Pawnee, used peyote and witnessed Ghost Dances among the Comanche and Wichita before bringing the doctrine to his own people in the autumn of 1891. He was known as a devotee of both movements.[40] A story is told of how on one occasion White, using the power of his crow feathers (in his version of the dance the crow was one of the birds that guided the visionary to the spirit land), divined the presence of a lost strap. Although the divination here may be only a coincidence, it is one of the old traditional uses for peyote.[41] John Wilson, a Delaware-Caddo not to be confused with Wovoka, was an important leader of the Ghost Dance among the Caddo who later performed the same function in the peyote cult.[42] In his report for 1896, the agent for the Southern Cheyenne and Arapaho mentions the opposition of "old men who are wedded to barbarous

39. John Lame Deer and R. Erdoes, *Lame Deer, Seeker of Visions* (New York: Simon and Schuster, 1972), 229.

40. A. Lesser, *The Pawnee Ghost Dance Hand Game: A Study of Cultural Change* (New York: Columbia University Press, 1933), 60–61, 76, 117–18.

41. W. LaBarre, *The Peyote Cult* (New York: Schocken Books, 1969), 23–25, 134.

42. Mooney, "Ghost-Dance Religion," 903–5; F. G. Speck, "Notes on the Life of John Wilson, the Revealer of Peyote, as Recalled by His Nephew, George Anderson," *The General Magazine and Historical Chronicle* 35 (1933):539–56; LaBarre, *Peyote Cult,* 151–61.

customs" who want only to draw rations and perform "ghost" dances
and use "the 'mescal.' "[43] Because the focus of the peyote cult was
peaceful accommodation to the existing white culture,[44] the movement
from the Ghost Dance to peyote would be a natural one for those in the
process of readjusting their expectations.

Wovoka's feedback to the supernatural (element 4). Specific evidence
for this element of the prophetic process is often difficult to find
because the prophet's own communication with the supernatural would
typically not be public in nature. What does seem clear is that as events
unfolded Wovoka's message underwent change, and the conclusion that
these changes were influenced to some extent by his own reflections on
his social and historical situation is difficult to avoid. (See the discussion
of additional revelations, element 5.) Because Wovoka understood himself to be a messenger of the supernatural, he must have considered
these changes—like the original message—to have their source in the
supernatural. Still, some strong input from his own understanding of
events is to be assumed. I am designating this intellectual component of
a prophet's activity "feedback to the supernatural."

Captain J. M. Lee's account of the teaching of Tavibo, the founder
of the Ghost Dance of 1870,[45] seems to imply this kind of a process.
Lee, who visited the Walker Lake reservation, reported that Tavibo's
teaching came in three stages, each of which was based on a revelation.
At first he said that within a few moons a great upheaval would swallow
up the whites but not their goods or the native Americans. This
message met with few believers and a number of vocal skeptics. Tavibo
then withdrew for a time. When he returned, he announced that both
native Americans and whites would be swallowed up in the coming
disaster, but in a few days the former would be resurrected to enjoy life
on a reconstituted earth. This message was popular for a while, but its
popularity waned as time passed. The prophet's final message was that
the Great Spirit was incensed at the lack of faith displayed by his people
and that only believing native Americans would be resurrected after the

43. A. E. Woodson, "Report of Cheyenne and Arapaho Agency," *Annual Report
of the U.S. Bureau of Indian Affairs* (Washington, D.C.: Government Printing Office,
1896), 250.
44. See, for example, B. Barber, "A Socio-Cultural Interpretation of the Peyote
Cult," *AA* 43 (1941):673–75.
45. On the question of this mistaken identity, see n. 16.

world catastrophe.[46] The conclusion is difficult to escape that the troubles experienced by the prophet were reported to the deity and were taken account of in a new revelation.

Additional revelations (element 5). When a prophet is the recipient of more than one revelation, we should be on the alert for some modification in the message. Major substantive changes are not necessarily implied, although such may certainly occur. The effect might just as easily be an orderly amplification of the original message. As nearly as we can tell, Wovoka's visions of 1887 and 1889 would fit the amplification category, as would the three visions that the Seneca Handsome Lake experienced in 1799 and 1800.[47] We know from the testimony of those who visited him that Wovoka continued to experience trances in which he visited the spirit world, but the effects of these trances, other than substantiating his original message, are uncertain.

We have already noted indications that after a time Wovoka began to alter some of the earlier elements of his message. His interview with Mooney is particularly revealing, for there he softens considerably the threat of supernatural destruction of the whites, denies any responsibility for the "ghost shirts" that became such a conspicuous feature of the dance among the Sioux, and denies the claim that he was Jesus, come this time to the native Americans. When we recall that this interview took place in January 1892, we can reasonably assume that behind these apparent shifts in doctrine lies a considerable amount of negative feedback arising from the historical situation.[48] We need to remember that at that time an excellent communications system existed between the native American tribes of the west, who regularly utilized the railroads and the mails for visiting back and forth and for keeping each other informed about current events.

Furthermore, the dance, particularly as it was manifested among the "hostile" Sioux, had been the subject of considerable journalistic sensationalism and had caused rising anxieties in many parts of the

46. Mooney, "Ghost-Dance Religion," 701–2.
47. Ibid., 771–74; A. F. C. Wallace, *The Death and Rebirth of the Seneca* (New York: Vintage Books, 1972), 239–62; see pages 61–62 of this book.
48. The fact that Mooney was a white may also have been a factor, but we will see that these alterations occur also in messages addressed to native Americans.

country.[49] Wovoka would have been aware of much of this, and, indeed, Bailey suggests that after Wounded Knee he became concerned that the government would hold him responsible for the actions of the Sioux dancers and order his arrest.[50] Thus Wovoka seems to have experienced strong negative feedback both from the military, directed against the antiwhite aspect of his message, and from his own followers as the result of the failure of the millennium to materialize. The increased emphasis on ethical admonition noted previously, with the corresponding deemphasizing of the apocalyptic elements of the message, may be a response. Given the nature of prophecy, we would have to assume that the resulting changes in his doctrine would need to be seen by the prophet and his followers as based on new revelation.

Additional proclamations (element 6). The original message of Wovoka apparently remained essentially unchanged through 1890, but certain shifts are discernible thereafter. Besides the evidence cited previously, other indications suggest an altered focus of the prophet's activity. When Sitting Bull the Arapaho and other Oklahomans visited Wovoka in October 1892, he told them he was tired of so many visitors and wanted them to go home and tell the people to stop dancing.[51] Furthermore, for several decades after the turn of the century, Wovoka carried on a regular correspondence with native Americans from several parts of the west, a main purpose of which was his sale of sacred red paint, eagle and magpie feathers, and other sacred objects. James O. Long of the Indian Service at Oswego, Montana, was familiar with the contents of some of this correspondence, and he wrote in 1938 that at no time did Wovoka "send instructions in the dance, or in any way give advice concerning the religion." The correspondence collected by Grace Dangberg also indicates that Wovoka was now functioning as a healer.[52]

In general, Mooney's interview suggests that early in 1892 Wovoka was already moving in the direction of accommodation with the dominant white culture. That this shift in emphasis continued is

49. E. S. Watson, "The Last Indian War, 1890–91—A Study of Newspaper Jingoism," *Journalism Quarterly* 20 (1943):205–19.
50. Bailey, *Wovoka the Indian Messiah*, 176ff.
51. Mooney, "Ghost-Dance Religion," 901.
52. G. M. Dangberg, "Letters to Jack Wilson, the Paiute Prophet, Written Between 1908 and 1911," *BBAE* 164 (Washington, D.C.: Government Printing Office, 1957), 286; see W. Z. Park, "Paviotso Shamanism," *AA* 36 (1934):107.

apparent in a letter dated January 17, 1909, from Fred Robinson, an Assiniboin who had been instructed in the Ghost Dance by Kicking Bear in 1902. Robinson sought Wovoka's aid in his task of telling the people "what they ought to do." Robinson goes on to speak of a "good road" and a "bad road" and says, "I want you to help to make the people straight thought."[53] In a letter dated April 8, 1909, Rufus Medicine sought the prophet's help in living on earth "to do God's Good Will," and asked him to "pry [sic] for me that I may know the Good ways towards God our Father."[54] Fred Robinson was responsible for the transmission of the dance to a small community of Sioux living in Saskatchewan, where it continued to be practiced into the 1950s. Of this surviving group of practitioners, Alice Kehoe says, "the Ghost Dance was taught there as primarily an ethical code for Indians, not merely a ritual."[55] All this is further evidence that as time passed other elements, in particular moral preachment, replaced apocalyptic at the center of Wovoka's message.

Although the stated goal of the early Ghost Dance doctrine was the reestablishment of the old life in a reconstituted world, Wovoka's message already contained the seeds of several far-reaching cultural changes. This adaptation is particularly evident in his forbidding of warlike activity and his call for the brotherhood of all native American tribes.[56]

Supernatural confirmation (element 7). This element in the model designates a more subtle kind of feedback in which the primary focus is on the supernatural: The people, having responded in a positive way to the activity of the prophet, now look for some indication that the promises he has proclaimed will be fulfilled. The trances in which many of the dancers visited the spirit world to converse with dead relatives and catch glimpses of villages of native Americans living in the old way should be understood as a kind of preliminary confirmation of the prophet's proclamation. Among the Pawnee, the visions of the dancers provided an even more concrete foretaste of the coming cultural restoration by making possible the revival of a number of old ceremonial

53. Dangberg, "Letters," 288.
54. Ibid., 289.
55. A. B. Kehoe, "The Ghost Dance in Saskatchewan," *Plains Anthropologist* 19 (1968):301.
56. Mooney, "Ghost-Dance Religion," 783.

activities that had fallen into disuse because knowledge of their correct performance had been lost.[57] Cures effected during the dances and the stories of various miraculous occurrences attributed to Wovoka would also have performed this function (see further, pages 47–48).

Wovoka's disciples (element 8). Sometimes a prophet may have particularly close associates whom we may call disciples. Such persons are of particular interest to us insofar as they are not simply companions but are directly involved in prophetic activities, for example, in transmitting and preserving what the prophet has said. Such disciples in fact had an important role in the spread of the Ghost Dance doctrine. From early 1889, delegations of Indians traveled to Nevada to visit Wovoka and returned to spread the Dance among the tribes to the east. Of the many who made these trips, some emerged as important disciples, notably Porcupine (Northern Cheyenne), Sitting Bull (not the famous Sioux chief but a Northern Arapaho who, after September 1890, was active in spreading the doctrine among the tribes in Oklahoma), and Short Bull and Kicking Bear (Sioux).

The presence of disciples requires a modification of our basic model of the prophetic process. The message of the prophet may now be transmitted to the people through an intermediary, and occasionally direct revelations to a disciple serve either to supplement the message he received from the prophet (e.g., Short Bull's advancing the time of the millennium) or to authorize the activity of a disciple who had never made the pilgrimage to Nevada (e.g., Bianki, a Kiowa; Frank White and Joseph Carrion, Pawnee).[58]

Figure 2 incorporates these additional elements and at the same time suggests some further complexities in the relationships among actors. For example, the prophet's message *(p)* may be filtered through the disciples before it reaches the people, perhaps already in somewhat

57. Lesser, "Cultural Significance."
58. Mooney ("Ghost-Dance Religion," 788–89) records the hostile speech in which Short Bull announced that because "the whites are interfering so much" he would advance the time of the millennium. This was a time of mounting tension between the dancers and the agents and white residents living on and near the Sioux reservations; within a few weeks the tension led to the sending of troops into the field. We seem to have here another instance of the operation of feedback in the alteration of a prophetic message. Accounts of the others' visions may be found in Mooney, "Ghost-Dance Religion," 909–11 (Bianki); A. Lesser, *The Pawnee Ghost Dance Hand Game,* 60–64, 78–80 (Frank White, Joseph Carrion).

altered form *(p')*; their feedback may follow the same path in reverse, but it might also be addressed directly to the prophet.

The development of the doctrine of the Ghost Dance was also influenced informally by feedback from the participants in the dances. Dancers frequently fell into trances, and their visions gave rise to ghost songs that were used in subsequent dancing. The prophecy initiated by Wovoka and transmitted by his disciples was carried on and developed by the people.

Instead of going back through all the relevant components of the process for each of the major disciples, we will focus in general terms on their development of the doctrine. This focus involves a discussion of the continuity of their message with that of Wovoka, of developments that serve only to amplify what the prophet taught, and of developments that introduce substantive alterations in that teaching. Changes arise in response to the situation in which the disciple operated and the way in which he interpreted what he had originally heard. The focus of our attention will be on Porcupine, Sitting Bull (the Arapaho), Short Bull, and Kicking Bear, the disciples of whose teaching we have the fullest accounts.

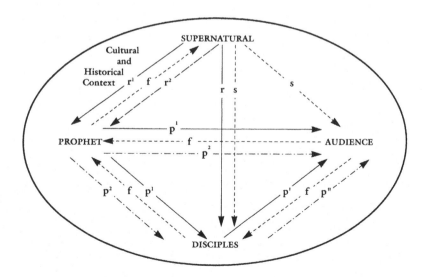

Figure 2

In general, the teaching transmitted by the disciples remained faithful to that of Wovoka as described in Captain Dick's account. However, the additional doctrinal elements that appear in the Southern Cheyenne-Arapaho messiah letter and the Mooney interview show more variation. None of the four disciples refers in the reports we have to Wovoka's claim to be able to control the weather. We must, however, be cautious about such an argument from silence. Both Porcupine and Short Bull are known to have attributed other miraculous deeds to Wovoka, and the weather-control element of the teaching was apparently not out of harmony with their view of him.[59] As noted previously, the ethical admonitions that the messiah letter and Mooney interview attribute to Wovoka show somewhat more variation. Only Porcupine and Short Bull take up this theme. Porcupine mentions specifically only one of the items attributed to the prophet (not to fight) and refers to a second (cooperation with whites) by implication. Short Bull mentions none of the admonitions on the original list but adds three of his own: the Indians are to farm, send their children to school, and follow Wovoka's "example." Because these three also point in the direction of cooperation with the whites and because Short Bull was a militant Ghost Dancer who would have had no reason to invent these admonitions, the conclusion seems reasonable that from the earliest time this element was present in some form in the prophet's teaching. In 1889 and 1890, however, moral preachment would have taken a definite subordinate position to the main apocalyptic focus of the message.[60]

Despite Wovoka's disclaimer to Mooney, the disciples tend to emphasize strongly the connection between the prophet and Jesus claimed in the messiah letter: "Jesus is now upon the earth. He appears

59. W. Z. Park notes that the strongest of Paviotso shamans were reputed to be able to control the weather. This was done not to bring about desired conditions, but "in order to demonstrate their supernatural power"; "Paviotso Shamanism," 108. In this light a report from the agent C. C. Warner concerning Wovoka is interesting: "He obtained his notoriety by telling the Indians that he would invoke the Great Spirit and bring rain (after there had been two years of drouth), and it so happened that his promised invocation was in the commencement of our severe winter of 1889, during which time it stormed almost incessantly from October to April. His success was rapidly spread abroad, and from that time on he has had many followers. Many Indians from distant tribes have been here and are now visiting him, and from eighty to a hundred have been to see him during the past six months"; "Report of Nevada Agency," in *Annual Report of the Bureau of Indian Affairs* (Washington, D.C.: Government Printing Office, 1891), 301.
60. Mair, "Independent Religious Movements," 126–30.

like a cloud."[61] Of particular interest are the subtle differences of interpretation that occur in connection with this element. Porcupine's tone is reverential throughout. He continually refers to Wovoka as the Christ and talks about the brotherhood of "all the whites and Indians." When he talks about the previous coming of the Messiah, his manner is matter-of-fact:

> In the beginning, after God made the earth, they sent me back to teach the people, and when I came back on earth the people were afraid of me and treated me badly. This is what they did to me (showing his scars). I did not try to defend myself. I found my children were bad, so went back to heaven and left them. I told them that in so many hundred years I would come back to see my children. At the end of this time I was sent back to try to teach them. My father told me the earth was getting old and worn out, and the people getting bad, and that I was to renew everything as it used to be, and make it better.[62]

The report of the Sioux delegates who visited Wovoka at the same time as Porcupine contains essentially the same claim about the prophet but in a context and manner decidedly hostile to the whites:

> When the soldiers of the white people chief want to arrest me, I shall stretch out my arms, which will knock them to nothingness, or, if not that, the earth will open and swallow them in. My father commanded me to visit the Indians on a purpose. I have came to the white people first, but they not good. They killed me, and you can see the marks of my wounds on my feet, my hands, and on my back.[63]

We will return to this hostile interpretation by the Sioux.

The main example of a development of the doctrine serving to amplify the image of the prophet and what the prophet taught occurs in reports of Wovoka's acts of power. We have noted that the early reports of his teaching contain a reference to only one item of this sort, the prophet's supposed ability to control the weather. In the accounts of the delegates, however, this motif is greatly heightened. Porcupine claimed that the prophet was in fact the creator of the world, that he could speak all languages, and that he had supernaturally "sent" for the delegates of

61. Mooney, "Ghost-Dance Religion," 781.
62. Ibid., 796.
63. Ibid., 797.

the various distant tribes to visit him.[64] The Sioux delegates reported
that Wovoka appeared to the visitors by descending in a cloud. He
instructed them in how to hunt buffalo so that the slain animal would
miraculously come to life again, and on the journey homeward they
successfully employed this technique. He also miraculously shortened
their journey home by transporting them "a great distance" while they
slept.[65] Such stories about the prophet seem to have become widespread and presumably functioned both to stimulate and maintain
belief in his message.[66]

The Sioux disciples introduced the most substantive alterations in
the prophet's message, and in general these changes lay in the direction
of an attitude of greater hostility toward the whites. We have already
noted their more hostile reading of the Jesus motif, although given the
apocalyptic focus of Wovoka's original message this change would seem
at most an amplification of his teaching. A problem also arises concerning the origin of the ghost shirts, those special garments that were
supposed to make the wearer invulnerable to whites' bullets. Bailey
notes that Wovoka disclaimed all responsibility for the ghost shirts but
suggests that, in light of his sale of shirts to his followers and the magic
"he performed to prove to his followers that he was inviolate and bullet-
proof, Wovoka can scarcely escape blame for the ghost-shirts of the
eastern Sioux."[67] At any rate, apparently only among the Sioux did the
disciples push the use of these shirts and relate that use to the possibility
of open hostilities between whites and native Americans. Thus on
October 31, 1890, Short Bull addressed his followers:

> If the soldiers surround you four deep, three of you, on whom I have put
> holy shirts, will sing a song, which I have taught you, around them, when
> some of them will drop dead. Then the rest will start to run, but their
> horses will sink into the earth. The riders will jump from their horses, but
> they will sink into the earth also. Then you can do as you desire with

64. Ibid., 795–96.
65. Ibid., 797.
66. For other examples, see G. B. Grinnell, "Account of the Northern Cheyenne
Concerning the Messiah Superstition," *JAFL* 4 (1891):66–67; Maus, "The New Indian
Messiah"; W. K. Moorehead, "Ghost-dances in the West," *Illustrated American* 5
(1891):333; Anonymous report, *JAFL* 4 (1891):162. This element of the miraculous is
discussed in chapter 4 below.
67. Bailey, *Wovoka the Indian Messiah*, 215 n. 57, 126–27. Park makes reference to
the supposed invulnerability of the strongest Paviotso shamans. He also reports that
Wovoka was known to be "an excellent doctor for gunshot wounds" in "Paviotso
Shamanism," 107, 109, 113.

them. Now, you must know this, that all the soldiers of that race will be dead. There will be only five thousand of them left living on the earth. My friends and relations, this is straight and true.[68]

Other indications show that the Sioux altered the doctrine in the direction of noncooperation with the whites and even outright hostility toward them. Only the Sioux delegates reported overt threats of hostile action against whites by the prophet himself.[69] Kicking Bear seems also to have counseled active hostility, saying that the bullet-proof ghost shirts meant that the native Americans now had the power to destroy the troops[70] and proclaiming that the whites would no longer be able to make gunpowder and that their remaining stocks would not work against the attacking Indians.[71] Furthermore, a prohibition was made against the use of metal objects in the dance, and the eventual elimination of all white trade goods was anticipated.[72]

Several factors in the historical-cultural situation of those times might have accounted for this hostile turn in the doctrine as it was preached among the Sioux. For a fifteen-year period ending with the Custer battle of 1876, the Sioux had been relatively successful in their military encounters with the whites. Many of the old chiefs, including Red Cloud, Sitting Bull, and Hump, were still alive. The treaty of 1868 had established a great Sioux reservation comprising the whole of the present South Dakota west of the Missouri River, but by 1889 significant portions of this area had been taken over by the whites, including all of the Black Hills and a broad corridor between that area and the eastern part of the territory. In addition the Sioux had a number of specific grievances relating to such matters as cuts in rations, delays in monetary compensations promised in the treaties, crop failures, disease, and boundary disputes. In an appendix on the "Causes of the Outbreak," Mooney presents a collection of documents illustrating these conditions,[73] and a history of the whole period is admirably presented by Utley.[74] One has the impression that for many of the Sioux the white

68. Mooney, "Ghost-Dance Religion," 789.
69. Ibid., 797, quoted above.
70. G. E. Hyde, *A Sioux Chronicle* (Norman: University of Oklahoma Press, 1956), 258.
71. McLaughlin, *My Friend the Indian*, 188.
72. Mooney, "Ghost-Dance Religion," 798, 800.
73. Ibid., 829–42.
74. Utley, *Last Days of the Sioux*.

conquest was not yet a psychological reality and that consequently the
so-called nonprogressive leaders could still command a large following.
On this point the statements by V. T. McGillycuddy, a former agent at
Pine Ridge, and American Horse, one of the so-called progressive
chiefs, are informative.[75]

We may conclude that the Ghost Dance doctrine as it was transmitted by the disciples was not a static entity. Rather, it underwent
shifts in response to feedback from the people and the specific historical
situation in which it was proclaimed. We have observed the development of stories about Wovoka's acts of power, arising at least in part
from the need of believers to have confidence in the power and promises
of the prophet. We also noted the changes introduced by some Sioux,
who found in the dance a vehicle for their more active hostility against
the whites.

Finally, a few words may be said about the transmission of the
doctrine by the people through the creation and use of Ghost Dance
songs. The trances into which dancers fell were a common feature of the
dance ceremonial. Fallen dancers were moved to a safe place, and when
they revived they announced to the people the content of their visions.
Often these visions formed the basis of new ghost songs that were used
in subsequent dancing. Because they are highly individual and short, we
would not expect these songs to provide us with a systematic view of
the doctrine of the dance, but comparison of the main elements found
in them with the doctrinal elements that we have been discussing is
interesting.[76] The two most frequent themes in the songs are the return
of the dead and the restoration of the game, both of which are central to
Wovoka's original teaching. Beyond that, their most striking feature is
the recounting of the old-time activities, particularly games, that the
dancers witnessed during their visionary trips to the spirit world. This
focus on the old way of life—soon to be realized again—is an elaboration of the prophet's message. The visions may therefore be viewed as a
preliminary supernatural confirmation of that message.

75. Mooney, "Ghost-Dance Religion," 831–33, 839–40.
76. Ibid. Mooney records a large number of Ghost Dance songs of the Arapaho,
Cheyenne, Sioux, Kiowa, Caddo, Comanche, and Paiute. Other sources of songs are
L. W. Colby, "The Ghost Songs of the Dakotas," *Proceedings and Collections of the
Nebraska State Historical Society*, series 2, vol. 1, no. 3 (1895); E. G. Eastman, "The Ghost
Dance War and Wounded Knee Massacre of 1890–91," *Nebraska History* 26
(1945):26–42; and Lesser, *The Pawnee Ghost Dance Hand Game*.

Anyone who wishes to study the Ghost Dance of 1890 has a significant body of evidence available. In this material, of course, are numerous perspectives on the dance, which may be seen as an episode in the history of a tribe, of relationships between native Americans and whites, or of the U.S. military. It can be discussed as an example of a millenarian movement or for the contribution it made to a particular tribe's culture. For those interested in examining it as an instance of prophetic activity and comparing it with other such phenomena, the challenge is to arrange the data in a way favorable to the achievement of that goal. Our model has proven to be useful in doing this, and we can observe what appears to be a rather close fit between the data available on the dance and the characteristics delineated in the model.

JEREMIAH

The known public activity of the prophet Jeremiah spans approximately the last forty years of the existence of the Palestinian state of Judah (626–586 B.C.E.).[77] For the century prior to this period, Judah had been an Assyrian vassal state, but by the time Jeremiah appeared on the scene the power of the Assyrians had begun to wane, particularly in the outlying regions of their empire. Under King Josiah (640–609 B.C.E.), Judah began to reassert its independence. Its political influence was extended northward into the Assyrian provinces of Samaria and Galilee, and accompanying this rebellion was a major reform of the Yahweh cult. Based on an old lawbook found during the remodeling of the temple in 622, this reform sought to reassert the traditional form of the covenant relationship between Yahweh and his people.

Although independent, Judah's geographical position placed it in the middle of an international struggle for power that made its situation precarious. Revolts in both Egypt and Babylon had contributed to the weakening of the Assyrian empire, but as the pressure on the Assyrians by Medes and Babylonians became more intense (614–610) Egypt,

---

77. This date has been disputed. W. L. Holladay, for example, has been an advocate of the view that 627/626 B.C.E. is to be understood as the date of Jeremiah's birth, rather than the date he began his prophetic activity; see *Jeremiah 1* (Philadelphia: Fortress Press, 1986), 1–10. I prefer, however, to accept the date as marking the beginning of his prophetic career; see T. W. Overholt, "Some Reflections on the Date of Jeremiah's Call," *CBQ* 33 (1971):165–84; idem, "Jeremiah," in *Harper's Bible Commentary*, ed. J. L. Mays (New York: Harper and Row, 1988).

hopeful of preserving a buffer state between itself and these new threat-
ening powers, came to the aid of its old enemy and joined Assyria in an
abortive attempt to recapture the city of Haran, near the headwaters of
the Euphrates. While Pharaoh Neco was on his way to this rendezvous
in 609, he met and killed Josiah in battle, and on his return from the
Euphrates three months later he deposed Josiah's successor and placed a
Judean of his own choice, Jehoiakim, on the throne in Jerusalem. Four
years later, in 605, the Babylonian king Nebuchadrezzar decisively
defeated the Egyptian army at Carchemish on the Euphrates, and Judah
again found itself squarely between two opposing powers.

    Of course, considerable factionalism arose in Judah over how best
to respond to this situation. During his reign, Jehoiakim and his
supporters among the princes adhered to a pro-Egypt policy and came
into open conflict with Jeremiah.[78] The king eventually revolted against
Nebuchadrezzar, and the result of this action was the capture of Jerusalem and the deportation of people and property to Babylon in 597.
Under Zedekiah, the last king of Judah, the same party dispute continued. The majority of the princes seem to have been solidly pro-
Egyptian, and the proclamations of Jeremiah became explicitly pro-
Babylonian in the sense that he interpreted Nebuchadrezzar's conquest
of Jerusalem as Yahweh's will and instructed the people to be obedient
to their Babylonian overlord (see Jeremiah 27—29). The king wavered
but ultimately threw in with the pro-Egypt group. Judah revolted
again, and Jerusalem was for a second time besieged and captured.
More of the population was exiled, and the city itself was destroyed and
the temple of Yahweh burned. The prophet elected to stay in Judah.
Shortly thereafter he was carried away to Egypt against his will by a
group of fleeing Judeans (see Jeremiah 37—44).

    This series of events presented the participants in them with a
complex political and theological problem. Decisions were required as
to the appropriateness of specific political and military actions, and in
this critical time some looked to the religious traditions of the people

    78. See Jeremiah 26 and 36. In all of this Jeremiah, too, had his supporters in
high places. Note particularly the references to members of the house of Shaphan in Jer.
26:24; 29:3; 36:10–13, 25; 40:5–6; 41:2. See J. A. Wilcoxen, "The Political Background of Jeremiah's Temple Sermon," in *Scripture in History and Theology: Essays in
Honor of J. Coert Rylaarsdam*, ed. A. L. Merrill and T. W. Overholt (Pittsburgh: Pickwick
Press, 1977), 151–66; B. Long, "Social Dimensions of Prophetic Conflict," *Semeia* 21
(1981):30–53.

for guidance. Prophets differed (see Jeremiah 28), however, and no single answer satisfactory to all emerged.

The data in the Book of Jeremiah are particularly well suited to interpretation in terms of our model because by comparison with other prophets in the Hebrew Bible our information about his activity is exceptionally full. In the Book of Jeremiah, extended narratives describe the prophet's activities, and two special categories of material also provide information. The first of these—the prophet's complaints to Yahweh—has been widely recognized and discussed, and it provides us with several specific instances of feedback, both from the people to Jeremiah and from the prophet to Yahweh.[79] The second—a collection of direct quotations from the people—has not received much attention, although James Crenshaw has pointed the way toward using them in a more dynamic description of the prophetic act. In particular he sees mirrored in them a "voice of the people" against which the prophets had to struggle.[80]

This body of direct quotations is remarkable both in size (nearly a hundred instances in Jeremiah as compared to approximately a dozen each in Amos and Hosea) and in distribution (instances occur in approximately eighty percent of the chapters and are scattered fairly evenly through the book). These quotations seem for the most part to

---

79. The usefulness of the complaints for understanding Jeremiah's feelings and the more individual aspects of his activity as a prophet has been seriously challenged by H. Graf Reventlow, who insists on seeing them as products of the prophet's official cultic function as mediator between Yahweh and the people, in *Liturgie und prophetisches Ich bei Jeremia* (Gütersloh: Gütersloher Verlag, 1963). He does not, however, discuss the three complaints that are potentially most damaging to his thesis (18:18–23; 20:7–13, 14–18). R. P. Carroll has also taken the position that the complaints do not give us biographical information about Jeremiah but reveal instead conditions of the Judean exiles projected onto the prophet, in *From Chaos to Covenant: Prophecy in the Book of Jeremiah* (New York: Crossroad, 1981), 123 (cf. 107–30). See also the relevant passages in his commentary *Jeremiah* (Philadelphia: Westminster Press, 1986). Reventlow's position has been criticized by J. Bright ("Jeremiah's Complaints: Liturgy, or Expressions of Personal Distress?" in *Proclamation and Presence*, ed. J. Durham and J. Porter [Atlanta: John Knox Press, 1970], 189–214) and J. Berridge (*Prophet, People, and the Word of Yahweh* [Zurich: EVZ, 1970], 114–83), who with Holladay (*Jeremiah 1*) wish to see the confessions as expressions of personal anguish. In my opinion the confessions can provide us with useful information about Jeremiah's activity. Although their use of the traditional language and form of the lament makes confidence in specific details difficult, the conflict mirrored in them seems entirely realistic; see Overholt, "Jeremiah," in *Harper's Bible Commentary*, esp. the short essay, "Jeremiah's Complaints" (618–19).

80. J. Crenshaw, *Prophetic Conflict* (Berlin: Walter de Gruyter, 1971), 23–48. See also W. J. Horwitz, who argues for using these quotations to help establish the historicity of the text, in "Audience Reaction to Jeremiah," *CBQ* 32 (1970):555–64.

be products of Jeremiah's rhetorical skill and not verbatim records of the speech of others. They may still be used to understand the kind of audience feedback he was receiving. In all probability, they accurately reflect Jeremiah's perceptions of how people were reacting to him; sometimes the reactions were tangible (Jer. 20:1–6; 26) but at other times much less so (11:18–19; 20:7–8).[81]

In applying our model to the interpretation of Jeremiah, we can conveniently combine several of the eight components in such a way as to allow us to focus on the dynamic interaction between the three main actors in the prophetic process. In what follows, then, we will speak of two interactive sequences: one centering on revelation, the other on proclamation.

The revelation-feedback-revelation sequence (elements 1, 4, 5). The conviction that the message of the prophet was based on revelation received from Yahweh is recurrent in the Book of Jeremiah. The superscription to the book as a whole defines the date and duration of Jeremiah's ministry in terms of when the word of Yahweh came to him (Jer. 1:1–3; cf. 25:1–3). In fact, the very first episode we encounter in the book is an account of the experience by which the prophet understood himself to have been called and commissioned as Yahweh's messenger (1:4–10). Furthermore, the call experience seems to be not the only occasion on which the prophet felt he had received a revelation from Yahweh. For example, prophetic utterances are introduced by the formulae: "And Yahweh said to me" (3:6, 11) or "The word of Yahweh came to me saying" (2:1). More importantly, we have recorded for us a number of apparent visionary and/or auditory experiences that, because of their content and context, cannot plausibly be assigned to a single occasion (1:11–12, 13–19; 13:1–11; 18:1–11; 19:1–15; 24:1–10; 31:26; 38:21).[82]

81. See T. W. Overholt, "Jeremiah 2 and the Problem of 'Audience Reaction,'" *CBQ* 41 (1979):262–73.
82. The relative weight as evidence to be assigned to any of the formulae or passages cited in this paragraph, and others that might be added to them, depends in part on one's view of the composition of the Book of Jeremiah. The problems here are great, and opinions differ widely. Three recent commentaries represent the main options on this issue: Carroll, *Jeremiah*; Holladay, *Jeremiah 1*; and W. McKane, *A Critical and Exegetical Commentary on Jeremiah*, vol. 1 (Edinburgh: T. & T. Clark, 1986). See my discussion of these commentaries in "Interpreting Jeremiah," *Religious Studies Review* 14 (1988):330–34. In my opinion, the Book of Jeremiah, although by no means a biography in the modern sense of the term, does provide us with useful information about the prophet.

The communication that took place in Jeremiah's revelatory experiences was not all one-way. Feedback from the prophet to Yahweh begins in the call experience itself with the protest that because of his youth he was not up to the task that was being imposed upon him (Jer. 1:6), and each of the six complaints also contains this element. These complaints focus on the problems Jeremiah had with remaining faithful to his prophetic office and give prominent place to feelings of ill will directed against his personal enemies. The wickedness of his enemies is stressed (12:4; 18:23), as is the unfairness of their continuing to prosper (12:1–2). The demand is made that they be punished by Yahweh (11:20; 12:3b; 15:15; 17:18; 18:21–23). Conversely, Jeremiah asserts his own righteousness and faithfulness to his office (12:3a; 15:16–17; 17:16; 18:20), complains bitterly about the burdens of being a prophet (20:7–9, 14–18), and even accuses Yahweh of acting unfaithfully (15:18; cf. 20:7–9).

We will return to the matter of the people's hostility toward the prophet. Here we need to point out that one factor in all this mutual hostility was the question of the validity of the prophet's revelation and the message based upon it. Jeremiah had announced that disaster would befall the people, not because he took delight in doing so but because he understood that to be the content of his revelation (Jer. 17:16). The people, who would not have been inclined in any case to accept such a judgment, at some point began to subject him to intense ridicule because what he had threatened had failed to occur (17:15; 20:7–8). Evidently Jeremiah also had his doubts about the validity of the revelation (15:18; 20:7), and these doubts were a main element in his feedback to Yahweh. Verses 5:4–5 may be another indication of this process by which the prophet reacted to his understanding of his revelatory experience.

Finally, the complaints also contain two examples of Yahweh's rejoinder to the prophetic feedback (Jer. 12:5–6; 15:19–21). These comments are clearly to be understood as "additional revelations," the burden of which was to confirm the message that the prophet had been proclaiming all along. We can assume that a similar feedback-response series lies behind that portion of the Hananiah episode (Jeremiah 28) in which Jeremiah was temporarily unable to dispute the message of his opponent, but "sometime later" was instructed by Yahweh to return and to condemn Hananiah as a liar (28:13–14). The dynamics of the prophetic process reflected in our model imply that prophets understand alterations in their message to be the result of additional revelations from the god. Insofar as passages in the Book of Jeremiah that seem to hold out hope for the people's future (e.g., 31:31–34, the new covenant, and 32:1–15) reflect the prophet's own message and not the views of an editor, they also imply further revelations.

The proclamation-feedback-proclamation sequence (elements 2, 3, 6). The passages just cited make clear that in large part Jeremiah considered his task as a prophet to be one of proclaiming to the people a message he understood to be based on a series of revelations from Yahweh. In general, his primary message was fairly consistent: because of their actions and the "falsehood" that pervaded their existence, the people were standing on the brink of a great national catastrophe. The message was also well known, and we know that it evoked considerable response. We now turn to this feedback from the people to the prophet.

Jeremiah's message clearly aroused a good deal of hostility. This opposition was sometimes stated in general terms: the prophets are windbags and their words not those of Yahweh (Jer. 5:12–13). More often it represented direct personal attacks on Jeremiah. He was derided because what he proclaimed failed to come to pass (17:15; 20:7–8), and the laments make clear that these attacks represented more than just a casual disagreement, because in some cases they gave rise to threats against his life (11:18–23; 18:18, 22; 20:10). On at least one occasion he was beaten and put into the stocks by a member of the priestly establishment (20:1–6; cf. 29:26–28). Following his temple sermon, the priests, prophets, and people attempted to engineer a death sentence for him (26:7–9). On another occasion the princes attempted to dispose of him by throwing him into an abandoned cistern (38:1–6). We also have references to other predicaments: he was pursued by the agents of an angry king (36:26), accused of treason (37:13–14; 38:1–4), and imprisoned (32:2–3; 37:15–16, 20–21).

Even this list does not exhaust the negative responses to Jeremiah's proclamation. The book abounds in references to prophets whose message, broadly characterized as one of "peace," stands in direct contradiction to that of Jeremiah. The classic example is the conflict with Hananiah described in Jeremiah 28. In several instances people refused outright to obey what he conveyed to them as the will of Yahweh (43:1–7; 44:15–19). On the positive side, we have references to individuals and groups who supported the prophet (26:16–19, 24; 36:13–19; 39:11–14; 40:1–6). On occasion he was sought out by someone who wished to learn Yahweh's will for the current situation (21:1–2; 38:14–16; 42:1–3). Many of these passages contain direct quotations from the people responding to Jeremiah's message.

No doubt about it, the feedback to Jeremiah's proclamation was mixed. We are led directly to the question of the criteria by which the people formed their judgment of his message. The question has been widely discussed under the rubric false prophecy, and this very notion highlights the problem of the nature of prophetic authority, for how could two prophets whose views conflicted with each other represent the same god? The tendency has been to seek more or less absolute criteria—the presence or absence of a prophetic call, the morals of the prophet, or the fulfillment of his predictions—for distinguishing between true prophets and impostors. In evaluating a specific person's activities, several criteria are usually employed simultaneously. Because the situations in which the prophets acted are known to have been fraught with crisis and ambiguity, however, such criteria do not work very well.

Earlier I suggested that a prophet's message could be evaluated by the general criteria that it is sufficiently grounded in cultural and religious traditions and relevant to the current sociopolitical situation. However, two people using these standards would not necessarily come to the same conclusions about what the prophet said. Both Jeremiah and Hananiah had a following, and the followers of each could find some legitimate grounds for believing that "their" prophet's message was faithful to the tradition and relevant to the current historical situation.[83] What is important to notice is the intensity and significance

83. See Crenshaw, *Prophetic Conflict*, on the ambiguities and tensions built into the prophetic situation (1–4), the influence of the "voice of the people" on the prophets (23–38), and the prophets' "desire for success" (65–66). See also T. W. Overholt, *The Threat of Falsehood: A Study in the Theology of the Book of Jeremiah* (London: SCM, 1970) 24–48, 86–104. Comparative data reveal a variety of criteria by which intermediaries have been evaluated, including whether there is a claim to have had a special commission from a deity, stereotypical behavior, a message that conforms to traditional customs and beliefs and is adequate to the specific circumstances, "successful" actions (fulfilled predictions, specific problems resolved, etc.), and whether the prophet is performing useful and acceptable social functions. For a brief discussion see Overholt, "Jeremiah," the short essay, "The problem of 'false' prophecy" (630–31). The texts in Overholt, *Prophecy in Cross-Cultural Perspective*, contain numerous examples of this evaluative process (consult the key to marginal notations, p. 22, and the "Index to Marginal Notations").

of the element of feedback in this segment of the prophetic process. Whatever else may be said, each prophet clearly had his own source of authority and moral support in a group of followers. Each had to defend his claims against those who would disavow them.

Finally, we must ask whether Jeremiah's message was affected by the nature of the feedback he received. Here the data are not so clear, but some tentative suggestions may be offered.[84] Recall again the dispute between Hananiah and Jeremiah. Contrary to what Jeremiah had been saying, Hananiah proclaimed that within two years Yahweh would break the power of the king of Babylon and bring about the return of the Judean captives from exile (Jer. 28:2–4). Jeremiah's response was that, although such an occurrence was desirable, Hananiah's message had broken with the tradition of prophecies of doom and could therefore be judged valid only if it were actually fulfilled (28:5–9). A criterion of judgment appears to have been introduced here, but Hananiah was not deterred by it. Also note that when Jeremiah himself later returned to resolve the conflict this criterion played no part in what he said. Hananiah then reasserted his position and emphasized his conviction by breaking the symbolic yoke bars that Jeremiah had been carrying on his neck. At this point Jeremiah "went his way" (v. 11), returning only "sometime later" (v. 12) to reassert his own message and condemn Hananiah.

The striking point here is the pause. Although the message of Jeremiah apparently did not change, he was for a period stymied and forced to retreat for some reconsideration and/or renewal of his conviction. The discussion of the prophet's feedback to Yahweh provides other indications that he resisted the kind of message he felt called upon to proclaim. Therefore, we can reasonably conclude that the intensity of the negative feedback he experienced caused him, at the very least, to pause and reconsider both the content of what he said and even his own continuance in the prophetic office (see Jer. 20:9).

---

84. Although prophets' messages may undergo certain alterations as a result of feedback from their audiences, such change need not necessarily occur. Jeremiah's preoccupation with what the people said indicates a certain need on his part to take their responses seriously. The evidence suggests that this feedback had an effect on him personally (discouragement, doubts about the plausibility of his own message, hopes that the message of his opponents was plausible in 28:6, etc.) but caused no major changes in his message.

Little can be said of the two remaining elements in the model. No clear examples of supernatural confirmation (element 7) occur in Jeremiah. In fact, Jer. 20:7–8 and 44:16–19 seem to echo disconfirming experiences. The absence of this element may be due in part to the preoccupation of the Book of Jeremiah with the negative reactions of the prophet's audience to him.

Finally, we know that Jeremiah had at least one disciple (element 8), Baruch the son of Neriah. He wrote down oracles at Jeremiah's dictation and once carried the resulting scroll to the temple on the prophet's behalf, there reading it to an assembled group of nobles (Jeremiah 36). Little else is known about Baruch (see 32:9–16; 43:1–7).

Postponing for the moment further discussion of the model itself, we move directly to another case and focus our discussion on the same interactive sequences used in our discussion of Jeremiah.

HANDSOME LAKE

The Seneca tribe to which the prophet Handsome Lake belonged had been a member of the famed Iroquois League, a closely knit confederation of tribes whose origin predates the arrival of Columbus.[85] During much of the eighteenth century, through a system of playing off the British against the French, this confederation was able both to maintain its territory and security and to benefit from the material goods of European culture. All that ended during the American Revolution. Neutrality was abandoned, and the confederacy split. Most of the Iroquois directed their loyalty to the British. The ultimate result was that nearly all of their villages from the Mohawk River to the Ohio country were destroyed and they were cut off from their allies to the west, who established their own confederacy separate from the Iroquois.

The reservation system that was gradually imposed upon the Iroquois during the last decades of the century created what Anthony F. C. Wallace calls "slums in the wilderness, where no traditional Indian

---

85. This brief historical sketch depends mainly on Wallace, *Death and Rebirth of the Seneca,* esp. 21–236. I first presented material on Handsome Lake in "Prophecy: The Problem of Cross-Cultural Comparison," *Semeia* 21 (1982):55–78.

culture could long survive and where only the least useful aspects of white culture could easily penetrate."[86] The Cornplanter grant on the Allegheny River in northern Pennsylvania was somewhat unusual among the reservations because of its relative isolation from white settlement. Although the influences of European material culture were considerable, many of the old social and political customs survived, and the annual cycle of traditional religious ceremonials was still observed. There Handsome Lake, Cornplanter's half-brother, resided. Of course, such isolation could only be relative, and the social pathologies that had been making inroads among the Iroquois for years were found also in Cornplanter's town. Excessive consumption of alcohol was a particularly serious problem.[87]

As in the case of Judah in Jeremiah's day, no unanimity of opinion existed among the Iroquois as to how to confront the problems inherent in their historical and cultural situation. Each reservation had its factions, the so-called progessives "advocating the assimilation of white culture" and the conservatives "the preservation of Indian ways."[88] Cornplanter may be reckoned with the former group, and by the time of Handsome Lake's vision his village had already come under the influence of Quaker missionaries. These missionaries were nondogmatic in their approach to religion and chose to concentrate on offering positive assistance to the Cornplanter Seneca in such practical areas as farming, carpentry, and education. By May of 1799 they had also persuaded the council to ban the use of whiskey in the village.[89]

86. Wallace, *Death and Rebirth of the Seneca*, 184.

87. The followers of Handsome Lake recounted a legend of how the "evil one" enticed an unsuspecting young European to bring a bundle of "five things" (a flask of rum, a pack of playing cards, some coins, a violin, and a decaying leg bone) across the ocean to the native Americans. This gift resulted in great misery and made necessary the "Good Message," or Gaiwiio; A. C. Parker, *The Code of Handsome Lake, the Seneca Prophet* (Albany, N.Y.: State Museum, 1913), 16–19. On alcohol abuse at Cornplanter's village, see ibid., 20–22; and Wallace, *Death and Rebirth of the Seneca*, 193–94, 228–36.

88. Wallace, *Death and Rebirth of the Seneca*, 202; R. F. Berkhofer, "Faith and Factionalism among the Seneca," *Ethnohistory* 12 (1965):99–112.

89. M. H. Deardorff, "The Religion of Handsome Lake: Its Origin and Development," in *Symposium on Local Diversity in Iroquois Culture*, BBAE 149, ed. W. N. Fenton (Washington, D.C.: Government Printing Office, 1951), 79–107; Wallace, *Death and Rebirth of the Seneca*, 221–36. Selections from the Code of Handsome Lake (the Gaiwiio) may be found in Overholt, *Prophecy in Cross-Cultural Perspective*, 101–22. In a somewhat different vein, R. Helms offers an interesting literary interpretation of the code; he views it as a "literary prophet-surrogate," the structure of which mirrors both the stages of Handsome Lake's career and the "form of the New Year festival," during which it is still recited; "'The Code of Handsome Lake': A Literary Study of Prophecy," *Genre* 4 (1971):18–38.

The revelation-feedback-revelation sequence (elements 1, 4, 5). The Gaiwiio ("Good Message"), a record of Handsome Lake's teachings that is still in use among followers of the Longhouse way,[90] begins by describing a "time of troubles" in Cornplanter village. The scene is at first communitywide. A party of native Americans had just returned from Pittsburgh, where they had traded skins and game for whiskey. A wild drinking party followed in which village life was disrupted and some families were forced to moved away for safety. The focus then shifts to a single sick man, who was held in the grip of "some strong power" and feared that he might die. Realizing that the cause of his illness was whiskey, he resolved never to use it again. Afraid that he would not have the strength to do this, he prayed to the "Great Ruler" and began to be confident that his prayer had been heard and he would live. The sick man was Handsome Lake.[91]

On June 17, 1799, the sick man appeared to die. His body was prepared for burial and relatives summoned, but he revived and reported he had had a vision of three messengers who had been sent to reveal to him the Creator's will and instruct him to carry it to the people. The vision also contained a threat, for Handsome Lake was shown the steaming grave of a man who had formerly been commissioned "to proclaim that message to the world" but had "refused to obey." On August 7 of the same year, the prophet received his second revelation in which he was guided on a journey through heaven and hell and given moral instruction. A third revelation occurred on February 5, 1800. Each of these visions was reported and discussed in a council of the people.[92]

Several passages in the Gaiwiio show that Handsome Lake expected to receive further revelations. In his initial vision the three messengers promised, "We shall continually reveal things unto you," and this promise was repeated in 1809 when in the midst of a personal crisis the messengers came to the prophet and said, "We understand your thoughts. We will visit you more frequently and converse with

90. See A. A. Shimony, *Conservatism among the Iroquois at the Six Nations Reserve* (New Haven, Conn.: Yale University Press, 1961).

91. Parker, *The Code of Handsome Lake*, 20–22.

92. This chronology was reconstructed by Wallace on the basis of the Simmons journal and other sources. The present form of the code as represented in Parker has some of the revelations out of context. See Wallace, *Death and Rebirth of the Seneca*, 359–60, n. 5.

you."[93] Although the present form of the Gaiwiio makes dating specific revelations difficult, some internal evidence suggests such a continuing sequence. Most conspicuous are the place names. The Gaiwiio specifically sets the initial vision in Cornplanter's village, but subsequent sections are said to derive from Cold Spring, Tonawanda, and Onondaga (all in New York).[94] These localities correspond to known periods of the prophet's activity. Furthermore, Wallace links at least four sections of the code to specific, dateable events: a derogatory reference to Chief Red Jacket arising out of a dispute over the sale of reservation land in 1801, a prophecy intended to discourage Iroquois participation in the "war in the west" (1811), and a composite section mentioning the people's reviling of Handsome Lake and his meeting with the Spirit of the Corn, which seems to mirror events that took place in the years 1809 and 1815.[95] The final sections of the code deal with the revelations and events immediately preceding the prophet's death, which occurred on August 10, 1815, at Onondaga.[96] These revelations clearly did not simply repeat what had gone before. They arose out of Handsome Lake's attempt to deal with new situations. He doubtless saw them to be divine responses to his own quest for a solution.

   The proclamation-feedback-proclamation sequence (elements 2, 3, 6). A summary of Handsome Lake's proclamation to the Iroquois has come down to us in the Gaiwiio. This narrative begins with an account of an episode of drunkenness and destruction in Cornplanter's village and of the prophet's sickness, death, and resurrection. In connection with the resurrection, the divine messengers revealed to Handsome Lake the four great wrongs by which "men spoil the laws the Great Ruler has made and thereby make him angry": drinking whiskey, using witchcraft, using "compelling charms," and practicing abortion. In the remaining sections of the Gaiwiio, considerable space is given to positive commands relating to social behavior (gossip, drunkenness, sharing, mourning customs, etc.), family life (the care of children, husband-wife relationships, the care of elders), and religion (the medi-

---

   93. Parker, *The Code of Handsome Lake*, 25, 47; Wallace, *Death and Rebirth of the Seneca*, 293–94.
   94. Parker, *The Code of Handsome Lake*, 20, 46, 47, 57, 60–62, 76–80.
   95. Ibid., 68, 65–66, 47; Wallace, *Death and Rebirth of the Seneca*, 260, 293–94, 318.
   96. Ibid., 278; cf. 239–302.

cine societies were ordered to disband, but a number of the traditional ceremonies are specifically sanctioned and regulated). In addition, the code deals in several places with the relationship between native Americans and whites (agriculture, schooling, and the Creator's protection of his people against extermination by the whites) and with the status of the prophet (disbelief is said to be due to the operation of an evil spirit and will be punished). A number of these themes are reinforced in the sections recounting the second revelation (the "sky journey"), where Handsome Lake witnessed the suffering of a variety of sinners (drunkard, wifebeater, gambler, etc.) in the house of the "punisher." Finally, the narrative expresses the apocalyptic themes of the sin of the world and the world's end and renewal.

Wallace understands the preaching of Handsome Lake to fall into two distinct phases. The first, covering the years 1799 to 1801, was characterized by an "apocalyptic gospel" in which the people were summoned to repentance and the recurring themes were world destruction, sin, and salvation. The second phase began in 1801 and featured a "social gospel" in which the main values that were stressed were "temperance, peace and unity, land retention, acculturation, and a revised domestic morality."[97]

As in the case of Jeremiah, the response to this message was mixed. In the early years he was able to exercise both political and religious power, and the council at Buffalo Creek in 1801 prohibited the use of liquor and appointed him "High Priest, and principal Sachem in all things Civil and Religious." Over the next few years, however, his political influence declined. In 1807 the Iroquois confederacy was reorganized and the great council fire established at Buffalo Creek, where one of the prophet's chief rivals, Red Jacket, was influential. Handsome Lake and Cornplanter also quarreled, and factions developed in the Allegheny band that caused the prophet to move out and locate first at Cold Spring and later at Tonawanda. Nevertheless, his religious influence remained strong. Preaching his gospel and winning converts, he made an annual circuit of visitations to other reservations.[98] As Wallace describes it,

> These conversions were not casual matters. The Indians traversed the same mystic path to Gaiwiio as white converts to Christianity; the

97. Parker, *The Code of Handsome Lake*, 76–80.
98. Wallace, *Death and Rebirth of the Seneca*, 260–61, 285–302.

converts retained an intense devotion to the prophet who gave them strength to achieve salvation. "One of the Onondagas, when asked why they did not leave their drunken habits before, since they were often urged to do it, and saw the ruinous consequences of such conduct replied, they had no power; but when the Great Spirit forbid such conduct by their prophet, he gave them the power to comply with their request."[99]

What one notices about the Gaiwiio is how directly it spoke to the situation that plagued the Iroquois of Handsome Lake's day. Addressing a people debauched and demoralized by contact with white culture and the loss of their own traditional ways, the Gaiwiio accused them of wrongdoing[100] and stressed evils disruptive of harmonious community life (strong drink, witchcraft, charms, and abortion).[101] In its commandments great emphasis was placed on the strengthening of family relationships and the regulation of social behavior. In response to the growing influence of white culture, it included explicit approval of farming, house building, animal husbandry, and, to a limited extent, education "in English schools."[102]

In real life, elements of this message evoked a negative response and caused the prophet trouble, particularly his determined attacks against witchcraft and supposed witch-inspired conspiracies. Reaction to the execution of one witch in 1809 forced him to leave Cold Spring, a situation reflected in the Gaiwiio:

> Now it was that when the people reviled me, the proclaimer of the prophecy, the impression came to me that it would be well to depart and go to Tonawanda. In that place I had relatives and friends and thought that my bones might find a resting place there.[103]

The Gaiwiio spoke to the current situation by advocating such important cultural innovations as the involvement of men in farm labor, limited acceptance of white education, and the dissolution of the totem animal societies. For all that, however, the Gaiwiio made sense in light of the traditions of the past. Social solidarity was stressed in the ethical

---

99. Ibid., 301; quoting from the *Evangelical Intelligencer* 1 (1807).
100. For example, "The Creator is sad because of the sins of the beings that he created. He ordained that mankind should live as social beings in communities,"; Parker, *The Code of Handsome Lake*, 36.
101. Ibid., 27–30.
102. Ibid., 38.
103. Ibid., 47; see Wallace, *Death and Rebirth of the Seneca*, 254–62, 291–94.

commandments of the code, and in particular the old religious values and ceremonies were for the most part retained. Its major new religious concept, the notion of judgment and afterlife in heaven or hell, was compatible with the old beliefs and was introduced "to insure the dedication of the people to conservative ritual." Handsome Lake "was in his own eyes as the messenger of God, necessarily the defender of the faith."[104] As Parker puts it, "Handsome Lake sought to destroy the ancient folk-ways of the people and to substitute a new system, *built of course upon the framework of the old*."[105] Eventually, a myth even developed to account for the origin of the conditions that made the Gaiwiio necessary and fix its place in the overall order of things.[106]

Feedback from the people to the prophet is clearly important both because of its potential for helping to shape the prophet's message and because their acceptance forms one of the bases of his prophetic authority. That the message of Handsome Lake gained such wide acceptance among the Iroquois in his own day would seem to be due largely to the skill with which he used the old traditions of the people in addressing himself to the crucial problems of the present. Only after his death (1815), when some of the traditional Iroquois leaders sought a way to counter the threats to community order posed by both sectarian Christians and disruptive nativists, did they call upon the memory of Handsome Lake in attempting to define the form and spirit of the old religion. At the religious council at Tonawanda in the summer of 1818, John Sky repeated a version of Handsome Lake's teaching and a minor prophet recounted a vision of confirming it. Similar incidents occurred over the next two decades. By the 1840s the text of the code was fixed. To this day it continues to be an important force in Iroquois life.[107]

Supernatural confirmation (element 7). In discussing specific instances of prophecy, we are always dependent upon the vicissitudes of historical reporting for our information. This dependence is especially evident in the case of "supernatural confirmation." We are dealing here largely with belief based upon circulating reports of individual experiences of a "supernatural" character; these pious tales easily escape the

---

104. Wallace, *Death and Rebirth of the Seneca*, 318; cf. 251–54, 315–18.
105. Parker, *The Code of Handsome Lake*, 114 (emphasis added).
106. See n. 87.
107. Wallace, *Death and Rebirth of the Seneca*, 330–37.

attention of the chroniclers of prophetic movements. Nevertheless, enough examples are available to suggest that this element could be important in the people's response to a prophet. Faith in Wovoka, the prophet of the Ghost Dance of 1890, was certainly enhanced by native Americans who returned from visits to his camp with tales of how he could control the weather and miraculously shorten the homeward journey of those who made the long trip from the northern Plains to western Nevada to visit him. In the case of Handsome Lake, the same dynamics can be seen at work in the Onondagas crediting the Great Spirit with giving them the power to abstain from alcohol and follow the Gaiwiio, as well as in the visions of other prophets confirming his message.

SOME REFLECTIONS

In this chapter I have attempted to illustrate the application of my model of the prophetic process by means of three case studies. All of these figures—Wovoka, Jeremiah, and Handsome Lake—have been called *prophet* by those who have studied them. Still, words can be slippery. We want to know to what kind of activity the term *prophet* refers and whether sufficient similarity exists among the three cases to warrant its application to all of them. Are all three prophets?

I have approached this problem by using a specific model of the prophetic process. The discussion has shown, I believe, that the data available about these three figures fit the model well; the three really are comparable. We can therefore say that the model works cross-culturally: it provides us with a tool for comparing the activity of intermediaries that is not unduly prejudiced by the obvious differences in their historical and cultural situations.

This result is important in several respects. In the first place, as we have noted, the processes of interaction that lie at the heart of prophetic activity have for the most part not been given their due by students of prophetic movements. Second, adopting this view of prophecy may enable us to gain perspective on certain social realities that are important to the functioning of prophecy, for example, the nature of prophetic authority, the nature and function of prophetic acts of power or miracles, and the nature of the situation in which the prophet operates (see chapter 4). Third, my model enables us to increase vastly the scope of our perception of what constitutes prophecy. Not only biblical prophets and founders of major movements of cultural renewal but also widespread institutionalized roles such as shaman and spirit medium share these characteristics. Fourth and finally, this expansion of scope extends our comparative base and enables us to be more confident in our understanding of the social dynamics of prophecy even in cases where the data are sketchy. If in such instances our model cannot generate "facts," then at the least it may make us more aware of the presence of theological or cultural veils in our sources and allow us to make well-educated guesses about what lay behind them.

I now want to bring these reflections to a close by posing a question. According to the Gospel of Mark, Jesus once asked his disciples about the people's view of his identity. The early to middle first century C.E. was characterized by social, economic, and political crisis, and eschatological expectation was intense. Leaders of several types— bandits, "kings," prophets—arose among the Jews in response to this situation.[108] In what way did the people of those times understand Jesus? The disciples responded that some thought he was John the Baptist, others Elijah, and still others "one of the prophets" (8:28; cf. 6:15). In another place the evangelist Mark has Jesus identify himself, at least implicitly, as a prophet (6:4). I do not wish to downplay the critical problems connected with assessing the historical accuracy of Mark's and the other Gospels' constructions of Jesus' life and of the reaction of his audiences to him. Nevertheless, on the basis of Mark's account, an interesting question might be what characteristics Jesus had that made *prophet* a natural designation, especially in a historical setting in which the conviction that he was a unique savior was not yet widespread.

The probable answer would seem to be that, whatever else he may have been, Jesus conformed to a cultural role identified by the term *prophet*. The role models at hand were, of course, the prophets of the Hebrew Bible, as Mark 8:28 makes clear. We might also wonder what about his activity suggested this identification. Precisely, I should think, those characteristics elaborated by our model: Jesus had an interaction with God that motivated an interaction with the people. Jesus' teaching

108. See R. A. Horsley and J. S. Hanson, *Bandits, Prophets, and Messiahs: Popular Movements in the Time of Jesus* (Minneapolis: Winston, 1985).

was experienced by members of his audience as authoritative (2:22), and this authority was confirmed in the minds of the people by his powerful acts.[109] Whatever else we may say about him, clearly Jesus functioned among his contemporaries as a prophet.

So in the search for prophets, our model encourages us to cast a rather wide net. In many societies over a wide range of times and places, human beings have been thought capable of interacting with the supernatural. What we have been calling *prophecy* is one type of this interaction and a rather widespread one at that. Although prophecy exists in many variations, nonetheless a similarity underlies all kinds of prophets.

---

109. Cf. the discussion of Jesus' prophetic role in D. E. Aune, *Prophecy in Early Christianity and the Ancient Mediterranean World* (Grand Rapids: Eerdmans, 1983), 153–69.

4

Features of
the Prophetic Process

The comparative point of view on prophecy as a social process has implications for the way we understand certain specific relationships, activities, and circumstances that are part of an intermediary's role. Here I discuss three of these: the intermediary's authority, miracles, and the kind of situations that elicit prophetic activity.

COMMANDING THE PROPHETS: THE NATURE
OF PROPHETIC AUTHORITY

The traditional answer to the question of the source of a prophet's authority is no doubt the simple assertion, "God."[1] The divine revelation prophets claim is, of course, important to their self-understanding (cf. Amos 3:8) and can be cited to justify their utterances (Jer. 26:12–15) and to condemn their opponents (Jer. 28:15–16). It is also an important element in the people's understanding of prophets. However, the structure of interrelationships specified in our model of the prophetic process suggests that the source of prophets' power over others is not exclusively their presumed contact with the supernatural world. Despite revelatory experiences, intermediaries cannot effectively exercise their roles unless at least some of their audience responds positively.

1. In common usage the word *authority* often refers to the right or power to enforce laws and exact obedience or to a person or group invested with such, but it has other connotations relevant to the argument of this section, namely, the power to influence and persuade and the claim that something should be accepted or believed. This section incorporates material from my "Commanding the Prophets: Amos and the Problem of Prophetic Authority," *CBQ* 41 (1979):517–32.

The model suggests that the authority of intermediaries has two aspects. On the one hand, the prophet makes the claim that the deity has authorized the proclamation of a certain message. The basis of this claim is usually a religious experience that is private and therefore essentially intangible and unverifiable by the members of the audience, who nevertheless assume that genuine prophets will have had such an experience.[2] Direct contact with a deity seems to be regarded as an absolutely crucial element in the constitution of a given occurrence of prophecy not only in ancient Israel but also in other cultures. On the other hand, prophets cannot be effective and cannot function as intermediaries unless the people acknowledge their claim to authority, and the social reality of prophecy depends upon this act. Members of an audience are free to choose whom they follow.[3]

To speak of authority in terms of acceptance is to acknowledge that the audience judges every instance of prophetic activity on the basis of certain tangible marks; that is to say, it knows in general what to expect of its intermediaries. Put differently, a stereotypical conception of what constitutes authentic prophetic behavior operates in each situation. To revert to the examples given at the beginning of this book, the participants at an Ojibwa shaking tent ceremony knew what spirits

2. Sometimes the alleged reception of revelation is accompanied by behavior that can be observed. For example, J. Mooney reports of Wovoka's "great revelation" that during an eclipse of the sun "he fell asleep in the daytime and was taken up to the other world. Here he saw God, with all the people who had died long ago engaged in their oldtime sports and occupations, all happy and forever young"; "The Ghost-Dance Religion and the Sioux Outbreak of 1890," *ARBAE* 14 (Washington, D.C.: Government Printing Office, 1896), 771. Wovoka's "sleeping" was behavior that was over the years witnessed by many. Porcupine, a Cheyenne who visited Wovoka in Nevada late in 1889, recounts that the assembled people "danced all that night, the Christ [i.e., Wovoka] lying down beside us apparently dead" (ibid., 795). Similarly, during the reception of his initial vision, Handsome Lake lay in a deathlike trance; A. C. Parker, *The Code of Handsome Lake the Seneca Prophet* (Albany, N.Y.: State Museum, 1913), 20–30. From the observer's viewpoint, however, such behavior is at best circumstantial evidence with respect to the existence of a communication from a deity and reveals nothing at all about its content.

3. Thus Burke Long: "The authority of a prophet was a vulnerable, shifting social reality—closely tied to acceptance and belief"; "Prophetic Authority as Social Reality," in *Canon and Authority*, ed. G. W. Coats and B. O. Long (Philadelphia: Fortress Press, 1977), 19. Similarly, R. Wilson: "Intermediaries do not operate in a vacuum. They are integral parts of their societies and cannot exist without social guidance and support"; *Prophecy and Society in Ancient Israel* (Philadelphia: Fortress Press, 1980), 51. At the level of communication theory, acknowledging of authority (or of some other relationship), whether conscious or unconscious, can be said to be part of every act of communication; see Paul Watzlawick, et al., "Some Tentative Axioms of Communication," in *Social Psychology and Everyday Life*, ed. B. J. Franklin and F. J. Kohout (New York: McKay, 1973), 195–96.

might be summoned and what type of response and assistance could be expected from each. Although the shamanic performance witnessed by Rasmussen no doubt contained novel elements, nevertheless the general pattern of possession behavior was familiar to all the villagers who witnessed it.

At the level of what is said, one mark of prophetic authority is the ability to clarify and articulate what audience members themselves have begun to feel about their particular situation: that this sickness is the result of witchcraft or the patient's (or some other person's) own misdeeds, this communal misfortune is the sign of a god's displeasure, and the like. Prophetic utterances are experienced as having explanatory power. Referring to millenarian movements, Kenelm Burridge says that the task of the prophet is to organize and articulate a new set of assumptions that suggests a way to make sense of the chaos of the present situation. In doing so, he concentrates in himself the people's own probings, and his revelation usually "echoes the theorizing and experimentation that has gone before."[4]

The people choose their prophets; that is, they attribute authority to them, because they perceive in the proclamation continuity with the cultural traditions sufficient to make what they say intelligible and at the same time innovations sufficient to offer the possibility of a new interpretation that will bring order out of what is perceived as chaos. Thus, another closely related mark of prophetic authority is the effectiveness, real or imagined, that seems to characterize the intermediary's activities. This effectiveness is perhaps most often experienced in the form of rhetorical skill (to his followers the prophet's message makes sense out of the current crisis situation), but marvelous acts, including instances of fulfilled prophecy, may also play a role.[5] Such seemingly supernatural occurrences help to confirm the authenticity of the prophet. They are accounted for in the model under the rubric supernatural confirmation and are dealt with in more detail later in this chapter.

From the point of view of audience reaction, then, the general criterion for the attribution of authority to prophets might be expressed as perceived effectiveness. The hearers do not by their act of attributing authority to prophets confer powers on them because, from one point

4. Burridge, *New Heaven New Earth* (New York: Schocken Books, 1969), 11–14, 111.
    5. See Long, "Prophetic Authority as Social Reality," 13–16.

of view, the claim to supernatural designation means that they already have, or are perceived to have, these powers. What they do, in effect, is confirm them in their role. The audience's affirmative response, necessary for intermediaries to exercise their role, is an act of commitment based on its recognition of that power. Although some positive response to their activity is necessary for prophets to perform their role, however, large numbers of supporters are not. James Crenshaw[6] has suggested about the biblical prophets that conflict with perhaps the great majority of those who heard them (even other prophets) was "inevitable" and that on the whole they had little impact upon their contemporaries. That they were accepted by some of those who heard them, however, is shown both by references to specific supporters (e.g., Isaiah's mention of his disciples, 8:16; the aid Jeremiah received from various members of the house of Shaphan, 26:24; 36) and by the very fact that their utterances were preserved, collected, and eventually committed to writing.

Perhaps one of the most striking examples of this role of the people is the case of Yali, a native leader in post-World War II New Guinea, of whom more will be said later in this chapter.

As a specific illustration of the problem I have been discussing, I now want to take up the following question: What was the authority by which Amos carried out his function as a prophet? At first glance the answer seems apparent, for in the account of his confrontation with the priest Amaziah at Bethel he is made to say, "Yahweh took me from behind the flock, and Yahweh said to me, 'Go, prophesy to my people Israel'" (7:15). That he considered himself to have been charged with the responsibility of delivering Yahweh's words to the people is further indicated by his frequent use of the formula "Thus says Yahweh" to introduce oracles (e.g., 1:3, 6; 2:6; 3:12; 7:17). In addition, the book even contains a statement of "theory" concerning Yahweh's relationship to the prophets:

> The lion has roared,
>   who will not be afraid?
> The Lord Yahweh has spoken,
>   who will not prophesy? (3:8)

To rest content with this answer, however, would be to overlook certain complications. For one thing, it is a theological answer and does

6. J. Crenshaw, *Prophetic Conflict* (Berlin: Walter de Gruyter, 1971).

not illuminate the social setting in which the prophet functioned. The effect is to define all those who do not respond positively to the prophet's message as at best callous or indifferent and at worst apostate. In turn we are left with the puzzle of trying to define the nature of "false" prophecy and explain the fact that, as Crenshaw has reminded us, the preaching of the prophets seems to have had relatively little positive impact on the behavior of those who heard them.[7]

Furthermore, passages within the Book of Amos point to a social component in the authorization of the prophet. According to Amos 2:11–12, Yahweh raised up prophets among the Israelites, but the people "commanded [them], saying, 'you shall not prophesy.'" In his confrontation with the priest Amaziah, Amos is told, "Oh seer, go, flee to the land of Judah and eat bread there and prophesy there, but do not continue to prophesy in Bethel, for it is the sanctuary of the king, and it is the house of the kingdom" (7:12–13). In both instances the prophets' opponents are quoted directly, and we see reflected public reaction against what the prophets are saying. The clear implication is that, sociologically speaking, such opposition could effectively deter the operation of prophecy by denying prophets the opportunity to speak and/or refusing to acknowledge their words as authoritative if they did.

These passages from Amos suggest that the authority prophets enjoyed in their public activity stemmed from two sources: (1) revelation from Yahweh and (2) acknowledgment within a particular social context by some segment of their audience. In arguing that prophetic authority does in fact have this double base, I first touch on the matter of the "social location" of Amos's activity and then move to an examination of 2:11–12 and 7:12–13. Finally, I take note of some comparative materials that may help us view this problem in a wider perspective.

The Social Location of
Amos's Prophecy

To raise the question of the social location of prophecy is to inquire after the particular cultural settings in which prophetic acts occur. The assumption is that these social contexts are likely to have some noticeable effects upon the functioning of the prophet. The phrase itself was used by the sociologist Peter Berger[8] in a study of

7. Ibid., 91–109.
8. P. Berger, "Charisma and Religious Innovation: The Social Location of Israelite Prophecy," *American Sociological Review* 28 (1963):940–50.

Israelite prophecy, and recently Robert Wilson[9] has examined the whole topic in a more comprehensive way.

The social location of Amos's prophetic activity has frequently been thought to be the cult, and Ernst Würthwein's early statement of this position is of particular interest.[10] Simply put, his thesis is that Amos began his prophetic career as a nābî[11] and ended it as a prophet of doom. The call to be a nābî, he tells us, is a call to an office like that of king, priest, or wise man, in which a fixed function—and not the specific tasks or attitudes of a given individual—is central. As a nābî, Amos's function would have been to undergird the welfare of the nation through acts of intercession (cf. 7:2, 5) and proclamations about the future (like the oracles against the nations in chapters 1—2). According to Würthwein, the series of visions recorded in Amos 7—9 step by step and against his wishes separated the prophet from his task of intercession and prepared him to be a prophet of doom. The assumption is that "one of the most important distinctions between nĕbî'îm and classical prophets lies in this bond to the function of the office and not in a personal commission." Thus, only when Amos spoke in a fashion "other than was expected from his office" was he banned from Bethel.[12] In the visions, Yahweh had revealed a new future to Amos, and this new knowledge did not cause him to stop thinking of himself as a prophet. For those who heard him, however, the break was clear. In their eyes, such a new message could not appear within the framework of an old office, and as a result Amos could no longer be acknowledged as a nābî in Bethel. In a word, Amos came under fire because he transgressed the expectations attached to the social role in which he was functioning.[13]

9. Wilson, *Prophecy and Society.*
10. E. Würthwein, "Amos-Studien," *ZAW* 62 (1950):10–52.
11. Würthwein (ibid., 24–28) uses *nābî* to designate a prophet with official ties to the religious establishment whose main function was the proclamation of "peace" in the broad sense of national welfare.
12. Ibid., 27–28.
13. Many others have assumed some form of connection between Amos and the cultic establishment. W. Brueggemann ("Amos 4:4–13 and Israel's Covenant Worship," *VT* 15 [1965]:1–15), J. Priest ("The Covenant of Brothers," *JBL* 84 [1966]:400–406), A. S. Kapelrud ("New Ideas in Amos," *VTSup* 15 [1966]:193–206), M. Fishbane ("The Treaty Background of Amos 1:11 and Related Matters," *JBL* 89 [1970]:313–18; "Additional Remarks on RHMYW," *JBL* 91 [1972]:391–93), and R. Coote ("Amos 1:11 RHMYW," *JBL* 90 [1971]:206–8) have all called attention to the presence of covenant language within the oracles. A. Bentzen ("The Ritual Background of Amos 1:2—2:16," *OTS* 8 [1950]:85–99), G. Farr ("The Language of Amos, Popular or Cultic?" *VT* 16 [1966]:312–24), J. Crenshaw ("The Influence of the Wise upon Amos," *ZAW* 79

The main alternative to the cultic view of the social location of Amos's prophetic activity centers on his presumed connections with the wisdom tradition. This idea was proposed by Samuel Terrien[14] and subsequently elaborated by Hans Walter Wolff,[15] whose interpretation is consciously directed against the view that Amos was connected in any formal way with the cult. Wolff's strategy is to take literally Amos's declaration that "Yahweh took me from behind the flock" (7:15) and to employ literary criticism to eliminate references to the old election traditions. This strategy allows him to argue that the characteristic themes of Amos's message (the "right" way, a positive attitude toward other nations, "justice and righteousness," concern for the poor and needy, warnings against extravagant life styles, etc.) reveal an orientation like that of a clan-based wisdom tradition.

Both of these views about Amos's social location have been criticized; neither has given rise to a consensus among scholars. Nevertheless, taken together they suggest several observations important to the problem of attempting to understand Amos's prophetic authority. First, social roles and expectations are understood to be culturally defined, which means that the social location in which a prophet carries out his activity is relevant to the problem of understanding the nature of his authority. Second, *social location* has to be defined broadly to include not just institutional settings in the strict sense but whole culturally determined patterns of expectation on the part of the prophet's audience as well.

Whether the classical prophets were themselves cultic functionaries has been a matter of intense debate. We may question whether the presence in their oracles of forms that are also known to function within a cultic context means that they themselves actually engaged in the activities of the official cult.[16] What is clear is that the prophets de-

[1967]:42–51; "Amos and the Theophanic Tradition," *ZAW* 80 [1968]:203–15), H. Gottlieb ("Amos und Jerusalem," *VT* 17 [1967]:430–63), and D. Christensen (*Transformations of the War Oracle in Old Testament Prophecy* [Missoula: Scholars Press, 1975]) have pointed to the prophet's use of cultic language. H. Reventlow (*Das Amt des Propheten bei Amos* [Göttingen: Vandenhoeck & Ruprecht, 1962]) and W. Brueggemann ("Amos' Intercessory Formula," *VT* 19 [1969]:385–99) have argued that the prophet actually performed a cultic function. This list is by no means exhaustive.

14. S. Terrien, "Amos and Wisdom," in *Israel's Prophetic Heritage*, ed. B. W. Anderson and W. Harrelson (New York: Harper, 1962), 108–115.

15. H. W. Wolff, *Amos the Prophet: The Man and His Background* (Philadelphia: Fortress Press, 1973).

16. See R. E. Clements, *Prophecy and Tradition* (Oxford: Blackwell, 1975).

pended on the older traditions. Whether or not they were cultic functionaries, many of the forms they used were, presumably, easily recognizable by the people who listened to their proclamations, and these
forms would therefore have provided a handy criterion by which the
prophets' activity could be judged. To put the matter differently, if an
audience were used to prophets functioning in a certain way (e.g., as
holder of a cultic office), then it might not be responsive to a change in
the style of operation or the content of the message, even though,
technically, a given prophet had separated herself or himself from the
traditional institutional context. To explore these matters further, we
look at two specific passages from the book of Amos.

Amos 2:11–12. The larger context of these verses is an oracle
against northern Israel, which is itself part of a series of eight "oracles
against the nations" characterized by a striking similarity of outline and
vocabulary. The utterances against Damascus, Gaza, Ammon, and
Moab display the basic pattern of these oracles. The formal features of
this pattern have been variously described, but the essential structure is
plain enough: a message of judgment expressed in formulaic language
and including both an accusation and an announcement of the coming
punishment is enclosed between opening and closing formulae.[17] The
oracles against Tyre, Edom, and Judah differ from the pattern in having
a slightly expanded accusation, a contracted announcement of punishment, and no concluding formula.

The oracle against Israel (Amos 2:6–16) stands by itself, both
because of its relatively greater length and because in it the common
pattern has been partially broken by the omission of some of the
internal formulaic language ("and I will send fire upon . . . and it will
devour the strongholds of . . ."), a considerable expansion of the accusation, and an alteration of the closing formula from the usual "says
Yahweh" to "utterance of Yahweh." The expansion of the accusation is
effected by incorporating a list of six specific kinds of wrongdoing,
involving both social injustice (vv. 6b–7a) and cultic perversions (vv.
7b–8), and by introducing a historical and theological review of Yahweh's past actions on behalf of the people and their response to these

---

17. See R. P. Knierim, "'I Will Not Cause It to Return' in Amos 1 and 2," in
Canon and Authority, ed. G. W. Coats and B. O. Long, 169; H. W. Wolff, *Joel and Amos*
(Philadelphia: Fortress Press, 1977), 135–44.

actions (vv. 9–12), which has no counterpart in the other oracles of the series. This review begins by recalling how Yahweh drove the Amorites out of the land (v. 9) and then seems to backtrack by mentioning the exodus from Egypt, the forty years' wandering in the wilderness, and (again) the conquest of the land (v. 10).

Some have questioned the integrity of this oracle against Israel. Werner Schmidt[18] suggests eliminating verses 10–12 from the larger oracle as a Deuteronomic addition, and Wolff agrees, taking up and expanding upon his arguments. These verses, says Wolff,[19] have a "predominantly prosaic style" and may be recognized as additions because of their shift from third person (v. 9) to direct address; their use of traditional language about the exodus, wilderness period, and conquest and their mention of the conquest, even though it has already been referred to in v. 9; their sermonic tone; and the fact that verse 12 takes up again the accusation against Israel, even though the transition from verses 6–8 to verse 9 seems to indicate that the prophet had already brought that portion of his oracle to completion. The content of these verses, he claims, seems best suited to a later period. In them the Deuteronomist is trying to drive home to the generation of the exiles the nation's guilt.[20]

This view is not without problems, however. If one of the criteria for judging verses 10–12 secondary is the switch to direct address, why is verse 13, where that stylistic feature is also present, not rejected, especially in view of the fact that in the other oracles of the series the announcement of punishment is couched in the third person? Furthermore, the whole unit (vv. 9–12) seems to be part of the accusation (the people have acted contemptuously despite Yahweh's deeds on their behalf[21]), and such an understanding eliminates the problem of having

18. W. Schmidt, "Die deuteronomistische Redaktion des Amosbuches," *ZAW* 77 (1965):178–83.

19. Wolff, *Joel and Amos*, 112–13, 141–42, 170–71.

20. R. Melugin ("The Formation of Amos: An Analysis of Exegetical Method," in *SBL 1978 Seminar Papers*, ed. P. J. Achtemeier [Missoula, Mont.: Scholars Press, 1978], 384–85) accepts the view of Schmidt and Wolff on vv. 10–12 and notes a number of close parallels between language contained in them and Deuteronomy. Wilhelm Rudolph (*Joel, Amos, Obadja, Jona* [Gütersloh: Mohn, 1971], 146–48) holds that v. 10 is an integral part of the oracle against Israel, but (following Schmidt) understands v. 12 as an intrusion referring to Amos's own fate.

21. See W. R. Harper, *A Critical and Exegetical Commentary on Amos and Hosea* (Edinburgh: T. & T. Clark, 1905), 57.

to explain how the accusation could come to an end in verse 8 only to
be resumed in verse 12.[22]

Verses 11–12 mention Yahweh's raising up of prophets and
Nazirites. The context suggests that—along with the exodus, wilderness wandering, and conquest—this raising up is to be seen as one of
his mighty acts on behalf of his people. The people's mistreatment of
these agents of Yahweh is symbolic of their rebellion against him, and
the report of it stands as the final item in the prophet's lengthy accusation against them. What is most important to us is the action that the
accusation presupposes. The people of Israel are here seen to exercise
direct control over the activity of Yahweh's prophets by commanding
them not to prophesy. Amos, of course, strongly disapproves of such
activity and announces that Yahweh also disapproves. He reports the
activity, however, in such a fashion as to make us believe that the people
felt that making such a demand was quite within their rights and
powers.

This reaction is not the usual Deuteronomistic view of the people's negative reaction to the prophets, according to which they are
pictured as ignoring to their own peril the warnings that Yahweh
persistently sent through his servants the prophets (2 Kings 17:13–14;
cf. Jer. 7:25–26; 35:15; 44:4–5). The latter view corresponds to the
general statement about the prophets in Deuteronomy that they would
speak Yahweh's word and that those who did not heed them would be
punished (Deut. 18:15–22). But what if the verses are, in fact, the
product of a Deuteronomistic editing of the book of Amos? We remember that the Deuteronomists interpreted the fall of Israel and
Judah as the result of the people's having broken their covenant with
Yahweh (cf. 2 Kings 17:1–23; 23:26–27; 24:18–20). These passages
emphasize the apparently historical fact that the people had worshiped
other gods besides Yahweh. The Deuteronomists interpreted this behavior as a perversion of the orthodox Yahwistic position to which they

22. Christensen sees the utterance as a transformation of a war oracle from the old
tribal league. Although he rejects v. 10, he considers v. 12 to be a description of Israel's
"fourth and final sin against Yahweh" and therefore genuine; *Transformations of the War
Oracle*, 71. G. Pfeifer sees in the oracle against Israel as it stands the same concreteness
and progression of thought that characterizes those against Damascus, Ammon, and
Moab and thus considers the verses genuine. He notes that Deuteronomistic thought
originated in the north and suggests the possibility that vv. 10–12 may indicate some
contact between Amos and that circle; "Denkformenanalyse als exegetische Methode,
erläutert an Amos 1:2–2:16," *ZAW* 88 (1976):66—69.

were personally committed. By analogy, then, if Amos 2:10–12 should be a Deuteronomistic rationalization of the message of doom announced by the prophet (2:13–16 and elsewhere) and subsequently actualized by the Assyrian conquest, we might reasonably assume that the people's actions depicted in these verses reflect a social reality of the same nature as the worship of other gods mentioned previously.

We can fairly say, then, that Amos 2:10–12 reveals the presence of two authorizing or enabling factors in the functioning of Israelite prophets: Yahweh raises them up, but the people are able to assert a measure of control over their actual functioning.

Amos 7:10–17. This passage, especially the prophet's statement in verse 14 that he is "not a prophet or the son of a prophet," has generated much discussion. As we have seen, Würthwein[23] proposes the hypothesis that Amos was called to the office of *nābî* and that over the course of his career he developed into a prophet of doom. He therefore sees Amaziah's rebuke as the expression of an official position and not a personal attack. In his oracle against Jeroboam (v. 11), Amos violated the expectation that a person in his office should be concerned to proclaim the welfare of the nation. The assumption that Amos was rebuked for his failure to function as expected in a well-known and defined office makes the best sense of Amaziah's action and of the puzzling apparent denial by the prophet of his prophetic vocation (v. 14). According to Würthwein, this action is not a denial at all. Rather, Amos asserted that to oppose his new functioning as a prophet of doom was to oppose Yahweh himself.[24] The implication of this interpretation is conflict—seemingly inevitable—between the two

23. Würthwein, "Amos-Studien," 19–28.
24. Rowley, upon whose work Würthwein draws in his interpretation of this passage, observes that Amos "was so like a prophet that Amaziah thought he was one, and he himself felt so like one that he could only use the term 'prophesy' for what he was engaged in doing" in "Was Amos a Nabi?," in *Festschrift Otto Eissfeldt,* ed. J. Fück (Halle: Niemeyer, 1947), 195. Amos's activity seems to have been perceived by Amaziah as falling within the bounds of a certain well-defined social role, and it was his lack of conformity to specific aspects of that role as it was understood by Amaziah that formed the basis of the conflict between them. Cf. J. Mays, *Amos* (Philadelphia: Westminster, 1969), 139. S. Lehming's attempt to refute Rowley and Würthwein seems to me to focus too narrowly on the use of the term *nb'* in Amos. In his zeal to preserve Amos's uniqueness vis-à-vis the guild prophets, he overlooks the force of Rowley's observation quoted above; cf. "Erwägungen zu Amos," *ZTK* 55 (1958):145–69.

sources of the prophet's authorization. The prophet, by the very nature of his message, was caught between Yahweh and his audience.

Other interpretations of this story of conflict between Amos and the priest of Bethel have been suggested. Wolff[25] thinks that the encounter depicted in these verses was probably historical and suggests that the subject of the narrative is really Amaziah the priest, who had supervisory functions at the state sanctuary at Bethel and who found himself caught "in a conflict of authorities." Faced with this dilemma, he neither criticized the content of Amos's words nor waited for instruction from Jeroboam but counseled the prophet to flee for his life.

Gene Tucker sees in these verses a "story of prophetic conflict" composed and preserved by disciples of Amos in order "to authenticate" his prophecies in the face of critics who claimed that the prophet had no right to speak where, when, and what he did.[26] Again, the question about the grounds for the opponents' challenge to Amos's authority must be raised. They must have had some reason to feel they could command the prophets, and an answer like that given to Amaziah (vv. 14–15) would probably not have satisfied them.

The passage does offer us some suggestions about an answer to this question. Bethel was a royal sanctuary (v. 13), and the ostensible ground for Amos's expulsion from it was his alleged plotting against the king. We can suppose that this incident was a cause of serious concern because in northern Israel the act of conspiring against a king is reported with some regularity and always ends in a change of dynasties (cf. 1 Kings 15:27; 16:9, 20; 2 Kings 9:14; 10:9; 15:10, 15, 25, 30). The king evidently had the right to control the operation of cultic personnel at this sanctuary, a right that he delegated to a subordinate official, Amaziah. The reaction against Amos on the part of Amaziah and those who agreed with Amaziah was probably motivated by both political considerations (a need to guard against subversion) and the prophet's failure to conform to a socially recognized pattern (prophets operating at a royal sanctuary were expected to support the state against its enemies).

Thus, in Amos 2:10–12 and 7:10–17 two different persons or groups are said to exert control over the prophets: the people of Israel

25. Wolff, *Joel and Amos*, 307–16.
26. G. Tucker, "Prophetic Authenticity," *Int* 27 (1973):423–34.

and a specific member of the political-religious establis
nation. This observation strengthens the impression tha
of commanding prophets we are squarely in the realm of social ｉ ｃ ａ ｉ ｉ ｃ ａ ｉ ｉ ｃ .
The question is, How are we to understand this authorization process?

Contexts for Commanding Prophets

The problem we face is that although the Hebrew Bible hints that
the process by which prophetic activity is authorized has more to it
than the reception of Yahweh's word, this additional something remains
for the most part hidden behind a veil of theology; that is to say, the
biblical writers emphasize assertions about the nature of Yahweh and
his relationship to his own and other people but are not overly concerned to lay bare the social dynamics of the authorization process.

In hopes of gaining insight into this problem, we turn our attention briefly to some instances of prophecy from other parts of the
world. Of course, considerable differences exist in time, geographical
location, and specific content between these figures and the biblical
prophets. Despite these differences, we have seen enough formal similarity in the activity of widely scattered prophetic figures to allow us
the reasonable hope that with the aid of comparative materials we can
arrive at a clearer picture of how this authorization process works. My
suggestion is that the type of phenomenon we are about to identify also
lies behind the passages in Amos we have been discussing.

Prophetic figures tend to appear in societies in times of crisis—in
situations at the personal, family, or some wider societal level in which
the normal order of things seems to be threatened with collapse. The
prime function of prophets is to address this situation with words and/
or deeds to which the audience will respond. Those favorably impressed
acknowledge the prophets' power, by which I mean primarily the
cogency of their interpretations of the current crisis and suggestions as
to how it can be resolved. The hearers attribute authority to prophets
insofar as they acknowledge and are prepared to act upon the truth of
their message. The fact that prophets claim to have had a revelation is
probably not the decisive factor in this acknowledgment. In many
native American cultures, for example, individuals commonly seek and
experience visions, and judgments about a prophet's validity would thus
be based primarily on an evaluation of his or her words and deeds.

I now briefly describe three non-Israelite prophetic figures whose careers may shed some light on the social dynamics of prophetic authority. With the first two, we return to somewhat familiar ground.

Wodziwob. In response to the deprivation resulting from years of increasingly intense contact with white civilization, a prophet named Wodziwob arose among the Paiute of Nevada and inaugurated a movement that came to be known as the Ghost Dance of 1870. The gist of his message was that the time was near at hand when the whites would be supernaturally destroyed, the now scarce game animals would be restored, and a general return to the conditions and practices of the traditional way of life would occur. Of special interest to us is the report of Captain J. M. Lee about the development of Wodziwob's doctrine. The prophet first announced that he had had revealed to him that the whites soon would all be destroyed, but their material goods would be spared at the time of the cataclysm. A few believed him, but in general the claim that native Americans could survive a natural catastrophe that would destroy the whites was ridiculed. His response to this negative reaction was to retire again to the mountains, where he received a second revelation. His message now was that both whites and native Americans would perish in the coming disaster but that the former would be eliminated permanently and the latter would come back to life within a few days and live forever on earth amid an abundant supply of game animals, fish, and pine nuts. This more reasonable message was popular for a time, but eventually support began to weaken. The prophet retired to the mountains and received a final revelation, that the "divine spirit" was angered at his people's lack of faith. As a consequence of this, only those native Americans who believed would be resurrected and happy, and others would perish forever along with the whites.[27] The history of the spread of this doctrine into California, Oregon, and Washington and of subsequent developments in it is a complex one. For our purposes we can simply note this example of the active role that the hearers of the prophet played in both enabling and shaping his activity.

27. Lee's account may be found in Mooney, "Ghost-Dance Religion," 701–2. On the origin of the 1870 Ghost Dance, cf. M. Hittman, "The 1870 Ghost Dance at the Walker River Reservation: A Reconstruction," *Ethnohistory* 20 (1973):247–78.

Handsome Lake. We have already discussed the career of Hand-some Lake, the Seneca prophet (see chapter 3). Although over the years of his activity his political influence waxed and waned, his religious influence remained strong. He made an annual circuit of the Iroquois reservations preaching his message, and those who accepted it derived from it the strength to shape their very lives:

> One of the Onondagas, when asked why they did not leave their drunken habits before, since they were often urged to do it, and saw the ruinous consequences of such conduct replied, they had no power; but when the Great Spirit forbid such conduct by their prophet, he gave them the power to comply with their request.[28]

Handsome Lake spoke convincingly to the current sociocultural situation of his people and advocated such important cultural innovations as the involvement of men in farm labor, limited acceptance of white education, and the dissolution of the totem animal societies. He condemned the individual autonomy and glorification that had been characteristic of the old Iroquois way and advocated instead family solidarity and restraint in social affairs. All his message was in response to the collapse of the old hunting and trading system under pressure from encroaching whites that forced the Iroquois into more intensive agriculture. Where gardening in the traditional culture had been the responsibility of the women, plow agriculture required male participation as well, and the yearly agricultural schedule demands a stable social order. The prophet therefore preached values that emphasized communal order over individual gratification.

To say that part of Handsome Lake's authority as a prophet stemmed from the positive response of many people to his message is but to suggest that they acknowledged the (god-given) truth of his analysis of the current critical situation and his formulation of the shape of the new order of things. Within a few years of his death in 1815, the process of institutionalizing his message had already begun. At a religious council in the summer of 1818, a version of his teaching was recited, and a minor prophet recounted a vision confirming it. Similar incidents occurred over the next two decades, and by the 1840s the text

28. A. F. C. Wallace, *The Death and Rebirth of the Seneca* (New York: Vintage Books, 1972), 301.

of the Gaiwiio, the code of Handsome Lake, was fixed. It continues to be an important force in Iroquois life down to the present day.[29]

Yali. Our final example takes us to the Madang District of northeastern New Guinea during the period preceding and following World War II.[30] The object of our interest is Yali, a reluctant prophet not so much because, like Jeremiah, his services were commandeered by God against his will but because he was proclaimed by his people to be a prophet without himself having made any claims to the role.

The prevalent form of prophetic movements in this area of the world is the cargo cults, which have occurred frequently and widely since roughly the mid-nineteenth century. The cargo referred to is in general Western manufactured goods. The natives had no real comprehension of how these goods were made or why they were distributed in the fashion they were, and the cults typically contained a myth accounting for the relationship of the Europeans and their goods to the native cosmos, as well as rituals that were thought to hasten the supernatural event by which the cargo would arrive and be turned over to the natives. Madang had had five successive cargo beliefs between about 1871 and 1950. The striking feature of this series is the conceptual continuity both in myth and ritual and in values and epistemology that the beliefs display.[31]

Peter Lawrence, who has chronicled this history so carefully, points out that the doctrines of the prophetic leaders of these cargo movements "were not accepted as 'true knowledge' until they had been substantiated by accredited claims of divine revelation."[32] Yali, however, made no such claims. Instead, he was involved after World War II in a quite secular rehabilitation scheme in cooperation with the Australian provincial administration. But when he

> tried to introduce a programme that did not include ritual activity . . . (it) got out of control almost at once. As Yali promised everything the people

29. See T. W. Overholt, *Prophecy in Cross-Cultural Perspective* (Atlanta: Scholars Press, 1986), 321–31.
30. The account of Yali is based on Peter Lawrence, *Road Belong Cargo: A Study of the Cargo Movement in the Southern Madang District New Guinea* (Manchester, England: Manchester University Press, 1964); see also Burridge, *New Heaven New Earth*; Overholt, *Prophecy in Cross-Cultural Perspective*, 295–308.
31. See Lawrence, *Road Belong Cargo*, especially chapter 1 and pp. 226–43.
32. Ibid., 245.

wanted, he got as quick and favourable a response as had his forerunners. Yet, because he did not take sufficient pains in explaining the scheme, was careless in his choice of words when relating his experiences in Australia, and did not clearly dissociate himself from general cargo ideology, the people distorted his propaganda by the end of the year. It had to be made consistent not only with their economic and socio-political aspirations but also with their intellectual assumptions. They could not understand that Yali intended to achieve his aims by means that were at least an attempt to evade cargo cult, even though he never denied its validity. They had to interpret him as a conventional cargo prophet before he and his teachings could be intelligible. Like his predecessors, he had to have received the charter for his programme from the cargo deity during some special experience. . . . He had seen the Hand of God, and the Light of God shone on his body.[33]

By the time of Yali, the cargo ideology seemed to have become "an intrinsic part of the culture of the southern Madang District."[34] It provided the interpretive framework in terms of which Yali's message could be understood, and it shaped the people's response. It enabled, indeed necessitated, their authorization of his activity as prophetic, even though he made no such claims for himself.

We can observe about these prophets that the decision of the people—and not revelation—is the crucial factor in their authorization.[35] The response of the audience can in effect force changes in the prophet's message (Wodziwob) or in the place of his activity (Handsome Lake); it is decisive in the long-term survival of the message (the Iroquois Longhouse), and it can even make a prophet of one who claims no revelation (Yali). None of these three prophets was part of a cultic or other fixed institutional setting. Nonetheless, in each case the people assumed they knew the nature of proper prophetic functioning and undertook to exercise a controling judgment over it. The case of Amos seems fundamentally the same: Although he claimed authority on the basis of his revelation (7:14–15), he was never truly independent of his audience. The people's attitudes about prophecy would inevitably

33. Ibid., 255–56.
34. Ibid., 269.
35. I take it that revelatory experience is an "obvious" and assumed factor in the authorization of a prophet in both the Israelite and the non-Israelite examples cited. That the role of the people in the authorizing process is less obvious in the Hebrew Bible than elsewhere is no doubt largely due to the fact that the comparative materials were recorded by outsiders to the native cultures who were more interested in social relationships and less susceptible to internal theological biases.

shape their responses to him and to other persons functioning as intermediaries. The virtue of Würthwein's view that Amos developed from a *nabi* to a prophet of doom seems to me to be that it accords well with the fact that the Israelites believed in prophecy but at the same time had certain ideas about its proper social location and shape.

The activity of "commanding the prophets" then seems to have two bases. The first is specific to the situation or institution: insofar as the prophet is attached to, say, the cultus or the court and performs a regular office there, he or she can be presumed to be under the direct control of superiors within the institutional structure. The second is process-specific and related to the specific nature of prophetic communication. The hearers assume that they know how real prophets ought to function, and they accept or reject a given prophet on the basis of these preconceptions. My contention is that this authorizing process is the social reality that lies behind Amos 2:11–12 and 7:10–17. The prophet, of course, responded negatively to it (7:18; 3:8), but precisely because this response mirrors his own deeply held theological conviction (as well as that of his followers) it obscures the underlying social reality.[36]

SEEING IS BELIEVING:
THE SOCIAL SETTING OF
PROPHETIC ACTS OF POWER

The seventh element in our model, supernatural confirmation, refers in large part to a fairly common phenomenon: the incorporation into prophetic behavior of occurrences referred to variously as shamanic tricks, miracles, and the like. Reports of these are often unsettling to modern readers, who tend to seek naturalistic explanations for them. In what follows I take a somewhat different tack by examining first the reports of such occurrences contained within the

36. The prophets have often been understood as "charismatic" figures with the implication that their peculiar power and authority is the result of a special "gift" from God. More recent discussions of charisma, however, have placed less emphasis on the personal qualities of charismatic individuals and, in line with the position taken here, more on the nature of the relationship between such individuals and groups within their societies; see T. W. Overholt, "Thoughts on the Use of 'Charisma' in Old Testament Studies," in *In the Shelter of Elyon: Essays on Ancient Palestinian Life and Literature in Honor of G. W. Ahlström*, ed. W. B. Barrick and J. R. Spencer (Sheffield: JSOT Press, 1984), 287–303.

Hebrew Bible and then appealing to examples outside Israel to suggest an appropriate social context for such reports. Put differently, the model suggests that we can expect supernatural confirmation to be a normal element of the prophetic process.

We generally think of the biblical prophets as speakers rather than actors, and as a consequence much more scholarly attention has been directed to the forms of their speech than to the patterns of their actions. Nevertheless, other kinds of behavior can be important in the performance of the prophetic role. Ioan Lewis[37] has recently suggested that some observable trauma must attend a prophet's call so that the audience may be aware at first hand of the nonverbal aspects of his or her power. Robert Wilson[38] puts the matter somewhat more broadly by focusing on the social aspects of both the selection of an intermediary and the intermediary's characteristic behavior.

My intention is to survey a specific category of prophetic actions that I refer to as "acts of power" and examine one subgroup of this category in more detail by asking in particular what these actions might suggest to us about the relationship between prophets and their societies.

Prophetic Acts of Power in
the Old Testament

"Acts of power" refers to reported actions of prophetic figures that in their narrative context appear somehow unusual, extraordinary, or miraculous. More than sixty instances of such actions are reported in 1 and 2 Kings and the prophetic books.

In terms of the relationship in which they stand to ordinary human activities, these reports can be divided into two broad categories. The first is acts that in themselves are fully within the capabilities of any person to perform. The naming of children (Isaiah 7; Hosea 1), the intentional breaking of a pot (Jeremiah 19), and the wearing or breaking of a yoke (Jeremiah 27—28) are not in themselves especially startling or indicative of power. Their context calls attention to them and makes them so. Similarly, anyone can walk the streets naked (Isaiah 20; Micah 1:8), although not many choose to do so. Such an act calls attention to itself, but the particular context gives it its significance.

37. I. Lewis, "Prophets and Their Publics," *Semeia* 21 (1981):113–17.
38. Wilson, *Prophecy and Society*, 48–51, 62–68.

Other actions may border even more closely on the exotic or bizarre—
Ezekiel's eating a scroll (3:1–3) and temporary dumbness (3:22–27;
24:25–27) or Hosea's marriage to a prostitute (1:2–3)—but are still
within the range of possible human activities.[39] These acts might be
called *symbolic* actions.

A second and smaller group of passages reports actions that
abrogate the laws of nature, by which I simply mean those that fall
outside normal expectations about what humans can accomplish. I do
not want to raise the question of whether anyone believed such things
could happen (presumably, some did so believe) but only suggest that
such acts would certainly be perceived as more special than normal.
Isaiah's causing the shadow of the sun on the dial to move backwards
(38:7–8 = 2 Kings 20:9–10) is an example, but the bulk of such
actions are to be found in the Elijah and Elisha narratives.[40]

Occasionally the report of a prophetic act of power gives an
indication of the actual or intended response of the audience. From
them we can see that some such acts seem to have encouraged those
who witnessed them toward a certain course of action (1 Kings 22:11;
Isa. 7:3–9; Hab. 2:2), but others provoked puzzlement that became
the occasion for a verbal exposition of the prophet's message (Jer.
16:10–13; Ezek. 12:8–16; 21:7 [Heb. = 12]; 24:19–24; 37:18–28).
Several times the actions evoked a hostile response (1 Kings 13:4; Jer.
28:1–4, 10–11, 12–16). Sometimes they led to the recognition that
Yahweh is God (1 Kings 18:39; Ezek. 24:24, 27) but more often to the
recognition that the prophet who performed them was an authentic
prophet (1 Kings 17:24; 19:20; 2 Kings 1:13–14; 2:15; 4:37; 5:15,
17–18; 8:4–6). Recognition is the predominant response in the Elijah
and Elisha stories, and possibly the contest between prophets recorded

39. The passages assigned to this category are: Isa. 7:3, 10–17; 8:1–4, 18; 20:3;
Jer. 16:1–9; 19; 27—28; 32; 35; 43:8–13; 51:63–64; Ezek. 3:1–3;
3:22–27/24:25–27; 4—5; 6:11–14; 12:1–16, 17–20; 21:6–7, 14–23; 24:1–2,
15–24; 37:15–23; Hosea 1:2–9; 3:1–5; Micah 1:8; Hab. 2:2; Zech. 6:9–14;
11:4–17; 1 Kings 11:29–30; 19:19; 20:37; 22:11. This section incorporates material
from my study "Seeing Is Believing: The Social Setting of Prophetic Acts of Power,"
JSOT 23 (1982):3–31.

40. The passages assigned to this category are: Isaiah 38:7–8 (= 2 Kings
20:9–11); 1 Kings 17:13–16, 19–22; 18:36–38; 2 Kings 1:10–12; 2:8, 14, 21, 24;
4:1–7, 25–37, 41, 43; 5:26–7; 6:6, 15–20. Cf. also Isa. 38:21–22. As the years passed,
some of these reports, like Elijah's and Elisha's raising of the dead boys, may have contributed to the development of widely held beliefs. See P. Lapide, *Auferstehung: Ein Jüdisches
Glaubenserlebnis* (Stuttgart: Calwer Verlag, 1977), 19–32.

in Jeremiah 27—28 should also be seen in this light. Here we should also take note of the Deuteronomistic assertion that, although the prophets may perform acts of power, they are still subject to a theological test to determine their authenticity (Deut. 13:1–5); that is, acts of power are not to be considered the final proof of a prophet's authority. The fact that the Deuteronomists felt the need to make such a stipulation seems to indicate that for some signs and wonders were enough to establish the authority of a prophet. The Deuteronomists could not allow such a practice to go unassailed because in their theologically conditioned view the true prophet was *the* mediator to whom Yahweh spoke directly and through whom Yahweh's true words were delivered to the people.[41] Although they had no use for such prophetic actions, apparently others did.[42]

Georg Fohrer has written the only full-length study of the prophets' actions, and it differs from the interpretation offered here in both the scope of the activities accepted for examination and the context within which they are interpreted. With respect to the former, Fohrer includes fewer specific episodes in his symbolic actions classification than I have in my initial broad categorization. This difference is most noticeable in Kings, where he finds only four such acts (1 Kings 11:29–31; 19:19–21; 22:11; 2 Kings 13:14–19). This narrowing of the field of inquiry is the result of Fohrer's distinction between magical and symbolic acts. He finds numerous examples of the former in the Hebrew Bible and considers magic to be the broader phenomenological context out of which symbolic acts arose. However, Fohrer contends that although in some of the prophetic actions the magical *element* is stronger than in others, none can be viewed as a magical *action*. The prophets overcame magic.[43]

This narrowing leads to the second difference. At the very outset Fohrer informs us that the symbolic actions need to be seen in the

41. See Wilson, *Prophecy and Society*, 157–66.
42. Very few of these acts of power—and none in the second group—are designated 'ôt or môpēt, the terms used in Deut. 13:1–5. Because the Elijah and Elisha narratives to which I will be turning my attention show very little influence of the Deuteronomists, this is perhaps not surprising. Because the Deuteronomists use these terms to designate both objects that serve as reminders (Deut. 6:8; 11:18) and manifestations of unusual power (Deut. 6:22; 7:19; 11:3; 26:8; 28:46; 29:2), we can reasonably assume that the reference in 13:1–5 is to acts like those under discussion.
43. G. Fohrer, *Die symbolischen Handlungen der Propheten* (Zurich: Zwingli Verlag, 2d ed., 1968), especially chapters 1 and 4.

broad phenomenological context of acts of magic and sorcery,[44] and his entire second chapter is devoted to examining parallels to the prophetic symbolic actions. The upshot of this effort is to show that the prophetic acts are not entirely idiosyncratic in external form. They have analogues in other cultures, an examination of which may shed some light on the underlying significance of the act. So, for example, when discussing 2 Kings 13:14–19 Fohrer points out the magical character of the act, refers to the shooting of arrows, bones, and the like to harm enemies, and cites specific examples from the Australian Aborigines, the African Bushmen, African stone age art, the Elephantine papyri, Jewish magic, Sweden, and Mexico.[45] His search for analogies is wide-ranging in both space and time.

This grounding of prophetic symbolic actions in magic is, however, only Fohrer's first assertion about them, not his last. As Fohrer makes abundantly clear, he considers the primary context for their interpretation to be theological. His claim is that the prophetic symbolic actions and their magical parallels are neither identical nor externally the same, the parallels between them being in "details," not in the "core." The magical elements are not simply abolished, leaving only the symbolic, as he holds to be the case with profane symbolic actions. Rather, an "inner and fundamental overcoming of the magical elements" occurs.[46] The characteristics of this prophetic alteration of the magical foundation may be stated as follows: the prophetic actions are undertaken at the command of Yahweh and not as the result of a human wish;[47] they are usually accompanied by an interpretation; and Yahweh's promise is given that the symbolized occurrence will take place. This promise provides a guarantee that is absent in magical acts and shows the prophets' dependence upon Yahweh. Profane symbolic actions symbolize and teach but do not establish a result; prophetic action is the bearer of divine revelation and is therefore certain of result. By the same token the magical is fundamentally overcome because the prophet is not working his own will but is expecting a special act of God, which

---

44. Ibid., 9–10.
45. Ibid., 23–25.
46. Ibid., 94–95.
47. For Fohrer a magical act is believed to carry its efficacy within itself, an act in which one seeks to grasp some secret, numinous power in the interests of wish-fulfillment. See "Prophetie und Magie," *ZAW* 78 (1966):27–28; and *Die symbolischen Handlungen*, 10–11.

by divine command he symbolizes. Nor is prophetic action to be considered a third possibility alongside profane and magical actions, for the symbol is not chosen by the prophet himself but commanded by God.[48] Thus Fohrer can speak of a broken or dialectical relationship of the prophetic symbolic action to magic.[49] Therefore, the apparently more "magical" acts (e.g., 1 Kings 17:14–16, 21) can be viewed rather as survivals of an earlier nomadic stage of Israel's social and religious development.[50]

My intention is not to offer a detailed critique of Fohrer's position. Instead, I will move directly to a consideration from a somewhat different perspective of a group of magical episodes in the Elijah and Elisha narratives, to see if something of their social functions can be discerned.[51]

The actions to be considered are those belonging to the category of acts that seem to abrogate laws of nature. About them we can make three observations. The first is that for the most part they occur in pairs: Both Elijah and Elisha miraculously provide for the sustenance of a widow (1 Kings 17:8–16; 2 Kings 4:1–7; cf. 4:42–44), bring a dead boy back to life (1 Kings 17:17–24; 2 Kings 4:18–37), and cause the waters of the Jordan River to part by striking them with a mantle (2 Kings 2:8, 14). Twice Elijah calls down fire from heaven (1 Kings 18:36–38; 2 Kings 1:9–16), and twice Elisha acts to eliminate poison from water or food (2 Kings 2:19–22; 4:38–41). Only four episodes, all of them attributed to Elisha, stand without parallel (2 Kings 2:23–25; 5; 6:1–7, 15–20). Clearly Elijah and Elisha are being depicted in a similar light.

We can in the second place observe that some of these episodes contain indications of a response to the prophet's action. After the raising of the widow's son, she said to Elijah, "Now I know that you are

48. Forher, *Die symbolischen Handlungen,* 94–98, 104–7.
49. Fohrer, "Prophetie und Magie," 46–47.
50. Ibid., 30, 46.
51. A. Rofé has divided the Elijah and Elisha narratives into three types: simple legenda, legenda which have undergone literary elaboration, and vita. His intention is to describe the stories as literary creations, and he has little to say about the effects the prophets' actions had on their society beyond the suggestion that the beneficiaries of the "simple miracles" (2:19–22, etc.) were "expected to respond with respect and veneration"; "The Classification of the Prophetical Stories," *JBL* 89 (1970):432. For our present purposes, we can lump these narratives into a single group because the actions themselves and not the nature of the accounts about them are our main concern.

a man of God and that the word of Yahweh in your mouth is truth" (1 Kings 17:24). When the Israelites assembled on Carmel saw the fire, they exclaimed, "Yahweh, he is God; Yahweh, he is God!" (1 Kings 18:39), and faced with a similar catastrophe the army captain recognized Elijah's power and prayed to be spared (2 Kings 1:13–14). The sons of the prophets, having witnessed Elisha splitting the waters of the Jordan, are said to have exclaimed, "The spirit of Elijah rests on Elisha" (2 Kings 2:15), and the woman whose son Elisha raised from the dead "came and fell at his feet, bowing to the ground" (2 Kings 4:37). Likewise Naaman, cured of his leprosy, acknowledged Yahweh's power and, implicitly, that of his prophet (2 Kings 5:15–19).

Two additional responses connected to other episodes are worth noting. Elisha responded to Elijah's casting his mantle on him by abandoning his home and following him (1 Kings 19:20). Even more suggestive is the episode in 2 Kings 8:4–6 where, at the king's request, Elisha's servant Gehazi tells of "all the great things that Elijah has done." During this telling, which included "how Elisha had restored the dead to life," the woman and her resurrected son appeared on the scene, and the king treated her even more favorably than she requested (cf. vv. 3, 6). We notice, then, the tendency to connect responses to accounts of prophetic acts of power.

Third, we observe the apparent social situations mirrored in the accounts of prophetic acts of power. Here considering the patterns of social relationships exhibited in the cycle as a whole can be useful. These patterns can be roughly diagrammed as follows (episodes containing prophetic acts of power are italicized; episodes containing responses have asterisks; a plus sign indicates ambiguity in the relationship depicted):

1. The prophet interacts with a king

   adversarial relationship: 1 Kings 17:1; 18:17–20; 19:1–3 (queen); 21:17–29; 2 Kings *1:1–16**; 6:24—7:20

   cooperative relationship: 1 Kings 18:41–46; 2 Kings 3:9–20; 8:1–6*; 9:1–13; 13:14–19

2. The prophet interacts with individuals and small groups (Israelite and other)

adversarial: 1 Kings *17:17–24** +; 2 Kings *1:1–16** +; *2:23–25*

cooperative: 1 Kings *17:8–16*; 18:7–16; 2 Kings *4:1–7,* 8–17, *18–37**

3. The prophet interacts with Israelite people (in sizable groups)

adversarial: none

cooperative: 1 Kings *18:21–40** +; 2 Kings *2:19–22*

4. The prophet interacts with "foreign" functionaries

adversarial: 1 Kings *18:21–40**; 2 Kings *6:8–23;* 8:7–15

cooperative: 2 Kings *5:1–19a**

5. The prophet interacts with his "servant" or with the "sons of the prophets"

adversarial: 2 Kings *5:19b–27*

cooperative: 1 Kings 18:41–46; 19:19–21*; 2 Kings *2:1–18**; *4:38–41, 42–44; 6:1–7*

In several passages the relationship depicted is difficult to cate- gorize as either adversarial or cooperative. For example, 1 Kings 17:17–24 begins with the widow accusing Elijah of causing her misfor- tune ("What have you against me, O man of God? You have come to bring my sin to remembrance, and to cause the death of my son!"), although the episode ends on a more positive note ("Now I know that you are a man of God, and that the word of Yahweh in your mouth is truth"). Similarly, in 2 Kings 1:1–16 Elijah is set against both the king and his troops, although the captain of the third group recognizes his power and prays for mercy. At the beginning of the Mount Carmel episode (1 Kings 18:21–40), the people are not overtly hostile, but neither are they actively supporting Elijah.

Now several things of interest emerge from this schematization of social relationships. With respect to pattern 1, although the tendency is to portray Elijah's relationships to the king as adversarial in nature, the opposite is true for Elisha.[52] Wilson[53] has suggested that Elijah was throughout his life a "peripheral prophet" attempting to reform the central cult, but Elisha, who began his career similarly, moved in the period after Jehu's rise to power in the direction of becoming a "central prophet" exercising social maintenance functions. We also note no acts of power in which the prophet interacts directly with the king and only one response attributed to a king (although the king is important behind the scenes in 2 Kings 1:1–16, his messengers and soldiers actually confront the prophet[54]). This lack of interaction is surprising, given the intensity of the relationships between king and prophet mirrored in the narratives as they have come down to us.

We notice about pattern 3 that only positive relationships are described between the prophets and groups. Interaction with large groups of people is clearly not the focus of attention in the narratives of this cycle.[55] Taken together, patterns 2 and 5 contain roughly two thirds of the acts of power and half the responses, suggesting that such actions were more at home in individual and small group situations.[56]

52. G. Hentschel believes that during the first part of his career the relationship between Elijah and Ahab was marked by cooperation rather than conflict. For his view of the developing relations between the prophet and the royal house, see *Die Elija-erzählungen* (Leipzig: St. Benno-Verlag, 1977), 275–323. On Elisha as a supporter of the monarchy, see M. Sekine, "Literatursoziologische Beobachtungen zu den Elisaerzählungen," *Annual of the Japanese Biblical Institute* 1 (1975):39–62.

53. Wilson, *Prophecy and Society*, 201, 206.

54. G. Hentschel believes that vv. 10–14 constitute a pre-Deuteronomistic expansion of an earlier narrative and points out that (1) they seem to convey a different picture of the prophet than the context (e.g., in v. 15 Elijah is no longer fearsome, but afraid), (2) the title "man of God" and the harsh treatment of opponents is reminiscent of the Elisha stories, and (3) v. 15 forms a good conclusion to v. 9. In his view the changing social situation brought about the change in the tradition. Thus, although the oldest tradition of the Ahaziah narrative was passed on among a north Israelite population faithful to Yahweh, the story later came to be transmitted in prophetic circles. The people were more interested in the sober facts of Elijah's encounter with the king, but the prophetic circles incorporated material about the prophet's experiences and turned the narrative into a miracle story. See *Die Elija-erzählungen*, 11–12, 202–8, 353–55.

55. In Hentschel's opinion, 1 Kings 18:21–40 was not originally part of the drought narrative. The oldest layer of tradition to be found in this passage is vv. 21, 30, and 40, with vv. 38–39 representing the next stage of development; ibid., 134–39.

56. With respect to 1 Kings 17:8–16, 17–24, Hentschel argues that these episodes were not originally part of the drought narrative but derive from a prophetic circle like that of Elisha. More interesting is his suggestion that an earlier form of the story of the prophet's raising the dead boy (identifiable in the dialogue-free core of the passage, vv.

As the diagram shows us, acts of power and responses to such acts may occur in both adversarial and cooperative situations, although their appearance is slightly more frequent in cooperative situations. They may thus be performed for the benefit of two kinds of individuals or groups, sometimes simultaneously (cf. 1 Kings 18:21–40): those inclined to be ill disposed and those inclined to be well disposed toward the prophet. However, the nature of the response is essentially the same in each case, namely, acknowledgment of the prophet's power and therefore his authority. The responses in patterns 3 and 4 are not really an exception to this. There the explicit acknowledgment is of the power of the prophet's God, but because it comes as a result of a successful act of mediation by the prophet, it also has the effect of acknowledging the prophet's authority. Finally, both acts of power and responses appear to be scattered throughout the prophets' careers, insofar as they can be known to us.

Differences of opinion exist over whether or not some of these episodes really refer originally to Elijah and Elisha. For example, Hans-Christoph Schmitt[57] argues that 2 Kings 4:8–37 and 6:8–23 were originally about an anonymous "man of God," whom the collector of the stories identified with Elisha. I am not fully convinced that this is the case, but even if it were, the hypothesis being presented here would not be altered. It might even strengthen the hypothesis because it would widen the scope of this type of prophecy beyond the figures of Elijah and Elisha.

Along somewhat different lines, Leah Bronner[58] sees the whole series of miracle stories as a product of a "well informed author" whose intention was to mount a polemic against Canaanite mythology in general and Baal worship in particular. However, the settings depicted in many of the stories themselves (e.g., actions within a group of supporters) do not reflect such a polemic. Thus, even if her suggestion contains some truth, this polemic does not appear to constitute the

---

19b, 21aa, bb, 22b, 23a) plays up the prophet's independent power, but later additions served to increase his dependence upon God; ibid., 93–98, 188–95, 271–73. If this should be correct, and if the original story was indeed connected with Elijah, our impression of the prophet as a powerful worker of wonders would certainly be strengthened.

57. H.-C. Schmitt, *Elisa: Traditionsgeschichtliche Untersuchungen zur vorklassischen nordisraelitischen Prophetie* (Gütersloh: Mohn, 1972), 89–91, 153–54.

58. L. Bronner, *The Stories of Elijah and Elisha as Polemics Against Baal Worship* (Leiden: Brill, 1968).

original function of the stories.[59] A similar point might be made about Alexander Rofé's classification of 2 Kings 5 among the "didactic legenda," in which the miracle itself is downplayed in order to stress something of deeper significance that transcends the immediate circumstances, namely, "to prove to foreigners" both that "there is a prophet in Israel" (v. 8) and that "there is no God in all the earth, but in Israel" (v. 15).[60] Rofé assumes the transformation of "popular, venerative" stories and considers the present version of Naaman's cure to be late, reflecting the dispersion of Israelites in Assyria after 721 B.C.E. We could grant such an interpretation and still maintain that the story had an earlier function, which the later author consciously moved into the background.

How are we to assess this evidence? The following proposition seems attractive: If these prophets demonstrated their power for both opponents and allies to see, if they did this at several stages of their careers, and if the typical response to these demonstrations of power was to acknowledge the power of the prophet and/or his God, then we could reasonably conclude that the social function of such acts of power was the legitimation of the prophets in the exercise of their office.[61] The biblical narratives themselves do not give us a very clear picture of this social process, however, and so examples from other cultures are useful in illustrating the logic of this suggestion.[62]

Acts of Power Outside Israel

That we do not know as much as we would like about the social setting of biblical prophecy is a truism. In that respect, as in others, the

59. Bronner's argument is sometimes forced; see, for example, her attempts to free Elijah and Elisha from any association with "magic" (ibid., esp. 105, 133).

60. A. Rofé, "Classes in the Prophetical Stories: Didactic Legenda and Parable," in *Studies in Prophecy*, VTSup 26 (Leiden: Brill, 1974), 145–48, 152–53.

61. Cf. B. O. Long, "Prophetic Authority as Social Reality," in *Canon and Authority*, 10–11; and Wilson, *Prophecy and Society*, 42–68. R. Kilian refers to Elijah's raising of the dead boy as a "proof-legend" *(Erweislegende)*, but because his interest lies in establishing that the Elijah narrative originated earlier than the version connected with Elisha, he does not pursue this observation; "Die Totenerweckungen Elias und Elisas—ein Motivwanderung?" *BZ* 10 (1966):44–56.

62. We ought to note Schmitt's reference to nonbiblical materials to interpret the function of the prophet Elisha observable in a group of miracle stories that Schmitt contends were connected with Gilgal (2 Kings 4:1–7, 38–41; 6:1–7). There the prophet appears not as a preacher but as a miracle worker concerned with the special welfare of his group of followers. Ecstasy is a central characteristic of these prophets, and Schmitt compares them to modern Islamic dervishes, whose numerous "paranormal capabilities" function as "signs of holiness"; *Elisa*, 162–69. Schmitt does not explain the social implications of this "special welfare" or the "signs of holiness," however.

concerns of the authors and editors did not match our own. Therefore, comparative materials can be useful in helping to bridge the gaps in our knowledge of the social context of Elijah's and Elisha's miracles. To this end we now turn to two examples of shamanic acts of power.

1. Our first example is a native American shaman, Wovoka, a Paiute of western Nevada whom we have already encountered as the prophet of the Ghost Dance of 1890 (chapter 3). Wovoka had a reputation for acts of power. Mooney[63] tells us that after his revelation he began to preach, "convincing the people by exercising the wonderful powers that had been given him." He goes on to say that Wovoka "occasionally resorts to cheap trickery to keep up the impression as to his miraculous powers. From some of the reports he is evidently an expert sleight-of-hand performer." Many of the native Americans, however, did not speak of Wovoka's powers in such negative terms.

A review of his reputation shows that Wovoka is said to have performed many wonders. He could reportedly control the weather, making the skies "rain or snow or be dry at will."[64] One document that came into Mooney's possession, an account of Wovoka's teachings to a delegation of Cheyenne and Arapaho in August 1891, written down by one of them on the spot, has him saying,

> I, Jack Wilson, love you all, and my heart is full of gladness for the gifts you have brought me. When you get home I shall give you a good cloud . . . which will make you feel good. . . . There will be a good deal of snow this year and some rain. In the fall there will be such a rain as I have never given you before.[65]

The agent of Wovoka's reservation, C. C. Warner, reported in a similar vein,

> The originator of this craze[66] is one of my Pah-Ute Indians. His name is Jack Wilson, and like all such cranks he is a fraud, but a pretty smart fellow. He obtained his notoriety by telling the Indians that he would invoke the Great Spirit and bring rain (after there had been two years of drought), and it so happened that his promised invocation was in the commencement of our severe winter of 1889 and 1890, during which time it stormed almost incessantly from October to April. His success

63. Mooney, "Ghost-Dance Religion," 772–73.
64. Ibid., 772.
65. Ibid., 781.
    66. The Ghost Dance came to be widely referred to among whites as the "Messiah craze."

was rapidly spread abroad, and from that time on he has had many followers.[67]

Wovoka could precipitate unusual events, making the "whole world" appear in his hat or appearing before the eyes of assembled delegates in a cloud.[68] Porcupine, a Cheyenne, found him to be clairvoyant (he could immediately discern any inattention among those to whom he was speaking) and capable of communicating his desires at a distance (native Americans came to visit him from distant reservations as a result of having been "sent for" by him[69]).

Though the western buffalo herds had long since vanished, Wovoka could provide game for his followers. He told a delegation of Sioux that, if they should meet and kill a buffalo on their journey home, they should cut off the head, tail, and feet and leave them behind so that the animal could resuscitate. They later reported that this happened, and a favorite ghost song used among the Kiowa refers to such an event:

> I shall cut off his feet (repeat).
> I shall cut off his head (repeat).
> He gets up again (repeat).[70]

The power of Wovoka to provide meat for his followers was confirmed in Ghost Dance ceremonies during which large groups of native Americans danced slowly in a circle and sang specially composed ghost songs. During these lengthy performances, individual dancers sometimes fell to the ground in a trance and visited the spirit world. According to Mooney,

> During the first year or two of the excitement, it several times occurred at Ghost dances in the north and south . . . that meat was exhibited and tasted as genuine buffalo beef or pemmican brought back from the spirit world by one of the dancers. It is not necessary to explain how this

67. *Sixtieth Annual Report of the Commissioner of Indian Affairs* (Washington, D.C.: Government Printing Office, 1891), I, 301. G. B. Grinnell reports a story that circulated among the Cheyenne to the effect that General Miles and his troops went to arrest Wovoka, who made it rain for seven days and nights, so that all but Miles himself were drowned; "Account of the Northern Cheyenne Concerning the Messiah Superstition," *JAFL* 4 (1891):67.
68. Mooney, "Ghost-Dance Religion," 775–76, 797.
69. Ibid., 795.
70. Ibid., 797, 1088.

deception was accomplished or made successful. It is sufficient to know that it was done, and that the dancers were then in a condition to believe.[71]

This belief had important consequences. One Sioux follower of Wovoka explained that the meat and other items brought back from the spirit world by the dancers were proof that their trances were authentic, and the trances were proof of Wovoka's power and authenticity.[72]

One group of Sioux delegates reported Wovoka promised that if they became tired on their long trip home and called upon him for help, he would shorten their journey. They did this one night, and in the morning awoke to find themselves "at a great distance from where we stopped."[73] Grinnell[74] found that in the autumn of 1890 enthusiasm for the Ghost Dance was revived among the Cheyenne by the report of some Shoshone and Arapaho who said that "while travelling along on the prairie they had met with a party of Indians who had been dead thirty or forty years, and who had been resurrected by the Messiah." Wovoka's public trances themselves were signs of his power, and the same was true for those of certain of his followers who became leaders of the dance among their own tribes.[75]

The power of Wovoka could even be said to have touched many of his followers in the trances of individual dancers. Many of the trance experiences were evidently induced by leaders skilled in hypnotic techniques,[76] but they were real enough to those who had them. Upon reviving, individuals commonly told of visiting the place where the dead were encamped. There they had met relatives and acquaintances living again the old native American life and saw herds of buffalo and other game.[77] What was seen in the trances affected the physical features of subsequent dance performances, and new songs, paraphernalia, and symbols were added in imitation of the visions.[78] These trances

71. Ibid., 991. For an eyewitness account of one such performance, see 916–17; cf. also Grinnell, "Account," 66.
72. Mooney, "Ghost-Dance Religion," 799; see E. Foster, *Sixtieth Annual Report of the Commissioner of Indian Affairs*, 427. Foster was agent at the Yankton Sioux Agency in South Dakota.
73. Mooney, "Ghost-Dance Religion," 797.
74. Grinnell, "Account," 61.
75. Mooney, "Ghost-Dance Religion," 795, 894, 904.
76. Ibid., 775–76, 798, 899, 922–26.
77. Ibid., 797, 904.
78. Ibid., 898–99, 916, 921, 923, 1075.

became a routine, institutionalized part of the dance performances and sometimes came so easily that hypnotic techniques were no longer needed.[79] Trancers were said to have died, which mirrors what was reported of Wovoka's own revelatory experience: "he fell down dead, and God came and took him to heaven."[80]

Comparatively speaking, not many of the adherents of the Ghost Dance met Wovoka face-to-face, but they knew of his acts of power. They knew through reports of those who had witnessed them, and they knew from their own trance experiences, which in their minds confirmed the prophet's power and his promise of a new world soon to come. Whether or not an individual had personally experienced a trance, however, the ghost songs based on trance visions and sung at every performance were testimonials to Wovoka's power. The dead relatives and friends, the artifacts of the old life, the game animals were all waiting, poised to return:

> The whole world is coming,
> A nation is coming, a nation is coming,
> The Eagle has brought the message to the tribe.
> The father says so, the father says so.
> Over the whole earth they are coming.
> The buffalo are coming, the buffalo are coming,
> The Crow has brought the message to the tribe,
> The father says so, the father says so.[81]

These songs were in effect personal confirmations of and testimonials to Wovoka's power and authenticity.

> My children, my children,
> Look! the earth is about to move (repeat).
> My father tells me so (repeat).[82]

Wovoka's acts of power were widely reported in his own day, although we have seen that native American and white attitudes toward

79. Ibid., 924.

80. Ibid., 772; see 795, 798, 922. Fr. J. Jutz says that this is the way the dancers themselves described the experience; "Der 'Ghost Dance' der Sioux Indianer," *Central Blatt and Social Justice* (St. Louis, May, 1918), 49–50.

81. Mooney, "Ghost-Dance Religion," 1072. "Father" refers to Wovoka.

82. Ibid., 973; 953–1103 contain an extensive collection of ghost songs and commentaries on them; see also L. Colby, "The Ghost Songs of the Dakotas," *Nebraska State Historical Society Proceedings and Collections*, Series 2, Vol. 1, no. 3, 1 (1895): 131–50.

them tended to differ considerably.[83] A biography by Paul Bailey[84] makes the claim that Wovoka consciously sought to become a "mighty magician" like Jesus (about whom he had learned through his contact with the Wilson family) and John Slocum, founder of the native American Shaker religion. To this end he consciously sought to build an image by holding séances at which he performed sleight-of-hand tricks and at the crucial moment staging a decisive miracle. An example of a miracle took place in the heat of midsummer and involved a prediction by Wovoka that at noon on the following day ice would come floating down the river. The event in fact occurred and became famous in the region. Local tradition persists that Wovoka was aided in his feat by the Wilson brothers, who were stationed upstream with a wagonload of ice that at the proper moment they dumped into the river.[85] Bailey also refers to other tricks performed by Wovoka—he made a block of ice fall from the sky, created a lode of gold by loading a shotgun with gold dust and shooting a rock face, contrived to prove his invulnerability by being shot with a gun loaded only with powder and dropping pellets from his hand onto the blanket on which he stood—each time emphasizing a naturalistic explanation and suggesting that the prophet willfully deceived his own people in order to enhance his own personal standing.[86]

By contrast Grace Dangberg's biographical sketch of Wovoka is much more balanced. She cites her sources faithfully and provides several lengthy quotations from an unpublished manuscript, "Wizardry—The Jack Wilson Story," written by E. A. Dyer, a white contemporary of Wovoka and his long-time friend and confidant. According to

83. All native Americans should not be assumed to have believed in Wovoka and participated in the dance; see J. Mooney, "Ghost-Dance Religion," 913–14, 926–27; T. W. Overholt, "Short Bull, Black Elk, Sword, and the 'Meaning' of the Ghost Dance," *Religion* 8 (1978):171–95.

84. P. Bailey, *Wovoka the Indian Messiah* (Los Angeles: Westernlore Press, 1957), 62–66, 211 n. 7.

85. See G. Dangberg, "Wovoka," *Nevada Historical Society Quarterly* 11 (1968):14 n. 11.

86. Bailey, *Wovoka*, 67–91, 121–28. Bailey has a second book, *Ghost Dance Messiah* (Los Angeles: Westernlore Press, 1970), which, although the fact is nowhere explicitly acknowledged, is an extensive revision of his earlier *Wovoka*. In the earlier edition, Bailey acknowledged his dependence upon written sources and informants and cited them in sixty footnotes. Despite that, the book has a certain novelistic quality, containing a great deal of dialogue that we must assume has been invented. The second edition is longer, cuts out all references to sources, and greatly expands the dialogue sections. In my opinion depending upon either to be an accurate biography of the prophet would be perilous.

Dyer, "Jack Wilson's trances were, at least to Indians, very impressive productions. . . . He wasn't shamming. His body was as rigid as a board. His mouth could not be pried open and he showed no reaction to pain inducing experiments."[87] Dangberg, whose ties with the Walker Lake area where Wovoka lived are long-standing, reports that "it was generally conceded by residents of Mason Valley that Wovoka correctly prophesied the 'hard winter' of 1889–90," and that some said he accurately forecast all storms during the period from 1886 to 1892. She reports two other episodes of interest. "Sometime during the 1880's the body of an Indian girl who had died was burned near Hawthorne. It is reported that 200 Indians saw Jack, as he had promised, raise the girl from the flames to 'God's house.'" Finally, Jack attributed having escaped injury in a haying accident to his being bullet proof.[88]

Much in these reports strikes us as bizarre, and we cannot rest content with simply narrating them. One of the good features of Dangberg's sketch is that she makes some attempt to relate Wovoka's actions to the larger context of Paiute shamanism, and we must do likewise if we want to see these acts of power in their proper perspective. Fortunately, we have at our disposal for this task Willard Park's study of shamanism in western North America.[89]

Among the Paiute a shaman is "one who acquires supernatural power through direct personal experience."[90] The Paiute believed that many among them possessed supernatural power through which they became more successful hunters, gamblers, or the like, but that the shaman possessed it in greater quantity and often demonstrated it in curing illness and in certain other characteristic performances. Such persons were thought to be able to control the weather,[91] to be bullet proof,[92] and/or to swallow heated arrow points.[93] Some had power over

87. Quoted in Dangberg, "Wovoka," 12.
88. Ibid., 12, 27, 30.
89. W. Park, *Shamanism in Western North America: A Study in Cultural Relationships* (Evanston: Northwestern University Press, 1938). Half of this book is devoted to Paviotso (i.e., Northern Paiute) shamanism, the other to the relationship of that phenomenon to the shamanism prevalent in surrounding cultures. See also Park's "Paviotso Shamanism," *AA* 36 (1934):98–113. Wovoka was a Northern Paiute.
90. Park, *Shamanism*, 10.
91. O. Stewart, *Culture Element Distributions: XIV, Northern Paiute* (Berkeley: University of California Press, 1941), 444; F. Riddell, "Honey Lake Paiute Ethnography," *Nevada State Museum Anthropological Papers* 4 (1960):70.
92. R. Lowie, *Notes on Shoshonean Ethnography* (New York: American Museum Press, 1924), 292–93; J. Steward, *Ethnography of the Owens Valley Paiute* (Berkeley: Uni-

the antelope and served as leaders of the communal antelope hunts that were an occasional feature of Paiute life.[94] Evidently Wovoka was not unique among Paiute either in performing acts of power or in the general nature of the acts he performed.

The shamans' strong power enables them to cure illnesses, and curing is their chief function among the Paiute. In some cases they are believed even to have brought the dead back to life by journeying into the other world, finding the departed soul of the person who had died, and inducing it to return to the body. The performances at which these healings took place differed from each other because of the differences in the experiences of the individual shamans,[95] but they were invariably social occasions in which everyone participated in some way (e.g., by singing) and in which the shaman's tricks played an important part:

> When Paviotso shamanism was in full swing, these performances, held in a small closely packed house, must have been exciting and impressive. The singing and the shaman's tricks appear to have excited the spectators to a high emotional pitch which was followed by a relaxation of tension attended often by a general feeling of satisfaction when control of the sickness was demonstrated by the return of the soul or the extraction of the disease-object.[96]

Park goes on to say that "legerdemain is not generally characteristic of the shamanistic performance. Apparently the shamans of today perform no tricks when curing, but several informants recall that in the past some practiced sleight-of-hand."[97] Among the tricks mentioned are making pine nuts mysteriously appear in a basket (a sign that the patient would recover), putting hot coals or a heated knife blade in the mouth, and licking the end of a bundle of burning reeds.

Some acts of power, especially control of the weather, seem to have served mainly a demonstrative function, proving "the shaman's rapport with powerful spirits, which give him power to cure the sick

---

versity of California Press, 1933), 310; B. Whiting, *Paiute Sorcery* (New York: Viking Fund, 1950), 28–30.

93. I. Kelly, *Ethnography of the Surprise Valley Paiute* (Berkeley: University of California Press, 1932), 192.

94. S. W. Hopkins, *Life Among the Paiutes, Their Wrongs and Claims* (Boston: Cupples, Upham and Co., 1883), 55–57; O. Stewart, *Culture Element Distributions*, 423; F. Riddell, "Honey Lake Paiute," 40.

95. Park, *Shamanism*, 40–41, 45.

96. Ibid., 47.

97. Ibid., 57.

and heal the wounded."[98] Occasionally, however, such power was used
for the benefit of the community, for example, by causing the ice to melt
in a river so that a run of badly needed fish could begin.[99] Although the
practice is not specifically reported among the Paiute, Park notes that
neighboring tribes commonly had midwinter performances of novice
shamans, one purpose of which was the exhibition of power.[100] Among
the Klamath, the novice shaman, after receiving power, waits until
winter to prove it; only then does he perform his first cure. We may
note that the repertoire of tricks attested for Klamath shamans has
many parallels with those of Paiute shamans.[101]

As to the social position of Paiute shamans, Park reports that not
every powerful shaman was a chief, but they were typically consulted in
secular matters. Specifically of Wovoka he says,

> [He] was a powerful and influential figure among the Paviotso. He was
> held in high esteem by members of all the bands, and five years after his
> death (in 1932), he was spoken of by nearly all Paviotso with admiration
> and respect. Perhaps some of the influence he enjoyed in later years
> among his own people can be traced to the demand by other Indians for
> his advice on religious matters.[102]

Yet in another place he says, "Prestige and status are expressions of
individual accomplishment, the result of personality and ability." Therefore, no generalization can be made about the social importance of
Paviotso shamans. "One shaman may be respected by the entire group
and consulted on a variety of problems involving personal affairs or
matters of importance to the group, another may be merely a practitioner who is more or less successful in treating the illnesses of members
of the tribe."[103]

Thus among a certain class of Paiute religious practitioners, acts
of power were expected, and one function of such acts was to engender
belief in the power and authority of the practitioner. In this respect

98. Ibid., 15.
99. Ibid., 60–61.
100. Ibid., 122–23.
101. L. Spier, *Klamath Ethnography* (Berkeley: University of California Press,
1930), 259–65.
102. Park, *Shamanism*, 70.
103. Ibid., 103.

Wovoka, although he advocated a doctrine with appeal far beyond the bounds of his tribe, is clearly recognizable as a Paiute shaman.

2. From western North America let us turn to the various Tungus peoples of Siberia, whose culture and beliefs have been so exhaustively described by S. Shirokogoroff.[104] *Shaman* (and its variants) is itself a term from the Tungus languages in which it "refers to persons of both sexes who have mastered spirits, who at their will can introduce these spirits into themselves and use their power over the spirits in their own interests, particularly helping other people, who suffer from the spirits."[105] Like their counterparts elsewhere, these shamans are reported to have performed acts of power, including self-infliction of wounds, various manipulations with fire, and ventriloquism (as western observers were wont to explain the voices heard during the performances).[106] Shirokogoroff remarks that such actions are frequently and erroneously portrayed "as imposture and tricking of the audience."[107] If we are to be fair, however, they should be seen from another perspective:

> As shown, the shamans, especially among the Manchus (under the Chinese influence, I suppose), use a great number of tricks for proving the presence of spirits. Such are e.g. all operations with fire. As a matter of fact, an inexperienced ordinary man cannot take into his mouth burning incense or step on a heap of burning charcoal, etc. without hurting himself. The shamans do it, sustaining sometimes only slight injuries which do not prevent them from going ahead with the performance.

104. S. Shirokogoroff, *Psychomental Complex of the Tungus* (London: Kegan Paul, Trench, Trubner, 1935).
105. Ibid., 269; see 271. On mastery as it relates to the shaman's trance and for a discussion of the communal context of the trance and an extensive bibliography, see L. Peters and D. Price-Williams, "Towards an Experiential Analysis of Shamanism," *American Ethnologist* 7 (1980):397–418. Selections from Shirokogoroff may be found in Overholt, *Prophecy in Cross-Cultural Perspective*, 165–202.
106. See M. Czaplicka, *Aboriginal Siberia* (Oxford: Clarendon, 1914), 228–33. A. Anisimov gives a vivid account of a shamanic performance among a related group of Siberians in which the manifestations of power included various sounds (screams, snorting of beasts, bird calls, whirring of wings) and walking on hot coals; "The Shaman's Tent of the Evenks and the Origin of the Shamanistic Rite," reprinted in Overholt, *Prophecy in Cross-Cultural Perspective*, 150–58. N. Chadwick quotes liberally from eyewitness accounts of shamanic performances, in the process calling attention to such phenomena as "ventriloquism," but her overall concern to highlight the "intellectual" aspect of shamanic activity and the shaman's "solemn religious function" causes her to subordinate the more dramatic aspects of the performances and not inquire into their social function; "Shamanism Among the Tartars of Central Asia," *JRAI* 66 (1936):93–102.
107. Shirokogoroff, *Psychomental Complex*, 331.

These facts are interpreted as due to the power of mastered spirits, and not to the shaman personally. If he succeeds in these tricks, the audience and himself believe that the spirit is actually present.[108]

In the same context he gives the example of a performance at which two members of the audience doubted the shaman's power. "The shaman took a coin from one of them and continued his performance. After a while he asked one of the skeptical men to open his hand and the man, to his great surprise, discovered the coin in his hand. Naturally, he, as well as the audience, were convinced of the great power of the shaman."[109]

This process can be put in a slightly different way. For a shamanic performance to be effective, the audience must be appreciative and sympathetic. When such is not the case, the shaman may have to utilize

108. Ibid. I. Casanowicz describes various shamanic "miracles" and comments, "shamans could hardly, for any length of time, keep up the belief in their superiority without convincing the people by 'miracles'—that is, by executing feats which exceed the power of the laity to perform or understand—of their supernatural endowments"; "Shamanism of the Natives of Siberia," *Annual Report of the Smithsonian Institution, 1924* (Washington, D.C.: Government Printing Office, 1925), 432.

109. Ibid., 331–32. B. Myerhoff writes of an occasion on which she witnessed the Huichol shaman (*mara'akame*) Ramon perform a death-defying series of leaps high up in a mountain canyon. Of the performance she says, "I could not be sure whether Ramon was rehearsing his equilibrium or giving it public, ceremonial expression that day in the barrancas. In societies without writing, official statements about a person's status and skill are often made in dramatic, public, ceremonial form. Whether seen as a practice session or as ritual, the events of the afternoon provided a demonstrative assertion that Ramon was a true *mara'akame* and, like all authentic shamans, a man of immense courage, poise, and balance"; "Shamanic Equilibrium: Balance and Mediation in Known and Unknown Worlds," in *American Folk Medicine: A Symposium*, ed. W. Hand (Berkeley: University of California Press, 1976), 101. W. Hoffman reports that Mide priests were able to make wooden beads, human effigies, and sacred bundles move. He considers these acts to be tricks that "present to the incredulous ocular demonstration of the genuineness and divine origin of the Midewiwin." When such acts are performed before candidates undergoing initiation, they have a "twofold purpose": to impress them with the supernatural power of the Mide priests and to divine whether the spirits are pleased with the contemplated initiation; "The Midewiwin or 'Grand Medicine Society' of the Ojibwa," *ARBAE* 7 (Washington, D.C.: Government Printing Office, 1891), 204–6. To give one further example, T. Beidelman has pointed out that "unlike priests, Nuer prophets must manifest anomalous, extraordinary attributes to demonstrate the validity of their claims to a new and unusual authority. . . . Confirmation of a prophet's calling is mainly through the public evaluation of the kinds of acts the nascent prophet claims to have performed after his strange behavior begins"; "Nuer Priests and Prophets," in *The Translation of Culture*, ed. T. Beidelman (London: Tavistock, 1971), 390. For a description of the miracles attributed to two well-known Nuer prophets earlier in this century, see C. Willis, "The Cult of Deng," *Sudan Notes and Records* 11 (1928):195–208; P. Coriat, "Gwek, the Witch-Doctor and the Pyramid of Dengkur," reprinted in Overholt, *Prophecy in Cross-Cultural Perspective*, 217–30; and A. Alban, "Gwek's Pipe and the Pyramid," *Sudan Notes and Records* 23 (1940):200–201.

various tricks to win over the audience. Over time some of these may become conventionalized and incorporated as a regular part of the ritual.[110] Some, like walking on coals or diving into the water and emerging out of a series of holes chopped in the ice, may become trials to test the power of new candidates. We may note in passing, as both the biblical and the Paiute materials contain examples, that Tungus shamans were thought to have the power to revive the dead.[111]

We ought to pay particular attention to the social support that formed the basis of a Tungus shaman's authority. When, for example, Shirokogoroff describes the formal characteristics of shamanism,[112] the reader is struck by the predominant place that society plays in them. The shaman is a "master of spirits"; indeed, he must have several spirits at his disposal, but they are for the most part spirits already known to the clan and the larger group. His knowledge is to an important extent limited by what the society already knows; if it does not conform sufficiently to this standard, he may not be recognized as an authentic shaman. Furthermore, the methods by which the shaman deals with the spirits and the paraphernalia he or she employs are for the most part traditional, as is the "general theory of spirits, their particular characters, and the practical possibilities of dealing with spirits" that form the "theoretical basis" of shamanic activity. Finally, most shamans are connected with the clan organization. Of all the persons who want to be or "pretend" to be shamans, only those acknowledged by the clan (or some other specific group) are considered to be authentic.[113]

These concepts are illustrated quite nicely by the election of a shaman among the Manchus in which public opinion is seen to play a decisive role, first in favoring the creating of a new shaman and then in a continuous evaluation of the performances of two candidates in terms of a rather well-defined set of communal expectations. Neither of the

110. Shirokogoroff, *Psychomental Complex*, 333–34, 339–40.
111. Ibid., 353, 320.
112. Ibid., 271–74.
113. On this latter point, see ibid., 348–50. Of persons who try to perform outside a proper social context, he says, "These are not shamans, because they cannot produce a real extasy [*sic*], especially without an audience, and they have no social functions, usually no paraphernalia, but they are either dishonest impostors or psychomentally affected people. By this I do not intend to say that they cannot become shamans, but I want only to indicate that they do not function as shamans, have no milieu and probably cannot assume the functions of shamans, because they are not recognized; this may be dependent, at least sometimes, on personal considerations" (350).

candidates was perfectly acceptable, but one was confirmed: although the new shaman did not know all of the spirits and could name only a part of them, he seemed to have reached ecstasy on the last day of the performance and fell down unconscious, "as white as paper, so that it was distressing to look at him," and the public opinion turned in his favour; he had "power" and for a long time the group had not had such a good shaman.[114]

Successful shamans form close bonds with their clients, and as the number of clients increases, they become more and more influential. If a shaman is perceived to have a "bad heart," however, the group often turns against him or her.[115] The audience has a stake in shamans and their performances and enters emotionally into performances. They do not remain aloof. Clan relationships generate sorrow and a desire to help the person for whom the performance is being staged. The performance itself is exciting; because the spirits the shaman controls and embodies are considered to be real, "emotive reactions are quite easy and natural." Further, "the rhythmic music and singing and later the 'dancing' of the shaman gradually involve every participant more and more in a collective action. When the audience begins to repeat refrains together with the assistants, only those who are defective fail to join the chorus."[116] If the audience contains too many individuals who are skeptical or not susceptible to ecstasy, "it may react too slowly to the shaman's suggestions, and the performance may therefore fail."[117] In a real sense, then, the community is in control, is itself, as Shirokogoroff puts it, "the acting agent."

> The issue of a performance depends on the personal ability of the shaman, in so far as his performing corresponds to the expectations of the community, and in so far as it is accepted and thus becomes effective. His individuality in the performance is thus greatly limited by the existing ethnographical and ethnical complexes. The performance must therefore have a form which would correspond to the ideas of the community about the performance and be in accordance with its susceptibility to the influence of suggestion, to hypnosis, and to ecstasy.[118]

114. Ibid., 358; see 353–58.
115. Ibid., 177–78.
116. Ibid., 331. A. Anisimov's account shows remarkably well the extent of the audience's active participation and the intensity of the ecstasy of both shaman and audience; "Shaman's Tent," in Overholt, *Prophecy in Cross-Cultural Perspective*, 150–58.
117. Shirokogoroff, *Psychomental Complex*, 333.
118. Ibid., 335; see 326, 328, 331, 343.

We appear, therefore, to be confronted with a movement that is circular in nature. Tungus society has a certain knowledge of the spirits and certain expectations of those who would claim to control them and manifest their power. The acts of power of a good shaman conform in a broad way to these expectations, with the result that the society accepts the authenticity of the shaman's calling. Tradition defines the actions, the performance of which proves the presence of authentic power.

Conclusion

The results of our three case studies may now be summarized. With respect to the Elijah-Elisha cycle, we have seen that the two prophets are depicted in a similar light, as perpetrators of acts of power. Accounts of these acts tend to be accompanied by responses from those who witnessed them, and such responses are always of essentially the same nature: they acknowledge the prophets' power and authority. Finally, these acts of power are directed at both those who were ill disposed and those who were well disposed toward the prophets. The observations on Wovoka and Paiute shamanism showed that among such individuals acts of power were to be expected; one of their functions was to engender belief in the power and authority of the shaman. Among the Tungus acts of power were expected. Such acts conformed in general to society's expectations for them and were taken as proof of the shaman's power and authority. Without such socially sanctioned proofs, the shaman either would never be confirmed initially or, having been confirmed, would stand in danger of rejection. The Tungus shaman faced the task of proving himself or herself to all members of the group, whether friendly, indifferent, or hostile.

The apparent congruence of these three cases suggests that supernatural confirmation is an important element in the social dynamics of prophecy. Therefore, we can reasonably conclude that the accounts of Elijah's and Elisha's acts of power, whatever else they may mean in the tradition and in the present form of the text, give us a glimpse of the process by which these early Israelite prophets were authorized. Elijah and Elisha are, of course, early Israelite prophets and not simply shamans in the Paiute or Tungus sense. The three display important differences as well as similarities. The differences lie primarily in the specific content of their beliefs, and the similarities are found predominantly in the structure of their relationships with the other members of their society.

Making a judgment about whether the specific acts of power attributed to any of these figures really happened is not particularly important to me. What is clear is that acts of power (or tricks, or miracles), whether witnessed or heard of, had a particular effect upon the relationship that existed between these religious functionaries and their societies. An interesting question is why so few miraculous acts of power occur in the Hebrew Bible outside the Elijah and Elisha cycle. Is this a localized or even individualized phenomemon? Did a certain segment of Israelite society not tolerate such actions, or (perhaps more likely) did a series of tradents not recognize or have interest in the original function of such accounts and therefore alter or ignore them? A study of the other broad category of prophetic acts of power (see n. 39) from the point of view of the conclusions arrived at here might throw some light on this problem.[119]

Finally, some additional words about the social setting of such actions and the stories about them are also in order. In my opinion Burke Long[120] has correctly emphasized that such stories are not to be understood as deriving primarily from circles of pious followers who sought to glorify the prophets. Citing parallels from other cultures, he observes that miracle stories are often encountered in societies where shamanism is in a state of decline and where one of their important functions is to reinforce belief in the institution of shamanism by recounting the feats of powerful shamans of the past, while at the same time allowing skepticism about specific individual shamans of the present. However, the fact that shamans and prophets find themselves the center of controversy and have their authority disputed does not neces-

119. The following proposition would be worth investigating. Begin with the assumption that one will not recognize an intermediary as authoritative without some reason to do so (even in societies where they are common, not everyone who might be considered an intermediary is so recognized). Now if in various societies intermediaries are to some extent dependent upon "acts of power" to motivate public acceptance, and if this dependence is also characteristic of certain biblical prophecy (Elijah and Elisha, at least), then perhaps the Deuteronomistic criterion of fulfillment as the standard for judging prophets can be seen as one development from an underlying belief that contact with the divine ought to result in manifestations, visible to the general public, of unusual ability.

120. B. Long, "The Social Setting for Prophetic Miracle Stories," *Semeia* 3 (1975):46–59.

sarily indicate that their particular religious function is in a state of decline, as Shirokogoroff's observations on the "present state and future of shamanism" make clear.[121] Be that as it may, such a setting would appear to me to fit a later use to which some such stories were put. In the case of Wovoka, his own power was recounted, not that of some more powerful predecessor. The same is true of the Siberian shamans.

Like Long and many others, I think of the Elijah-Elisha cycle as a complex literature in which several stages of development may be evident. In their original setting, the prophetic acts of power seemed to serve primarily to legitimate the authority of the prophet, but subsequent tellings of the story could serve to bolster that authority, whether in a given situation the influence of the prophets was waxing or waning. At later stages of the tradition, of course, the stories could be taken over altogether into the service of larger points of view.[122] In this respect I find myself in closer agreement with Long's more recent remarks on prophetic signs, in which he suggests that certain actions by Elijah and Elisha served to demonstrate their legitimacy and reinforce their claims of authority.[123]

All this having been said, the basic conclusion remains: seeing *is* believing (or should be), at least as far as the relationship of intermediaries to their societies is concerned.[124]

---

121. Shirokogoroff, *Psychomental Complex*, 391–94, 399.

122. R. Carroll, for example, suggests that "the compilers of the books of Kings" were influenced in their selection of stories about Elijah and Elisha by a desire "to draw attention to the resemblance" between these prophets and Moses; "The Elijah-Elisha Sagas: Some Remarks on Prophetic Succession in Ancient Israel," *VT* 19 (1969):412–13.

123. Long, "Prophetic Authority as Social Reality," 11, 15. See also idem, "2 Kings III and Genres of Prophetic Narrative," *VT* 23 (1973):337–48, where the present shape of some of the stories is shown to be "defined by" a specific literary schema in the service of "demonstrative theology," although this represents a reworking and not their original function; and along somewhat broader lines, idem, "Social Dimensions of Prophetic Conflict," *Semeia* 21 (1981):31–53.

124. That a certain way of looking at the world is presupposed in such a relationship is nicely suggested by B. Toelken's turning of a familiar phrase: "If I hadn't believed it, I never would have seen it"; "Seeing with a Native Eye: How Many Sheep Will It Hold?" in *Seeing with a Native Eye,* ed. W. Capps (New York: Harper and Row, 1976), 23.

THE CULTURAL AND HISTORICAL CONTEXT
OF PROPHETIC ACTIVITY

The elliptical boundary in Figure 1 (page 23 above) is intended to suggest that the interactions that constitute the prophetic process take place within a particular cultural and historical setting. Given the widespread distribution of prophetlike phenomena, a great deal of variation can be expected in the details of this context.

With respect to the Hebrew Bible, two general observations can be made about the context in which prophecy took place: First, for all practical purposes it is coterminous with the monarchy. Second, at least as far as named, independently operating prophets are concerned, it appears only in times of special crisis, either domestic (e.g., the transition to the monarchy) or international. The insight that prophets tend to appear in times of crisis has also been applied to the many millenarian movements that have developed within both the Jewish and Christian cultural tradition and in many other cultures. Indeed, Weston LaBarre's major review of the literature on these movements bears the title "Materials for a History of Studies of Crisis Cults."[125]

We might possibly adopt the notion of crisis as a common factor in the context of prophetic action, but such a move must be made with caution. The model with which we have been working has enabled us to identify a wide variety of people involved in social behavior that can be described as prophetic. Similarly, crisis wears many faces. For Jeremiah and Wovoka, the crisis took the form of outside military intervention (threatened or actual) on a large scale, with the potential for major disruptions in the prophet's culture, including the loss of political independence. The focus of the prophet's activity was this national threat. Among the Shona of Zimbabwe, spirit mediums were traditionally called upon in times of wider community crisis, for example, when drought threatened or questions arose as to the succession to a chiefship. M. Daneel, a European who was allowed to consult the high-god Mwari through his medium at Matonjeni, found him to be concerned with the conflict that had arisen as the result of contact between native and white cultures.[126] The period of political and social unrest

125. W. LaBarre, "Materials for a History of Studies of Crisis Cults," *Current Anthropology* 12 (1971):3–44.

126. M. Daneel, *The God of the Matopo Hills: An Essay on the Mwari Cult in Rhodesia* (The Hague: Mouton, 1970); see T. W. Overholt, *Prophecy in Cross-Cultural Perspective*, 234–41.

during the late 1950s and into the 1960s in what was then called Southern Rhodesia saw a rise in African nationalism that was accompanied by an increase in native beliefs and practices. At the level of the whole culture, spirit mediums provided one affirmation of traditional cultural values, but the matters on which they were consulted tended to be of more individual, or strictly local, significance, for example, the various physical afflictions of specific clients.[127]

Several levels of crisis are evident here. In the history of a people, national crises occur or come to a head intermittently. At the individual level, crises recur because life goes on—relationships become strained, people become sick and sometimes die, and the like. That the Innuit shamanistic performance observed by Rasmussen was occasioned by a purely local crisis in the form of an unusually savage storm or that a given Ojibwa shaking tent ceremony might be concerned with the health of a single individual should not be allowed to obscure the underlying similarity of their cultural situation with that of Wovoka or Jeremiah.

Why should prophetic activity be most evident in times of crisis? Presumably at such times humans feel most vulnerable, least in control, and more in need of explanations that will make sense of a seemingly chaotic world. The anthropologist Clifford Geertz has spoken of religion as a symbolic system that "attempts to provide orientation for an organism which cannot live in a world it is unable to understand."[128] The prophetic situation, then, might be described as one in which the basic religiocultural understanding has been undermined. In what did the integrity of the Seneca male reside when the game animals were depleted and he could no longer go to war? To be able to subsist, more emphasis had to be put on farming, which was women's work! What could be more damaging to the system of beliefs about Yahweh's election and protection of his people Israel than the death of "good king Josiah" and the subsequent conquest of Jerusalem by the Babylonians? In these situations people found chaos breaking in upon them but heard as well prophets like Jeremiah and Handsome Lake proclaiming an interpretation that promised a new order.

---

127. P. Fry, *Spirits of Protest: Spirit-Mediums and the Articulation of Consensus Among the Zezuru of Southern Rhodesia (Zimbabwe)* (Cambridge: Cambridge University Press, 1976); see T. W. Overholt, *Prophecy in Cross-Cultural Perspective*, 241–48.
128. C. Geertz, "Ethos, World View, and the Analysis of Sacred Symbols," in *The Interpretation of Cultures* (New York: Harper and Row, 1973), 140–41.

A word of caution is in order. No consensus exists as to why some crises become the occasion for prophetic activity and others do not.[129] Our observations about crisis must therefore be taken as descriptive and not as implying anything specific about cause.

The scope of the crisis probably has some effect on the content of the prophet's proclamation, especially on the amount of innovation it contains. Accounts of shamanistic cures give the impression of highly stereotypical activities with a somewhat restricted scope for individual differences among shamans within the same culture. During a séance, shamans may relay to their audience messages from the spirit world.[130] Still, in many cases emphasis on communication of an explicit message is minimal.[131] In instances of major cultural crises, the situation is likely to be reversed, with great emphasis placed on verbal communication.

With respect to how much old and how much new material we might expect to find in a prophet's message, no neat formula is available. Clearly, the message must have recognizable roots in the traditional but now threatened cultural synthesis for it to be understood and acceptable. In Burridge's scheme the millennial prophet is central to a process by which a people moves from a time when the old rules of the society remained intact, through an interim period of no rules, and to a final synthesis of a set of new rules.[132] Thus a consistent theme in Handsome Lake's preaching was condemnation of the individual autonomy and glorification that had been characteristic of the old Iroquois way, lately fallen into the chaos of social pathology, with advocacy in its place of restraint in social affairs. Elizabeth Tooker suggests that what the prophet was trying to do was "to introduce a value system . . . consistent with the economic system that was also introduced at the same time."[133] With the collapse of the old hunting-trading system, the Iroquois were forced into more intensive agriculture, but plow agriculture required male participation and the yearly agricultural schedule demands a stable social order. Therefore, the values he selected empha-

---

129. See K. Burridge, "Reflections on Prophecy and Prophetic Groups," *Semeia* 21 (1981):99–102.

130. See A. Anisimov, "Shaman's Tent," in Overholt, *Prophecy in Cross-Cultural Perspective,* 154.

131. A good example may be found in Boas's texts relating to shamanism among the Kwakiutl of the Pacific northwest; see ibid., 23–58.

132. Burridge, *New Heaven New Earth,* 165–69.

133. E. Tooker, "On the New Religion of Handsome Lake," *Anthropological Quarterly* 41 (1968):187.

sized communal order over individual gratification. If these values were similar to those of the white society, the reason was primarily that both were agrarian.

That the message of the biblical prophets arises out of and is in dialogue with the religious traditions of their people is well known.[134] For his part Jeremiah stood within the old exodus-election tradition of Judah (cf. for example, 2:1–8). His accusations against the people make clear that from his viewpoint (i.e., that of a "pure" Yahwist; the question arises of how many such Yahwists were among his compatriots) the present period had no rules, at least in the sense that the people had chosen to ignore important aspects of their covenant with Yahweh. Put differently, we might say that he was interpreting the fruits of a long process of acculturation in the land of Canaan as apostasy. Yet in the future he saw the institution of a new covenant, recognizable in terms of the old but operating on the basis of new assumptions about the nature of the relationship between Yahweh and Israel (31:31–34).[135]

Almost inevitably when we look at a prophet we consider first the content of the proclamation. Having adopted this approach, we are likely to be most impressed by the differences from all other prophets about whom we know. The argument of this book has been that when we go beneath the level of content to that of process, significant similarities begin to emerge. Having learned something about the underlying similarities of specific prophets like Wovoka, Jeremiah, and Handsome Lake, we have, I believe, gained at least some understanding of all other prophets as well.

---

134. See R. Clements, *Prophecy and Covenant* (London: SCM Press, 1965); and idem, *Prophecy and Tradition* (Oxford: Blackwell, 1975).

135. The specific social functions of particular intermediaries (e.g., upholding the established social order, encouraging social change, diagnosis and curing of sickness, etc.) depend upon the circumstances and needs of this larger sociohistorical context. They are also influenced by the prophets' relative position within society, that is, whether they are associated with the establishment or with some peripheral group. On the distinction between "central" and "peripheral" possession, see I. Lewis, *Ecstatic Religion* (Baltimore: Penguin, 1971); and R. Wilson, *Prophecy and Society*, 32–88 passim.

5

Prophecy and Divination

Prophets are intermediaries whose primary business is to facilitate communication between a divine reality and a human audience. However, they do not have a monopoly on this function. In ancient Israel as well as in other societies both ancient and modern, diviners were an important source of knowledge about "the purposes, will, or attitudes of the gods."[1]

Divination may be thought of as "a technique of communication with the supernatural forces that are supposed to shape the history of the individual as well as the group"[2] or an "attempt by men to gain access to the knowledge which only the spirits, as omniscient beings, possess about the source of those social and physical ills which may afflict a community."[3] Commonly, a diviner making an inquiry of a god employs some physical technique, such as casting lots or examining the entrails of a sacrificial animal.

Students of ancient Israelite religion have typically stressed the *differences* between prophets and diviners. The former are seen as agents who take the initiative in addressing the words of Yahweh to the people and through whom the deity speaks freely. The latter are consulted and must make formal inquiry to discover the deity's will. However, this difference should not blind us to important *similarities* between prophets and diviners, similarities that can contribute to our understanding of the nature of prophetic activity.

1. B. Long, "Divination," *IDBSup*, 241.
2. A. L. Oppenheim, *Ancient Mesopotamia* (Chicago: University of Chicago Press, 1964), 207.
3. J. Mack, "Animal Representations in Kuba Art: An Anthropological Interpretation of Sculpture," *Oxford Art Journal* (November 1981):53.

EVIDENCE FOR DIVINATION
IN ANCIENT ISRAEL

The Hebrew Bible has six prominent terms designating persons who practice divination. A generic term covers *diviner* and/or *divination* (*qsm/qesem;* cf. Isa. 3:2, Mic. 3:7). The others seem to label more specialized functions: *soothsayer* (*'nn,* literally, one who "causes [a spirit?] to appear"; cf. Mic. 5:12), *augur* (*nḥš,* one who looks for omens; cf. Lev. 19:26), *sorcerer* (*kšp;* cf. Mic. 5:11), *spirit of the dead* (*'ob;* Lev. 19:31), and *familiar spirit* (*yiddě'ōnî;* Lev. 19:31). The original meanings of these terms are not always clear,[4] but the fact that in some contexts several of them are mentioned together indicates that some differences of function were recognized (cf. Deut. 18:9–14, which adds charmer and necromancer to the above list; 2 Kings 17:17; 21:16; Jer. 27:9).

In addition to these terms, references to specific acts of divination are made. Sometimes Yahweh's will is sought by consulting him with the Urim and Thummim (Num. 27:21; 1 Sam. 14:41; 28:6), inquiring of an ephod (1 Sam. 23:9–12; 30:7–8), or casting lots (Prov. 16:33; Josh. 18:6, 8, 10; Judg. 20:9). Several texts refer to messages derived from omens, as in the case of the selection of Rebekah (Gen. 24:12–14, 21, 26–27) and Jonathan's decision to attack the Philistines (1 Sam. 14:8–12; cf. also 2 Sam. 5:22–25; Num. 17:1–13 [MT 16–28]; Isa. 7:11–12).[5] Yahweh can communicate through dreams (Gen. 31:10–13, 24, 29; 41; 1 Sam. 28:6) or through a ritual ordeal (Num. 5:11–31). Hosea speaks of the people inquiring of a thing of wood (4:12).

Several texts narrating events from the premonarchic and earliest monarchic periods of Israelite history give us some details about how and why divination was employed. We first consider three that describe a process of selection using lots: 1 Samuel 14; Joshua 7; and 1 Sam. 10:17–27.

1 Samuel 14. This text contains the most elaborate of these accounts. The narrative is set in the context of continuing hostilities

---

4. Cf. I. Mendelsohn, "Divination," *IDB,* vol. A-D, 856–58.
5. Cf. A. Guillaume, *Prophecy and Divination among the Hebrews and Other Semites* (London: Hodder and Stoughton, 1938), 118–27, gives examples of omens among tenth-century C.E. Arabs.

between the Israelites under King Saul and the Philistines, and it contains references to four occasions on which Yahweh was consulted (or almost consulted) for instructions on what to do. First of all, Jonathan, acting on his own and without Saul's knowledge, looked for a sign that would reveal whether or not Yahweh would grant him success in his planned attack against the Philistine garrison (vv. 8–12). The answer was affirmative.[6] Next, Saul, noticing something wrong in the Philistine camp and discovering that Jonathan and his armor-bearer were missing, summoned Ahijah the priest to bring the ephod.[7] Events were unfolding rapidly, however, and Saul ordered the priest to break off the consultation and hurried into battle (vv. 18–20). Later, Saul proposed a nighttime pursuit of the routed Philistines. It is noteworthy that on this occasion the priest took the initiative by intervening and suggesting a consultation (vv. 36–37). Saul complied, posing his questions about the success of the plan in such a way that they could be answered either yes or no (cf. 1 Sam. 23:11; 30:8; 2 Sam. 5:19). Clearly, the expectation was that Yahweh would answer because when he did not Saul assumed that someone among the people had sinned, and he initiated another consultation to determine where the guilt lay (vv. 38–39). In this final consultation (vv. 40–42), the Urim and Thummim[8] were employed to render a series of choices between alter-

6. Cf. ibid., 164–76. At the end of his discussion, Guillaume asks how, if there are recognizable techniques for producing the results of divination, the words that accompany its announcement, "Thus says Yahweh," can be justified. He continues, "The answer, I think, is that to the Hebrews God was the immediate cause of every act in the universe, and therefore sights and sounds which fell upon the senses of the prophet at the moment of prophesying were 'signs' communicated by God at that particular moment to indicate his will. A similar explanation may be given to the oracles of the Beduin. Originally they rested on a belief in the power of a heathen god; in Islam they were believed to rest on a knowledge of Allah's purposes. In Islam, as in Judaism, there is no immediate agent between God and Creation" (183).

7. LXX substitutes *ephod* for MT's *ark*. R. W. Klein accepts this reading on the grounds that "during Saul's reign" the ark was "stationed at Kiriath-jearim" and that the language corresponds to references to consulting the ephod in 1 Sam. 23:9 and 30:7; *1 Samuel* (Waco: Word Books, 1983), 132; cf. H. P. Smith, *A Critical and Exegetical Commentary on the Books of Samuel* (New York: Scribner's, 1902); P. K. McCarter, *I Samuel* (Garden City, N.Y.: Doubleday, 1980).

8. Although it is clear enough in this passage that the Urim and Thummim were one mechanism for arriving at conclusions by "lots," the few references to them give no information about what they were, apart from the fact that they were small enough to be kept in a pocket of the "breastplate of judgment," one of the priestly garments (Exod. 28:30; Lev. 8:8). E. Robertson has argued plausibly that the Urim and Thummim were small objects upon which were written letters of the Hebrew alphabet. Because letters also stood for numbers, these could be drawn from the breastplate to render decisions by

natives that culminated in the identification of the guilty party.[9] The language is that of casting lots: in the first round, Saul and Jonathan "were taken," and the people "went free"; in the second and final round, Jonathan "was taken."

Two of these four consultations have as their purpose the acquisition of information about the outcome of a future event, specifically, a battle (1 Sam. 14:8–12, 36–37). Presumably, the aborted consultation (vv. 18–19) had a similar goal. The last (vv. 40–42) seeks to identify the person guilty of a particular infraction. All are directed to Yahweh and assume that he is capable of and willing to provide the desired information. All are structured in such a way that the deity is given the means (a sign, lots) to choose the correct one of two alternatives.

We need to keep in mind that communication is, by definition, a two-way exchange. In general we might say that if prophetic oracles are a natural way for a deity to initiate communication with a human audience, then divination is a natural way for human beings to initiate communication with a god. However, some cases do not fit neatly into this scheme. In 1 Sam. 14:36–37 we hear of a priest who takes the initiative in suggesting a consultation. As in the case of prophets who come forward to address an audience, he presumably had reason to believe that Yahweh had something to say in the present situation. Then again, we frequently hear of people consulting the prophets, a topic to which we will shortly return.

Joshua 7. This text contains the narrative of an unsuccessful Israelite attack on the city of Ai and the subsequent attempt by Joshua to determine the reason for the failure and to take corrective action. One striking feature of the narrative is that it depicts a period of direct, verbal communication between Joshua and Yahweh immediately following the debacle. The question of why Yahweh allowed his people to be defeated (vv. 6–9) is answered with the revelation that someone has violated the covenant requirement to destroy captured persons and

---

means of odd-even discriminations; "The Urim and Thummim; What Were They?," *VT* 14 (1964):67–74.

9. Modern translations (e.g., RSV, NEB, JB) and commentators (e.g., Smith, *Samuel*; McCarter, *1 Samuel*; Klein, *1 Samuel*; cf. A. Toeg, "A Textual Note on 1 Samuel XIV 41," *VT* 19 [1969]:493–98; E. Noort, "Eine Weitere Kurzbemerkung zu 1 Samuel XIV 41," *VT* 21 [1971]:112–16) tend to follow the longer LXX text in v. 41. The shorter version found in MT is presumably the result of an error of the eye, the copyist accidentally skipping material between the first and the last occurrence of the word *Israel*.

booty (vv. 10–12). Yahweh then provides a general prescription for remedying the situation (v. 12), specific directions for how to identify the culprit by lot (vv. 13–14), and an appropriate punishment to be imposed (v. 15). Despite all this, he does not verbally identify the guilty party. For this he seems to prefer speaking through the sacred lots. Indeed, according to the narrative, Yahweh initiates the divinatory procedure (v. 14).

As in 1 Sam. 14:40–42, the goal of the divination was to identify a guilty party, and the procedure by which this was done was much the same. Here groups were apparently brought before Yahweh one at a time. Those he designated innocent were (it is implied) set free; the guilty were "taken." The main difference between the accounts is that 14:40–42 adds the detail that the Urim and Thummim were used in the selection process.

1 Samuel 10:17–27. This story—how Saul was chosen by lot to be Israel's first king—has strong parallels to the narratives just discussed. Samuel is said to have convened an assembly of Israelites for the purpose of conducting the divination (v. 17), but, as in 14:36 and Josh. 7:14, Yahweh is ultimately the initiator of the action; Samuel is here speaking as a prophet (vv. 18–19), and the selection process is undertaken as a result of Yahweh's decision to accede to the people's request for a king. The account of the selection is couched in the familiar language of "bringing near" and "taking."

The meshing of prophetic oracle and act of divination in this story could be the result of editorializing by a prophetic narrator who wanted to suggest that having a king must be seen as a kind of judgment against the people.[10] Be that as it may, the function of the divination is to discover whom Yahweh had chosen (v. 24).

A second consultation is required to complete the process because when the field was finally narrowed to Saul, he was nowhere to be found (v. 21). In this case, however, direct verbal communication occurs: Yahweh was asked about Saul's whereabouts, and he responded by naming the hiding place (v. 22). The parallel to Joshua 7 is obvious. Apparently, lots are the accepted way to get information of a certain type, namely, which of two alternatives Yahweh prefers. Whether this

10. McCarter, *1 Samuel.*

passage is a single story or a conflation of two episodes, the narrative suggests that it was natural to consult Yahweh in these ways. Nor is the passage negative about this resort to divination or, for that matter, about the kingship.[11]

1 Sam. 9:1—10:16. Two additional narratives from the life of Saul describe divinatory procedures. In 1 Sam. 9:1—10:16 Samuel identifies and secretly anoints Saul to be prince over the Israelite people. Although this anointing is the focal point of the story, divination plays an important role in the development of the action, in which Samuel is pictured as a well-known diviner, and the initial contact between the two occurred when Saul sought his services.

As the narrative begins, Saul and a servant have been sent by his father to retrieve some asses that had wandered off and become lost. Their initial lack of success prompts the servant to suggest that they seek the aid of a local "man of God" whose qualifications appear to be that he is "held in honor" and that everything he says "is sure to happen" (1 Sam. 9:6). The purpose of the visit is to be put on the right track with respect to the task of finding the lost asses (vv. 6b, 8b). We will see that divination for the purpose of finding lost property is fairly common in a number of cultures, and resorting to it seems an altogether natural stratagem in this narrative. Even the author of the editorial explanation in v. 9 takes it for granted and labels the procedure with the rubric "to seek God."[12]

Saul and his servant proceed to the seer's city and ask directions for how to find him. Meanwhile, the narrator adds parenthetically that on the previous day Yahweh had revealed to Samuel that Saul would be coming and should be anointed prince, so that he could save the Israelites from their Philistine enemies (9:15–16). When Saul comes into view, Yahweh identifies him to Samuel as the man about whom he had spoken (v. 17). The men meet, identities are established (vv. 18–19 show that Saul and the servant had previously known Samuel only by reputation), and Samuel gives Saul instructions about what he should do (v. 19). Samuel also volunteers the information that the lost asses have been found (v. 20a). This verse marks the end of the divinatory consultation. Without being asked, the seer answers the question the

11. At least not in its original form; cf. McCarter, *1 Samuel*; Klein, *1 Samuel*.
12. Cf. McCarter, *1 Samuel*, 177.

client brings, and the narrative action moves on toward Saul's anointment. The abruptness of the announcement about the asses may seem surprising, but it can be understood in the context of a convention in some forms of divination according to which the client conceals from the diviner the purpose of his or her visit.

The question has been raised whether Samuel or some anonymous "man of God" was being sought out to perform a divination. The identity of the diviner is clear enough in the narrative as it stands, but ambiguity arises when the tradition history of the passage is considered. The story may in fact be a composite in which a folktale about the recovery of lost livestock has been meshed with an account of Saul's anointing. A series of tensions within the narrative gives evidence that this is the case. For example, at the beginning of the story the "man of God" and/or "seer" is unknown to Saul by name (1 Sam. 9:6–13), yet in 9:14 the narrator suddenly identifies him with Samuel, a well-known figure (cf. 10:14–16). Again, according to 9:19 Samuel sends Saul on ahead to the high place, but 9:22 indicates that Samuel in fact escorted him to the sacrificial meal.[13]

According to Bruce Birch, an editor "influenced by prophetic tradition" worked the two stories together. He believes, however, that Samuel was already identified in the folktale, the "theme" of which is "Saul's unwitting encounter as a youth with Samuel."[14] H. W. Hertzberg maintains the anonymity of the diviner in the folktale.[15] In fact, despite widespread recognition that the passage is composite, no consensus has developed on the exact verses to be assigned to each of the stories.[16] What is important to notice is that the transformation of the folktale did not result in denying, obliterating, or criticizing Saul's recourse to divination. Rather, the account is accepted and utilized by the narrator, whose apparent desire is to show that Saul, directed by divine providence, found more than he sought.[17] Furthermore, according to this composite narrative, the diviner is not simply a technician who in some mechanical way answers the query of a client, but rather a

---

13. Cf. further B. Birch, "The Development of the Tradition on the Anointing of Saul in I Sam. 9:1–10:16," *JBL* 90 (1971):56.

14. Ibid., 67; cf. P. K. McCarter, *1 Samuel*, 186–87.

15. H. Hertzberg, *I & II Samuel: A Commentary* (Philadelphia: Westminster Press, 1964), 79.

16. Cf. Klein, *1 Samuel*, 84.

17. Cf. McCarter, *1 Samuel*, 176, 185.

person through whom Yahweh speaks and who is free to enlarge the scope of the consultation beyond what the client originally intended.

The final result is a narrative in which Samuel appears in a role readily recognizable to students of divination in other cultures. Samuel is sought out to provide information about the location of lost property and receives a fee for his services (1 Sam. 9:7–8). His reputation as a diviner depends upon the accuracy of the information he provides (v. 6). Hertzberg comments on the initial meeting in which Samuel gives Saul information about the lost asses: "The servant was right; this seer knows his business."[18] Finally, the diviner knows without having to be told the reason for the consultation.

1 Samuel 28. We come finally to the story of Saul's consultation with the spirit medium at Endor (1 Samuel 28). The narrator at once shows that Saul has two problems. First, the Israelite army is threatened by an apparently superior force of Philistines (vv. 4–5). Second, although consulting Yahweh is normal in such situations, the usual means for doing so have become unavailable: Samuel is dead; Saul (presumably acting as a loyal Yahwist) has banished "the (images of) ancestral spirits and ghosts"[19] from the land (v. 3); and Yahweh has refused to speak by such usual means as dreams, Urim, and prophets (v. 6).

Saul instructs his servants to seek out a woman who is a medium for ancestral spirits,[20] and they inform him that such a person is at Endor. Although he is said to have banished these diviners from the land (1 Sam. 28:3), this one remains, and her location is well known to them. Disguised, Saul visits her at night, and the narrative gives the impression that the procedures for consulting such a person are familiar. He knows what he wants and what to ask the woman to do: "Divine

18. Hertzberg, *I & II Samuel,* 83.
19. Cf. Klein, *1 Samuel.*
20. In H. Hoffner's opinion, the term 'ôb refers to a pit dug to give spirits of the dead temporary access to the upper world; "Second Millennium Antecedents to the Hebrew 'ôb," *JBL* 86 (1967):385–401. Subsequently, J. Lust argued persuasively that the 'ôbôt are neither pits nor wizards, but "the spirits of the deceased fathers living in the netherworld" and also "the instruments representing them" (in 2 Kings 21:6 and 23:24, they are apparently material objects); "On Wizards and Prophets," *VTSup* 26 (1974):139, 142. Leviticus 20:27 appears to suggest that mediums may be possessed by one or more of these spirits ("a man or woman in whom there is an ancestral spirit ['ôb] or a ghost [yiddě'ōnî]"), although the translations (RSV, NEB, JB) obscure this. In 1 Sam. 28:3, 9, as in Lev. 20:27 and elsewhere, these two terms occur as a pair; Klein (*1 Samuel,* 270) understands the latter to refer to "ghosts or their images."

for me," he says, "by means of an ancestral spirit, and bring up for me the one whom I tell you" (v. 8). He requests the spirit of Samuel (v. 11). This work is done, and a dialogue follows (vv. 15–19). The experience leaves Saul flat on his face in fear (v. 20).

Calling up ancestral spirits is a specific form of the generic operation, divination. Exactly what the woman did is unclear. The most obvious interpretation would be that she somehow summoned Samuel's ghost and allowed Saul to converse directly with his deceased counselor. J. Lust suggests that vv. 13–14 show that Saul did not himself see Samuel's ghost, and thus the ghost's words (vv. 15–19) "must logically be considered as the witch's interpretation for Saul of what she heard in her vision."[21] In any case, W. A. M. Beuken's argument to the effect that Samuel appears as a prophet and in doing so does not allow the woman time to conjure a ghost[22] has to be rejected as a piece of apologetic that does not come to terms with the underlying religious phenomenon.

The diviner does not seem to have been limited by the question posed by her client. Even allowing for some editorial expansion, Saul gets more than he requested. Saul came seeking guidance for action in war (v. 15) but got instead a prediction of defeat and death (v. 19).[23] Lust points out that the "structure and wording" of accounts of persons consulting prophets is "practically the same" as 1 Samuel 28: someone in a situation of urgency goes to a prophet (or sends a messenger), puts a question to Yahweh through the prophet (only information is asked for, not help), and the man of God answers with an oracle.[24]

ATTITUDES TOWARD DIVINATION
IN ANCIENT ISRAEL

The Old Testament presents conflicting evidence with respect to the place of divination in Israelite religion. On the one hand, we have

21. Lust, "On Wizards and Prophets," 141 n. 7.
22. W. Beuken, "I Samuel 28: The Prophet As 'Hammer of Witches,'" *JSOT* 6 (1978):8.
23. McCarter (*1 Samuel*, 423) understands vv. 17–18 to be part of a pre-Deuteronomistic stratum of the text; Klein (*1 Samuel*, 270) considers vv. 17–19aa to be Deuteronomistic.
24. Lust, "On Wizards and Prophets," 142; cf. 1 Kings 14:1–16; 22:5–6; 2 Kings 8:7–15.

already examined a number of passages that suggest a matter-of-fact acceptance of various forms of divination.[25] On the other hand, some references to divination brim with hostility. A classic example is Deut. 18:9–14.[26] Here various types of divination are prohibited, along with child sacrifice. The rationale for the condemnation is that these things were practiced by the nations whom Israel dispossessed (v. 9, 14), and Yahweh prohibits them. The Deuteronomistic bias in favor of prophecy is also in evidence here because the text turns immediately to the promise of a prophet like Moses who will speak the words that God will put in his mouth and who is, therefore, to be heeded (18:15–22). Similar prohibitions appear in Lev. 19:26 and 19:31.

Other passages condemn divination in a less systematic or specific way. The text of 1 Sam. 15:23, assigned by McCarter to the "middle stage in the growth" of 1 Samuel,[27] equates rebellion with "the sin of divination." Several kinds of divination are included in the catalogue of evils by means of which Manasseh angered Yahweh (2 Kings 21:6), and the prophets sometimes speak disapprovingly of divination (Hos. 4:12; Isa. 2:6; 8:19; 19:3; 44:25; 47:13; Jer. 27:9; 29:8). Jeremiah and Ezekiel accuse their prophetic opponents of uttering false divinations and the like (Jer. 14:14; Ezek. 12:24; 13:1–7, 23; 21:29; 22:28), but the content of what these opponents said and not divination itself seems to be under attack.

Thus, there is strong evidence that in some periods, or in certain circles, divination was recognized and accepted as a part of Israelite life, while in other times, or among different groups, it was rejected. Given the evidence that Yahweh was sometimes consulted by divination and made his will known through its results, we are led to ask on what grounds some could condemn it. The fact that passages criticizing divination are found largely in Deuteronomistic and prophetic contexts suggests that ideology and vested interests had a role to play. Broadly speaking, the goal of prophecy and divination were the same: to facilitate communication between Yahweh and his people. The Deuteronomist believed, however, that the Mosaic prophet was "the only legitimate channel of communication between Yahweh and the peo-

25. Such acceptance is probably also implied in passages like 2 Sam. 16:23 and Isa. 3:2–3, where diviners are simply mentioned in a list of official roles.
26. Cf. R. R. Wilson, *Prophecy and Society in Ancient Israel* (Philadelphia: Fortress Press, 1980), 160–66.
27. His "prophetic history"; McCarter, *1 Samuel*, 18, 20.

ple."[28] Furthermore, the reason commonly given for rejecting divination is that it is a foreign practice,[29] which is in harmony with the Deuteronomist's polemic against the native Canaanite culture (e.g., Deut. 7:1–5).

For their part, the prophets would have had an interest in establishing their authority over against any who might challenge them. In prophetic texts the thing under attack sometimes seems to be not so much divination itself as particular communications that the prophet considered false and misleading (cf. Jer. 14:14; 29:8; Ezek. 13:1–12, 20–23; 22:28) or that had been performed opportunistically for personal gain (Mic. 3:5–7, 11).[30] In these texts the generic term for divination (*qsm*) is used, and the precise nature of the activity is difficult to discern. A reasonable suggestion would be that the reference is to the practice of "consulting" (inquiring of, *drš*) Yahweh through a prophet in order to obtain information and advice. Such consultations are reported with reasonable frequency in the historical and prophetic books. For example, Jeroboam I sent his wife to Ahijah to inquire about the health of their son (1 Kings 14:1–18); in response to Jehoshaphat's request, Ahab sought from the prophets Yahweh's word about the advisability of going to war (1 Kings 22:5, 7, 8); and Zedekiah asked Jeremiah to inquire of Yahweh on the matter of Nebuchadrezzar's attack (Jer. 21:1–7; cf. 37:3).[31]

DIVINATION AS A SOCIAL PROCESS

As in the case of prophecy, the Hebrew Bible does not set out to give us a description of the social role of diviner or of the actual process

28. Wilson, *Prophecy and Society*, 162.
29. E.g., Deut. 18:9, 12; 2 Kings 9:22; 17:17 (cf. vv. 7–8, 15); 21:6; Isa. 2:6; 8:19; cf. Isa. 19:3.
30. Because there is no evidence that the prophets mentioned in the Jeremiah, Ezekiel, and Micah passages were employing any technical means of divination, possibly *divination* is used here in a general sense to refer to communication between God and humans. That divination itself is not under attack is, nonetheless, revealing.
31. Other examples may be found in 1 Sam. 9:9; 2 Kings 3:9–20; 8:7–15; 22:11–20; Ezek. 14:7 (where coming to a prophet to inquire of Yahweh is spoken of as a routine occurrence); 20:1–2; Mic. 3:6–7 (which implies that under normal conditions prophets could be expected to have visions and divinations). Note that 2 Kings 1:2, 3, 6, 16 assumes that inquiring of both Baal and Yahweh is normal practice, although in Israel the latter is to be preferred (the consultation is not said to be through a prophet, but Elijah is the one who eventually supplies the requested information, v. 16). Isaiah 31:1 and Jer. 10:21 both condemn Judah for not inquiring of Yahweh in the process of planning foreign policy; prophets are not explicitly mentioned in either passage.

of divination in which such persons engaged. Nevertheless, at least a partial picture of this activity can be assembled from available evidence.

We learn nothing about how people came to be diviners, but evidently in Israel, as in other cultures, diviners were entitled to receive a fee for services rendered. In the story of Saul and the lost asses, a small amount of silver is mentioned as the appropriate payment (1 Sam. 9:7–8), and Mic. 3:11 speaks of prophets who "divine for silver." The narratives tell of "fees for divination" brought to Balaam by the elders of Moab and Midian (Num. 22:7) and of forty camel loads of goods brought to Elisha by Hazael of Damascus (2 Kings 8:7–9). Despite the last example, one does not hear of rich diviners, which agrees with the situation found in other cultures. Divination is usually not a profitable profession, and diviners certainly cannot earn a living from such a talent.

Even in societies that accept diviners as performers of a legitimate social role, members of the public evaluate the skill and effectiveness of individual practitioners by various largely informal tests. Several texts, mainly in the prophetic books, speak of such critical evaluation. As we might expect, the prophets most often dispute the "worthless divination" of their opponents on the basis of preconceived ideas about what Yahweh was likely to say to his people. Thus, Jeremiah rejects their message of peace (14:13–15), their encouragement of revolt against Nebuchadrezzar (27:9–10), and their prediction that the exile would be short (29:8). Ezekiel also rejected the message of peace (13:6–10; probably 21:29), and he condemned those he understood to be encouraging wickedness (13:22–23; 22:27–31). Micah 3:5–7 mentions the prediction of peace but adds a motivational criterion, asserting that the contents of these prophets' speeches were determined by self-interest. These criteria are obviously subjective. A more objective criterion is whether what the diviner says proves to be accurate. Use of this standard is explicit in 1 Sam. 9:6 and implicit in Joshua 7. Convinced that the defeat at Ai was the result of some infraction of the rules of combat, Joshua cast lots to determine the identity of the guilty party, who was subsequently executed. Ai was attacked again, this time successfully. We can safely assume that the victory would have been understood as a proof of the divination's validity.

Divination is understood to be one way in which gods can communicate with their human devotees. Among both Israelites and their neighbors, the client most frequently initiates such communication. We have numerous examples:

Joshua (Num. 27:21)

Saul (1 Sam. 9:5–10; 14:41–42; 28:7–8; 1 Chron. 10:13)

Balak (Num. 22:4–7)

Philistine rulers (1 Sam. 6:2)[32]

This pattern is not invariable however. After the defeat of the Israelites at Ai, Joshua, their leader, prayed to Yahweh and was instructed by him to divine (Josh. 7:6–15). In both 1 Sam. 10:17–24 and 14:36, the person who ultimately performed the divination (Samuel and a priest, presumably Ahijah, respectively) initiated the process. In these cases Yahweh, working through a diviner, might be said to initiate the contact.[33] Similarly, note that in the narrative of the lost asses Saul initiated the consultation, but Samuel had an independent message that dramatically broadened its scope (1 Sam 9:15–20; 9:27—10:8).

The texts indicate divination was used by Israel and its neighbors in ways that correspond to what we know about its use in other cultures. Divination is commonly employed when the situation requires a selection from among alternatives or a decision about some course of action. Thus, lots were used to apportion the land (Joshua 18–19), select between goats on the Day of Atonement (Lev. 16:6–10), identify a guilty party (Josh. 7:14–18; 1 Sam. 14:41–42), decide who would go into battle (Judg. 20:8–11), and choose a king (1 Sam. 10:20–24). Information gained by divination was used to decide the time or route of a march (Num. 27:21; Ezek. 21:21–23), as well as whether to pursue the enemy or flee to safety (1 Sam 23:9–12; 30:7–8; cf. 14:37).

A closely related motivation for divination was to gauge the probability of future success (1 Sam. 14:8–10, 37; 28:15; 30:7–8; 1 Kings 20:33). Diviners could be enlisted to help recover lost property or information (1 Sam. 9:5–10, Neh. 7:65)[34] or to discover the cause of some circumstance (Gen. 30:27; Josh. 7:14–18; 1 Sam. 6:2; Jonah 1:7).

---

32. Cf. also Lev. 20:6; Isa. 8:19; 19:3.

33. In the last case Yahweh is said not to have responded to the divination (1 Sam. 14:37). We could still argue that Yahweh initiated the contact, however, because when in response to the silence Saul redefined the problem, there was an answer (vv. 38–42).

34. Cf. Gen. 44:15, which seems to refer to Joseph's ability to know that his possession had been "stolen."

The kind of knowledge communicated in divination follows from these purposes. The seeker learns the cause of a present state of affairs (1 Sam. 6:1–9; Gen. 30:27), the identity of a guilty party (Joshua 7; 1 Sam 14:41–42), what to do in the future (1 Sam. 28:15; at least this is what Saul sought), or what will happen in the future (1 Sam 28:19). On one occasion the divination served to legitimate a sociopolitical innovation, the monarchy (1 Sam. 10:17–24).

The biblical texts give us some insights into how divination works. We notice first of all some indications that it is rulebound, eliminating discretion on the part of the diviner. Mechanisms are employed that seem to ensure that results, because they are free from human manipulation, represent what God intends. Thus, the cows pulling the cart upon which Yahweh's ark had been placed were left to choose their own way (1 Sam. 6:7–9), and Yahweh identifies the guilty party through the random fall of Urim and Thummim (1 Sam. 14:41–42). Sometimes the circumstances are more ambiguous, as in the case of spirit mediums, who might be in a position to manipulate the apparitions they call up (cf. 1 Sam. 28:11–19).

Proverbs 16:33 may be taken as a general statement of the theory of such divination: humans cast the lots, but God decides.[35] Micah seems to allude to this explanation when he says that seers and diviners are shamed when Yahweh does not answer (3:7). 1 Samuel 10:24 explicitly states that Saul, selected by lot to be Israel's king, was chosen by God (cf. Josh. 7:14; Judg. 20:18).

We have already encountered a formal element well suited to such a theory, namely, the format of a choice between two alternatives that is employed in some divination. So, the Philistine cows will either take the ark to its own land or not (1 Sam. 6:9); Yahweh takes one of the groups presented to him and lets the other go (Josh. 7:14–18; 1 Sam. 10:17–24; 14:41–42);[36] and the Babylonian king consults his diviners about which of two roads to take (Ezek. 21:21–22).

This rule is not hard and fast, however. The account in Joshua 18–19 about how land was apportioned among seven tribes seems to

35. Cf. also Prov. 16:10 ("divination is upon the king's lips / his mouth is not unfaithful in judgment"), which rationalizes the king's authority by trading on the assumption that the results of divination are determined by God.
36. Cf. 14:36–37; 23:9–12; 30:7–8; Lev. 16:8–10; and, by implication, Num. 27:21; Neh. 7:65.

suggest the use of a separate token for each. When Saul and his servant went to consult the diviner (1 Samuel 9), they wanted to know the whereabouts of the lost asses. A yes-no pattern of inquiry pursued deftly and at length might well have yielded this information, but it was not used. Again, Saul asked the spirit medium an open-ended question about what he should do (1 Sam. 28:15).

The more general question in this regard is whether in the process of facilitating communication between Israelites and Yahweh the diviners had an active or a passive function. Did they shape the outcome, or were they conduits for the transmission of information? The evidence just cited suggests the latter, but, as usual, the matter is not that simple. In the Balaam narrative, Balak's request (Num. 22:6–7) implies that the diviner can manipulate the outcome of the divination in the client's favor. The wording of Balaam's response (23:21–23) seems to imply that such manipulation is possible, although he makes what must have been the diviner's standard assertion: what is communicated is solely the deity's will (cf. Num. 24:1; once the deity's will is ascertained, divination stops). Similarly, Isa. 47:9, 12 seems to suggest that the Babylonians used several types of divination ("sorceries," "enchantments") to ensure (military) success. In the consultation about the lost asses, Samuel seems to have gone beyond the matter at hand to utter an additional message based on revelation (1 Sam. 9:15–20; 9:27—10:8). Of course, when mediums (1 Samuel 28) or prophets are consulted, the process is by its very nature much more open-ended. Again, examples from other cultures show how interpretation, even the interpretation of texts, can be part of the function of a diviner.

ISRAELITE AND NON-ISRAELITE DIVINATION

Over the centuries and around the world, divination has played an important role in many societies. In addition to the sheer scope of its distribution, anyone studying divination is impressed by the variety of techniques employed. Even societies where one form has gained special prominence, say, the inspection of livers from sacrificial animals (hepatoscopy) in ancient Babylon or the casting of palm nuts (Ifa divination) among the Yoruba of west Africa, acknowledge and use other techniques as well. Evidence for several kinds of divination in

Israel—among them signs (1 Sam. 14:8–12), lots (Joshua 7; 1 Sam. 10:20–21; 14:40–42), consulting with ancestral spirits (1 Samuel 28), and inquiring through prophets (1 Kings 14:1–18)—is therefore not at all unusual.

Divination not uncommonly coexists with other forms of inter-mediation. Prophets and diviners may be found in ancient Israel, in Islam,[37] and among the Seneca.[38] Siberia[39] and tribal India[40] have both shamans and diviners, and Uganda[41] has diviners and spirit mediums. The roles are not always clearly distinguishable and sometimes are practiced by the same person.

Viewed against the background of non-Israelite practices, the divination mirrored in the Hebrew Bible appears quite normal. The social process is a familiar one, as is the underlying assumption upon which it is based, namely, that such acts are a valid form of communication with the divine. This normalcy can be illustrated by viewing the characteristics of Israelite divination just described in the context of non-Israelite practices.

Diviners typically receive some remuneration for their services. As in the case of Samuel (1 Sam. 9:7–8), the fees are often modest.[42] However, sometimes diviners make a living at their profession,[43] and sometimes they are not paid at all.[44]

37. R. Serjeant, "Islam," in *Oracles and Divination*, ed. M. Loewe and C. Blacker (Boulder, Colo.: Shambhala, 1981), 215–32; cf. A. Guillaume, *Prophecy and Divination*, 130–31.

38. T. W. Overholt, *Prophecy in Cross-Cultural Perspective* (Atlanta: Scholars Press, 1986), 101–22.

39. Ibid., 150–58.

40. Ibid., 249–84.

41. P. Rigby, "Prophets, Diviners, and Prophetism: The Recent History of Kiganda Religion," *Journal of Anthropological Research* 31 (1975):116–48.

42. J. Beattie, "Divination in Bunyoro, Uganda," *Sociologus* n.s. 14 (1964):46; B. Colby and L. Colby, *The Daykeeper: The Life and Discourse of an Ixil Diviner* (Cambridge, Mass.: Harvard University Press, 1981), 121, 127, 137; W. Hammond-Tooke, "The Initiation of a Bhaca Isangoma Diviner," *African Studies* 14 (1955):20–21; E. McClelland, *The Cult of Ifa Among the Yoruba*, vol. 1, *Folk Practice and the Art* (London: Ethnographica, 1982), 97; P. Rigby and F. Lule, *Divination and Healing in Peri-Urban Kampala, Uganda* (Kampala, Uganda: Makerere Institute of Social Research, 1971), 28, 42, 50–54; A. Shelton, "The Meaning and Method of Afa Divination among the Northern Nsukka Ibo," *AA* 67 (1965):1444; V. Turner, *Revelation and Divination in Ndembu Ritual* (Ithaca, N.Y.: Cornell University Press, 1975), 319, 321; Overholt, *Prophecy in Cross-Cultural Perspective*, 93–95.

43. W. Bascom, *Ifa Divination: Communication Between Gods and Men in West Africa* (Bloomington: Indiana University Press, 1969), 87–88; C. Radha, "Tibet," *Oracles and Divination*, 6; E. Ramponi, "Religion and Divination of the Logbara Trive of North-Uganda," *Anthropos* 32 (1937):851.

44. Radha, "Tibet," 6. Divination was part of the regular duties of Tibetan lamas.

Audiences are no more passive with respect to diviners than they are to prophets, and diviners' activities are evaluated in a variety of ways. One criterion is whether the outcomes of the divination are accurate and effective. If they are, the reputation of the diviner will be enhanced (as in 1 Sam. 9:6).[45]

Diviners may also be judged on the basis of stereotypical expectations that are, of course, culture-specific, but the process is the same as in Israel. These expectations sometimes involve procedural details. For example, the first verse recited by Ifa diviners should not relate directly to the client's problem,[46] and they should not be too facile in their recitation of the verses associated with the sign revealed by casting the palm nuts.[47] However, conformity to expectations goes beyond this. According to A. Irving Hallowell, Ojibwa shaking tent "conjurers" successfully played a role that had been prescribed by their culture and in the process strengthened belief in the reality of the spirits.[48] The society may want to know that the diviner has had the proper dreams or visions and has been certified by an established diviner.[49] What he or she says should be in correspondence with sentiments of the group.[50] Furthermore, diviners are subject to critical evaluation by their peers (cf. Mic. 3:11), who may be present at a divining session,[51] or a client may consult another diviner to check the accuracy of the first or to try to obtain a more favorable result.[52]

On this matter of evaluation, note that factors may predispose people to believe in the results of divination and therefore offset any errors and inaccuracies. One such factor is the belief that the gods are responsible for the existence of, or otherwise stand behind, the system

45. Colby and Colby, *Daykeeper*, 71, 136–37; D. Merkur, *Becoming Half Hidden: Shamanism and Initiation among the Inuit* (Stockholm: Almqvist and Wiksell International, 1985), 115; J. Morrison, "The Classical World," in *Oracles and Divination*, 103–4; Overholt, *Prophecy in Cross-Cultural Perspective*, 70–71; Radha, "Tibet," 6–7; Rigby and Lule, *Divination and Healing*, 50–54.

46. Bascom, *Ifa Divination*, 79.

47. McClelland, *Cult of Ifa*, 57–58.

48. Cf. the texts reprinted in Overholt, *Prophecy in Cross-Cultural Perspective*, 67–74.

49. Colby and Colby, *Daykeeper*, 71; M. Fortes, "Religious Premises and Logical Technique in Divinatory Ritual," *Philosophical Transactions of the Royal Society of London*, B, 251 (1966): 414; Hammond-Tooke, "Initiation."

50. Radha, "Tibet," 35.

51. McClelland, *Cult of Ifa*, 57–58.

52. S. Whyte, *Misfortune and Divination in Bunyole* (Kampala, Uganda: Makerere Institute of Social Research, 1971), 6–7.

134

134 CHANNELS OF PROPHECY

of divination.[53] For example, that the god Ifa "himself set up the system" of divination that bears his name is assumed,[54] and the formula "Ifa says . . . ," is frequent in the verses.[55] Another factor is that the nature of the problems dealt with (e.g., a Yoruba client's wish to know where to build a new dwelling) may make accurate assessment of results difficult and invite after-the-fact rationalizations like "Had I not divined, things would have turned out worse."[56] Sometimes procedural safeguards make it unlikely that the diviner could manipulate a result. For example, the Yoruba client routinely withholds from the diviner information about the problem that motivated the consultation.[57]

Divination may in fact play a centrally important role in a given society.[58] About the Late Assyrian Empire, Jana Pečírková has said that it was "an inseparable part of the political ideology and the practical politics of the state."[59] In such situations the tendency is to focus any suspicions that might arise on individual diviners, not on the system itself.[60]

In both Israel and elsewhere, the client normally takes the initiative, but this practice should not of itself lead us to a negative evaluation of divination, and on this matter, as elsewhere, ambiguity exists. In examining the biblical evidence, we noted a case where the diviner-priest took the initiative in suggesting a consultation (1 Sam. 14:36–37), and in several narratives Yahweh appears to be the one who set the process in motion (Josh. 7:10–15; 1 Sam. 10:17–21). In other passages Yahweh's intention is freely announced with respect to some

53. W. Bascom, "The Sanctions of Ifa Divination," *JRAI* 71 (1941):44–45, 52; J. Clarke, "Ifa Divination," *JRAI* 69 (1939):235; Fortes, "Religious Premises," 416; E. Idowu, *Olodumare; God in Yoruba Belief* (London: Longmans, 1962), 77; H. Junod, *The Life of a South African Tribe*, II. *Mental Life*, 2d rev. ed. (London: Macmillan, 1927), 570; Mack, "Animal Representations"; E. McClelland, "The Significance of Number in the Odu of Ifa," *Africa* 36 (1966):423–24.
  54. McClelland, *Cult of Ifa*, 41.
  55. Bascom, *Ifa Divination*, 141ff.
  56. Bascom, "Sanctions of Ifa," 44–45, 69–70; McClelland, *Cult of Ifa*, 56.
  57. Bascom, "Sanctions of Ifa," 48–52. Such secrecy is also attested among the Arabs (Guillaume, *Prophecy and Divination*, 118, 126–27), as well as the Zezeru of Zimbabwe and the Navajo (cf. Overholt, *Prophecy in Cross-Cultural Perspective*, 94, 243).
  58. Bascom, *Ifa Divination*, 12, 60–62, 91–99, 118; McClelland, *Cult of Ifa*, 13, 95; G. Park, "Divination and Its Social Contexts," *JRAI* 93 (1963):195–209; Shelton, "Meaning and Method," 1454.
  59. J. Pečírková, "Divination and Politics in the Late Assyrian Empire," *Archiv Orientalni* 53 (1985):155.
  60. Bascom, "Sanctions of Ifa," 53, 70–71; Junod, *Life of a South African Tribe*, 569; Overholt, *Prophecy in Cross-Cultural Perspective*, 71.

matters but must be divined for matters of another type (Josh. 7:10–12, 13–21; 1 Sam. 10:20–21a, 21b-23). Elsewhere, possession of the medium by a god might be understood to mean that the deity has responded to the people's initiative by becoming available to them. Above all, the consensus among those utilizing divination—that it is a divinely sanctioned mode of communication—should alert us to its great importance.

Gods are often assumed to have specifically established divination as a way to communicate with humans,[61] and divinatory acts may begin with an invocation of gods.[62] C. J. Gadd speaks of an assumption among the Babylonians that an "understanding of the world-order" is possible to humans only if it is granted by the gods. "Divination," he says, "is the process (or one process) by which this communication is maintained, when the god's attention has to be ascertained, and is not freely announced."[63] According to A. Leo Oppenheim, the ancient Mesopotamians assumed that the gods were able and willing to communicate their intentions and that they were "interested in the well-being of the individual or the group."[64] For the Yoruba, Ifa, the god who speaks through the verses, was empowered and commissioned by the high-god, Olorun.[65] We should not overlook the testimony of diviners themselves who say that such activities represent "a communication with the gods."[66]

This communication is not limited to the specific information or advice received during a consultation. Sometimes, particularly when game is scarce, the Montagnais-Naskapi native Americans of the northeastern woodlands divine by scapulimancy (i.e., the interpretation of spots and cracks on shoulder blade bones that have been held in a fire) as part of their preparations for a hunt. This operation is motivated by a

---

61. Bascom, *Ifa Divination*, 109; O. Gurney, "The Babylonians and Hittites," in *Oracles and Divination*, 146; McClelland, *Cult of Ifa*, 13, 41–42.

62. Bascom, *Ifa Divination*, 37–38; Clarke, "Ifa Divination," 239; W. Lambert, "The 'Tamitu' Texts," *La divination en Mésopotamie ancienne et dans les régions voisines* (Paris: Presses Universitaires de France, 1966), 120; E. Reiner, "Fortune-Telling in Mesopotamia," *JNES* 19 (1960):24–25; Turner, *Revelation and Divination*, 274–75.

63. C. Gadd, "Some Babylonian Divinatory Methods and Their Inter-Relations," in *La divination en Mésopotamie ancienne*, 22.

64. A. L. Oppenheim, *Ancient Mesopotamia* (Chicago: University of Chicago Press, 1964), 207; cf. his "Perspectives on Mesopotamian Divination," *La divination en Mésopotamie ancienne*, 36.

65. Bascom, *Ifa Divination*, 119.

66. Colby and Colby, *Daykeeper*, 229–30; McClelland, *Cult of Ifa*, 87.

desire not only to locate animals but also "to re-establish harmony between individual hunters and the supernatural world believed to control the game supply."[67] By performing divination, the Montagnais-Naskapi do not abandon their own judgment about where animals might be found, although this interpretation has sometimes been offered. Divination, rather, is part of a whole "cycle of communications between men and spirits." This cycle begins before the hunt and lasts through disposal of the dead animals' remains; it comes to awareness especially in the killing of special animals (e.g., bear, moose, beaver), which involves special rites. "The use of divination is the sign that a spiritually important hunting event is imminent." Divination provides "a theatrical representation" of a normally "hidden aspect of the killing of animals"; it affirms a relationship and starts a "cycle of exchange."[68]

Each culture has a standard set of motivations for divination and of expectations about what knowledge may be obtained through it. Frequently—as in 1 Sam. 14:8–12, 36–37 and in 1 Kings 22:5–6, 15 (where prophets are consulted)—a client seeks guidance for future actions[69] or wishes to learn whether a proposed enterprise will be successful.[70] Diviners often assist in locating lost or stolen property or identifying thieves,[71] which is reminiscent of 1 Sam. 9:5–10. They also may be called upon to diagnose illness.[72]

Often gods are assumed to speak through prophets freely, but in divination speech is assumed to be filtered through some form of mechanical technique. Communication with the divine by means of

67. L. Vollweiler and A. Sanchez, "Divination—'Adaptive' From Whose Perspective?" *Ethnology* 22 (1983):193–94.
68. A. Tanner, "Divination and Decisions: Multiple Explanations for Algonkian Scapulimancy," in *The Yearbook of Symbolic Anthropology*, ed. E. Schwimoner (London: C. Hurst, 1978), 97.
69. Bascom, *Ifa Divination*, 51, 118; J. Boston, "Ifa Divination in Igala," *Africa* 44 (1974):350; S. Dornan, "Divination and Divining Bones," *South African Journal of Science* 20 (1923):506, 508; Radha, "Tibet," 4–5.
70. W. Eiselen, "The Art of Divination as Practised by the BaMasemola," *Bantu Studies* (1932):10; Junod, *Life of a South African Tribe*, 561; Radha, "Tibet," 4–5.
71. Beattie, "Divination in Bunyoro," 45; Colby and Colby, *Daykeeper*, 223; Dornan, "Divination and Divining Bones," 505; Mack, "Animal Representations"; Overholt, *Prophecy in Cross-Cultural Perspective*, 74–76; Radha, "Tibet," 4–5; Shelton, "Meaning and Method," 1447–49.
72. 1 Kings 14:1–20. Cf. Colby and Colby, *Daykeeper*, 223, 231; Junod, *Life of a South African Tribe*, 550–51; Mack, "Animal Representations"; Overholt, *Prophecy in Cross-Cultural Perspective*, 91–94, 279–82; Radha, "Tibet," 4–5; Ramponi, "Religion and Divination," 851; Turner, *Revelation and Divination*, 214, 230.

divination is, therefore, both limited and subject to subjective manipulation by the diviner. Basing a judgment about the comparative worth of prophecy and divination on such a supposition is dangerous, however. On the one hand, proving that the prophet's words are the unaltered words of the god would be difficult. On the other hand, divination tends to be rulebound, and the diviner's discretion, if not eliminated, is at least severely curtailed. One piece of evidence for this lack of discretion is the tendency for questions asked during divination to be phrased in such a way that they can be answered yes or no, the god being left to make the choice between alternatives.[73]

In Ifa divination, the diviner casts palm nuts, which are either loose or arranged on a chain, and then recites a series of verses associated by tradition with the resulting pattern. The activity proceeds according to strict rules, deviation from which is noted and criticized by both clients and other diviners. Subjective manipulation of the loose nuts or the chain would be difficult and is protected against by the fact that clients often keep the reason for the consultation secret and themselves select from the recited verses the one appropriate to their situation.[74] The Ifa verses form a body of tradition so important that they are in effect the unwritten scriptures of the Yoruba.[75] This kind of textual regulation of the results of divination can be found in ancient Mesopotamia, where omen lists and the like existed in written form. The result was a collection of generally accepted rules that introduced a degree of regularity into the interpretation of omens.[76]

Some forms of divination are apparently much easier to manipulate than Ifa. A Navajo diagnostician, arm trembling, may silently recite

73. J. Aro, "Remarks on the Practice of Extispicy in the Time of Esarhaddon and Assurbanipal," *La divination en Mésopotamie ancienne*, 109–17; Bascom, *Ifa Divination*, 51; idem, *Sixteen Cowries: Yoruba Divination from Africa to the New World* (Bloomington: Indiana University Press, 1980), 5–7; C. Blacker, "Japan," *Oracles and Divination*, 69; Gurney, "Babylonians and Hittites," 149–50; Lambert, "'Tamitu' Texts," 121; McClelland, *Cult of Ifa*, 49; Morrison, "The Classical World," 96–97, 99–100.

74. Bascom, *Ifa Divination*, 12, 50, 54, 68–71, 77.

75. Ibid., 11.

76. Gurney, "Babylonians and Hittites," 166–67; S. Hooke, *Babylonian and Assyrian Religion* (London: Hutchinson's University Library, 1953), 87–91; E. Leichty, "Teratological Omens," in *La divination en Mésopotamie ancienne*, 131; A. L. Oppenheim, "Divination and Celestial Observation in the Last Assyrian Empire," *Centaurus* 14 (1969):98, 121; idem, "A Babylonian Diviner's Manual," *JNES* 33 (1974):197–220; Pečírková, "Divination and Politics," 157, 167–68; Reiner, "Fortune-Telling in Mesopotamia," 31. Cf. also M. Jackson, "Sacrifice and Social Structure Among the Kuranko," *Africa* 47 (1977):123–24; M. Loewe, "China," *Oracles and Divination*, 48–49, 53.

a list of diseases, causes of disease, or curing ceremonials; when the arm ceases to tremble, the correct choice has been reached.[77] Among the Kuba of Zaire, the diviner recites a list of names or formulae while rubbing a disk on the back of a carved figure that has been anointed with oil. The word being uttered at the moment the disk sticks is understood to be the answer to the client's question. In addition, the diviner personalizes the recited list by utilizing knowledge of the client's activities, social situation, and the like.[78] In such cases the diviner would seem to have a certain amount of control over the result, but this is not what the diviners say or (at least most of) their audiences believe. For example, the Navajo diviner Gregorio describes his trembling arm as acting compulsively and outside his control.[79]

Even given stronger controls, we should not think of the diviner as trapped by an inflexible technique. In Ifa, for example, divine control (Ifa himself selects the figure and is the source of the verses) and human interpretation (the client selects as applicable one of the verses the diviner has memorized for that figure) are balanced. The client's interpretation of the results of the divination is affected by the number and kind of verses the diviner has memorized for a given figure. The diviner may attempt to influence the interpretation by improvising a verse or supplying a verse connected with another figure and also has some discretion in prescribing the required sacrifice, a standard part of the content of every message received through divination.[80]

Other examples of divination display a similar balance between prescription and interpretation. Among the Ixil Maya, the diviner selects a series of "day names" by scooping up a handful of seeds and laying them out on a cloth in a pattern of rows and columns. This process would be difficult to manipulate subjectively. Once the pattern of day names has been established, however, the diviner chooses from among the meanings associated with each of the days the one most appropriate for the present situation. In this the diviner may utilize knowledge of both the situation that prompted the consultation and the way the world runs.[81] Similarly, BaMasemola diviners interpret the pattern into which the cast bones fall, probably using their knowledge

77. Overholt, *Prophecy in Cross-Cultural Perspective*, 92, 95–96.
78. Mack, "Animal Representations."
79. Overholt, *Prophecy in Cross-Cultural Perspective*, 92.
80. Bascom, *Ifa Divination*, 11, 69–71, 76; McClelland, *Cult of Ifa*, 41–50.
81. Colby and Colby, *Daykeeper*, 230–33.

of tribal and personal affairs in the process.[82] One type of Tibetan divination involves the practitioner grasping a Buddhist 108-bead rosary. The beads between the two hands are counted, and formulae yield the general meaning of the number of beads between grasping hands, as well as texts giving detailed answers to questions for various combinations of numbers. However, the diviner's "intuitive feeling for the situation" is said to introduce an element of "creation or inspiration" into the process.[83] Again, in scapulimancy the cracks and scorch marks on the bone are generated randomly, but the diviner has to interpret them. This interpretation can be affected by how the bone is held in relation to the surrounding geography. In addition, various interpretations of any given pattern are possible.[84]

Finally, consider the matter of inspired intermediaries divining. In the Hebrew Bible, we hear of persons consulting prophets, and we can note examples of similar activity in other cultures as well: A. Anisimov reports that after a curing séance, a Siberian shaman divined with rattle and reindeer scapula to answer clanspeople's specific questions about the future.[85] In Japan, local guardian deities may reveal through a possessed villager the prospects for the coming harvest.[86] Among the Hill Saora, shamans divine while in trance, and V. Elwin reports that visitors drop in when a shaman is known to be in trance because consulting him or her then about one's personal affairs is economical .[87] Handsome Lake, the Seneca prophet, divined in a case of suspected murder.[88]

This overlapping of functions can be nicely illustrated with an example from Kiganda society (Uganda), which has both diviners and prophets.[89] Occasionally single individuals combine both roles, espe-

82. Eiselen, "Art of Divination," 28–29.
83. Radha, "Tibet," 15–16.
84. Vollweiler and Sanchez, "Divination," 199–201.
85. Cf. the text reprinted in Overholt, *Prophecy in Cross-Cultural Perspective*, 157.
86. Blacker, "Japan," 80–83.
87. V. Elwin, *The Religion of an Indian Tribe* (London: Oxford University Press, 1955), 277–78; for traditional Ugandan societies, cf. Rigby and Lule, "Divination and Healing."
88. Overholt, *Prophecy in Cross-Cultural Perspective*, 114.
89. Along with mediums, diviners function mainly to "aid the common man to order and safeguard his future, and . . . give him a means of acting to achieve these ends"; their primary orientation is toward the future. Prophets are associated with national gods at national and royal shrines. The priests at these shrines are primarily oriented toward the past, and prophets speak mostly to "the king and a few senior chiefs and notables." P. Rigby, "Prophets, Diviners, and Prophetism," 131.

cially during times of crisis, such as the period when colonial rule was coming to an end. Peter Rigby supplies a case study of one such person, Kibuuka Kyobe Kigaanira (i.e., Kigaanira the medium of Kibuuka Kyobe, one of the important national hero-gods), who, after he was already "involved in the divinatory aspects of Kiganda religion,"[90] was possessed by Kibuuka and instructed to establish himself in the god's national shrine. There he carried on a dual role, divining throughout his career but also performing national prophetic functions (e.g., he advocated the restoration of Buganda glory, the expulsion of the whites, the return of the king, and the return to the old religion).[91] He was jailed because of his activity but released after Uganda achieved its independence in 1963. After his release, "he returned to divination and the mediumship of Kibuuka."[92] Divination is portrayed here as an indigenous base from which prophecy can emerge when needed (in a time of crisis) but that it never really transcends.

PROPHECY AND DIVINATION

Our knowledge about the development of prophecy in Israel is sketchy. For instance, the relationship between early and writing prophets is debated, with many seeing a sharp division between them. Yet the biblical narratives designate both by the same terms (prophet, seer) and describe them in such a way that the reader is aware of a continuity of message and speech forms between the two.[93] Although the use of writing may have had some effect upon prophetic behavior,[94] early prophets need not be considered inferior to later ones; both served as intermediaries between their people and Yahweh and could affect the lives of individuals and groups.

90. Ibid., 134.
91. Ibid., 135–36.
92. Ibid., 139.
93. Cf. R. Wilson, "Early Israelite Prophecy," *Int* 32 (1978):3–7; H. Huffmon, "The Origins of Prophecy," in *Magnalia Dei, The Mighty Acts of God,* ed. F. Cross, et al. (Garden City, N.Y.: Doubleday, 1976), 181; J. Porter, "The Origins of Prophecy in Israel," in *Israel's Prophetic Tradition,* ed. R. Coggins, et al. (Cambridge: Cambridge University Press, 1982), 12–31; R. Rendtorff, "Erwägungen zur Frühgeschichte des Prophetismus in Israel," *ZTK* 59 (1962):145–67; S. Herrmann, *Ursprung und Function der Prophetie in alten Israel* (Wiesbaden: Westdeutscher Verlag, 1976).
94. M. Haran, "From Early to Classical Prophecy: Continuity and Change," *VT* 27 (1977):385–97.

We do not need to trace some sort of genetic development from divination to prophecy. Rather, the focus should be on the importance of communication between God and humans. The underlying assumptions about the possibilities and nature of divine-human communication—that such communication is possible, that the deity is ready and willing to engage in it, and that it is normally carried on through intermediaries—seem to provide the foundation for belief in both prophecy and divination. If we define *religious intermediation* as a process of communication between the human and the divine spheres in which messages in both directions are channeled through one or more individuals who are recognized by others in the society as qualified to perform this function, then both are intermediaries. Just as early Israelite prophets are not inferior to later prophets, so diviners are inferior to neither. Their activities are, however, somewhat different.[95]

To speak of divination and prophecy as in some respects "different" implies an emphasis on the observable activities of the bearers of these roles (physical techniques over against "direct" inspiration, waiting to be consulted over against taking the initiative, etc.). To speak of them as the "same" assumes that the most relevant point of comparison is the social function of intermediation/communication. To speak of an area where the differentiation is "fuzzy" (e.g., diviners taking the initiative, prophets being consulted) resembles the first approach more than it does the second. Note that there are differences in mode of operation between early and canonical biblical prophets (the former sometimes formed groups, they did not leave a written deposit of their words, they addressed mostly kings and not a larger audience), but their "sameness" is more important.

We should realize that assigning names is not a neutral activity. Serge Moscovici[96] points out that "naming" bestows upon something "a settled position in the culture's *identity matrix*." Further, naming "is not a purely

95. Cultures may display a preference for intermediaries of a certain type. Available evidence suggests that in the Mesopotamian heartland, divination was of great importance, but prophecy was not. There were prophets at Mari on the western "periphery of Mesopotamia" (cf. Wilson, "Early Israelite Prophecy," 10), although H. Huffmon suggests that the requirement, or sometimes suggestion, that their oracles be confirmed by technical divination (extispicy) shows that they "were not regarded as a fully acceptable means for divine revelation by the royal administration"; "Prophecy in the Mari Letters," *BA* 31 (1968):109; cf. 121–22. In the Hebrew Bible as it has come down to us (much influenced in the historical and prophetic books by Deuteronomistic theology), prophets appear as the preferred form of intermediary.

96. S. Moscovici, "On Social Representation," in *Social Cognition*, ed. J. Forgas (New York: Academic Press, 1981), 196–97.

intellectual operation enhancing clarity or logical consistency: it is an operation that is subservient to a social purpose." As a result of naming, the thing can be described and qualities imputed to it, it can be distinguished from other things, and "it becomes subject to a convention between those who use it and share the same convention."

"Prophet" and "diviner" are the equivalents in English of category designations already present in the Hebrew Bible. To some extent the distinction must be based on observable behavior (e.g., there are different Hebrew terms designating various specialized roles within these broad categories), and categories serve the useful function of reducing "the complexity of the social environment." But the creation of separate categories results in a masking of similarities, and this may in part be intentional. Categorization tends to protect "the value system which underlies the division of the surrounding social world."[97]

Roles presuppose "some essential characteristic" defining membership in the category.[98] But which characteristic is considered "essential" no doubt depends upon the point of view of the person describing the role. So, to talk about the difference between prophets and diviners in terms of direct contact with Yahweh versus manipulation of physical objects already displays a certain prejudice. It also has the effect of making the distinction between these roles appear quite large. If intermediation/communication is taken as the essential characteristic, then this impression of difference fades.

The differences have tended to dominate the discussion of biblical prophecy and divination. For example, Herbert Huffmon understands the prophet to be "a person who through non-technical means receives a clear and immediate message from a deity for transmission to a third party." This definition highlights the contrast "with learned, technical divination and the use of interpretative skills."[99] Insofar as "interpretative skills" refers to the ability, learned through formal training, to read the signs displayed in the entrails of sacrificial animals, or the like,[100] this difference seems accurate enough, but we must not assume that prophetic speech was simple reporting that involved no interpretation at all of the supposed direct contact with deity. What lies behind the debate between Jeremiah and Hananiah (Jeremiah 28), two Yahweh prophets who came to opposite conclusions about a particular specific

97. H. Tajfel and J. Forgas, "Social Categorization: Cognitions, Values and Groups," in *Social Cognition*, 116–23.
98. R. Brown, *Social Psychology* (New York: Free Press, 1965), 154.
99. Huffmon, "Origins of Prophecy," 172.
100. Huffmon, "Prophecy in the Mari Letters," 103.

historical circumstance, if not interpretations of experience based on differing understandings of the relationship of Yahweh to his people? More recently, Huffmon has argued that the results obtained in Israelite priestly divination by lots, like similar forms in modern cultures studied by anthropologists, are not really random but are manipulated by the diviner so that they express the group consensus and legitimate an already obvious course of action.[101] This assertion may to a certain extent be true, although he seems to underestimate the safeguards against arbitrary interpretations already discussed (one of his examples is Ifa divination). However, we might also ask whether the utterances of prophets are not similarly open to manipulation. When Micah (3:5–12) and Jeremiah (6:14; 14:14–15; 23:16–17) rail against false prophets, we infer that they are accusing them of saying what people wanted to hear, but did the true prophets like themselves do any differently? Were they not saying what a certain group "wanted" (i.e., thought it appropriate) to hear? Given the social dynamics, how free and spontaneous the words of any prophet can be is an open question. Kenelm Burridge has argued that "a prophet carries the interpretative role of the diviner out of an established framework into a quite new ambience of awareness. . . . He must articulate thoughts and aspirations and emotions that are immanent in the community to which he speaks if he is to be acceptable as a prophet."[102] Here again the dividing line between divination and prophecy is blurred.

True, the words of the biblical prophets were often at odds with the religion of the majority of the people they addressed and therefore "more often than not . . . played a destabilizing rather than a validating role in the religious life of their contemporaries."[103] This fact does not, however, undermine the validity of Burridge's observation. Insofar as prophets, by definition, had to have supporters, they could surely have been giving expression to the convictions of a portion of the population.

101. Huffmon, "Priestly Divination in Israel," in *The Word of the Lord Shall Go Forth,* ed. C. Meyers and M. O'Connor (Winona Lake, Ind.: Eisenbrauns, 1983), 355–59.

102. K. Burridge, *New Heaven New Earth: A Study of Millenarian Activities* (New York: Schocken Books, 1969), 154–55.

103. J. Blenkinsopp, *A History of Prophecy in Israel* (Philadelphia: Westminster Press, 1983), 15. Cf. M. Bourdillon, who contrasts nationalistic Israelite prophets with Shona oracles, in "Oracles and Politics in Ancient Israel," *Man* 12 (1977):124–40.

Robert Wilson[104] also stresses the difference between the two roles when he says that "unlike diviners and priests, prophets come into direct contact with the divine, either when they are possessed by the divine or when they supernaturally transcend the human world to enter the divine realm. Prophets are therefore channels through which divine messages reach the ordinary world and through which humans can gain direct access to the divine." Note that the last sentence makes two statements about prophets. The first fits diviners as well because they are also channels for messages from the divine world. We have seen that in both ancient Israel and elsewhere the results of divination are considered to reveal the will of the god, a point Prov. 16:33 states directly:

> The lot is cast into the lap,
>   but the decision is wholly from the Lord.

If Yahweh's will can be revealed in longer oracles, certainly it can also be revealed in a simple yes or no.

Wilson's second statement, that prophets provide "direct access to the divine," suggests a more promising criterion for separating the two but is not unambiguously true. Distinguishing clearly between prophet and diviner is difficult because of the fuzzy area between them. For example, because spirits speak through them, African spirit mediums and Ojibwa shaking tent shamans seem, like prophets, to offer direct access to the divine. Yet both are sought out for answers to questions and problems that are typical of consultations with a diviner.[105] These examples are not unlike the biblical accounts of consulting prophets. The medium at Endor no doubt employed a technique for summoning "gods" (1 Sam. 28:13),[106] but the result on this occasion was a direct experience of an ancestor spirit, Samuel. In 1 Sam. 10:17–24 we are privy to an occasion on which Samuel functioned both as a prophet and as a diviner.[107]

104. Wilson, "Early Israelite Prophecy," 8.
105. For examples of consulting shaking tent shamans for the purpose of diagnosing and curing illness, cf. Overholt, *Prophecy in Cross-Cultural Perspective*, 63–66.
106. Cf. M. Hutter, "Religionsgeschichtliche Erwägungen zu `ĕlōhîm in 1 Sam. 28, 13," *Biblische Notizen* 21 (1983):32–36.
107. Especially in his chapters on divinatory prophecy and dreams and visions, Guillaume points to close parallels in technique between Israelite prophecy and more recent Arabic modes of divination (omens, dreams, visions). For Guillaume, who operates within the framework of an evolutionary view of religion, the uniqueness of the

H. M. Orlinsky's differentiation between diviners and prophets is even stricter: only the canonical prophets are to be considered really prophets; all the rest (Samuel, Gad, Elijah, Elisha, and others) are to be classed as diviners.[108] Huffmon criticizes Orlinsky's assertion that in Israel no development leads from divination to prophecy and says that this view seems to assume the latter originated in something like "a miraculous mutation in the people of Israel."[109] Orlinsky does acknowledge some similarities between the earlier diviners (whom he calls *seers*) and the canonical prophets: for example, the activities of both may involve ecstasy and the messages of both are grounded in Yahweh monotheism. However, the differences between the two are stressed: seers were members of guilds, but prophets received a spontaneous calling against their will; seers "predicted the future and attempted to control it," and prophets did not; the seer was "a man of action," but the prophet "a man of words."[110] These characterizations are not well documented and are sometimes—as in the case of the claim that seers were sought out for advice, for which they were paid, and prophets were not—inaccurate. Furthermore, they ignore what I have taken to be the major point of comparison: both were important and conventional means by which the people communicated with Yahweh.

The model of prophetic activity introduced in chapter 2 and used throughout this study represents the social dynamics of intermediation as a process of communication. Speaking of God as the initiator of this process has been convenient for us although we have seen in this chapter that that is not invariably the case. The dynamics of divination can also be illustrated by a version of the model. The communication is still dialogical, but this time it is normally (again, exceptions exist) initiated by the client (or audience).

Figure 3 diagrams the act of consulting a diviner. Such a consultation begins when the client, motivated by a problem or question,

---

Israelite prophets lies elsewhere, namely, a "more profoundly spiritual view of life" than was attained by "heathen" diviners; *Prophecy and Divination*, 364–65. On the general topic of shamanistic elements in the Hebrew Bible, cf. A. Kapelrud, "Shamanistic Features in the Old Testament," in *Studies in Shamanism*, ed. C.-M. Edsman (Stockholm: Almqvist and Wiksell, 1967), 90–96; and K. Goldammer, "Elemente des Schamanismus im alten Testament," *Ex Orbe Religionem: Studies in the History of Religions* (Supplements to *Numen* 22 [1972]:266–85).

108. H. Orlinsky, "The Seer in Ancient Israel," *Oriens Antiquus* 4 (1965):153–74.

109. Huffmon, "Origins of Prophecy," 183.

110. Orlinsky, "Seer in Ancient Israel," 155–60.

presents himself or herself to a diviner (1). The diviner performs a technical operation, perhaps preceded by an invocation of the deity (2), observes the god-given result of the action (3), and communicates that result to the client (4). The client responds (5) by accepting the result and acting on it or perhaps by rejecting it or seeking another opinion.

The acts of divination reported in 1 Samuel and Joshua 7 are relatively straightforward instances of this process. Take, for example, 1 Sam. 14:38–46. Saul, needing to determine who was guilty of sin, initiated a consultation (1). The identity of the diviner is not clearly indicated, but presumably it was a priest (14:36). The diviner cast lots (2), and the guilty person was taken (3). Saul was made aware of this result (4) and took action by confronting Jonathan (5). The whole occurrence may have lasted only minutes.

By contrast, clients of an Ifa diviner may seek detailed advice about their problem by asking a series of questions. Such consultations may be quite long, even requiring several sessions to complete.[111] The pattern is, however, exactly the same, the length being accounted for by the large number of repetitions of the basic elements. For example, the client approaches a diviner (1), who invokes the god, Ifa, and casts the palm nuts (2). Observing the placement of the nuts, he identifies the figure (3) and recites the verses he has memorized for it (4). The client chooses one of these verses as applicable to his or her own case (5) and then asks additional questions (1). The diviner casts the nuts to determine the answer (yes or no) to each of these (2, 3) and reports the result to the client (4); this sequence may be repeated many times. Finally, the

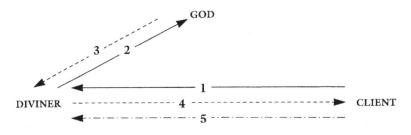

Figure 3

111. McClelland, *Cult of Ifa*, 50.

client accepts the result and makes preparations to offer the required sacrifice (5).

This process takes place within a particular social setting. As with divination, so too with prophecy: it is at home in a situation of crisis, ambiguity, or the like. In many of the occasions on which people resort to divination, the crisis is real and immediate: someone is ill, or a decision must be made about whether to go into battle. In others—planning to build a new house or to go on a journey—it is more nebulous, with at most a vague threat, a possibility of misfortune, that must be investigated. This difference suggests that the sense of crisis has powerful psychological roots. As we have already noted in the case of prophecy, a situation is a crisis for those who imagine it so.

In terms of their social role and function, then, diviners must be considered alongside prophets as legitimate intermediaries between Israelites and Yahweh.

6

The End of Prophecy:
*No Players without a Program**

The problem of the end of prophecy has in recent years been a topic of interest to students of the Hebrew Bible. The dominant opinion on this matter seems to be that Israelite prophecy came to an end in the early postexilic period. At the very least, prophecy after that time was transformed into something else. In light of what has already been said about the social dynamics of intermediation, however, such a view does not seem to me altogether satisfactory. My intention in this chapter is to move the discussion of the end of prophecy onto different ground.

One difficulty with many approaches to this problem is that they focus on a search for bearers of a particular social role, the classical Israelite prophet. With the possible exception of Haggai and Zechariah, no figures like these are to be found in the biblical literature of the postexilic period; the problem is to determine what became of prophecy. However, we might ask, if the surviving literature preserves the utterance of no such prophets, then does this absence mean that none existed? Furthermore, how did a society that for centuries assumed and acknowledged the existence of prophets suddenly find itself without bearers of that social role?

The approach I intend to take to the problem of prophecy's end may be illustrated by an analogy. At the theater, a concert, or an athletic contest, the audience is commonly provided with a program booklet, the function of which is to enable members of the audience to identify performers by name. Whether the audience knows these names or not,

*This chapter is a slightly modified version of an essay by the same title that appeared in *JSOT* 42 (1988):103–115.

however, the play or concert or game goes on. Players exist even
without a program. My title for this chapter suggests that in the case of
a social process like prophecy no performance at all can take place—
and, consequently, no players (in this case, prophets) can be identified—apart from a conceptual program in the collective consciousness
of a society. Such a program allows a given performance to be recognized and therefore authorizes it. Even obvious and unavoidable social
roles such as parent are subject to judgments based on such conceptual
programs about the competence of individual bearers of them. Is, for
example, an adult observed administering a severe beating to one of his
or her offspring recognizable as a "parent"?

BIBLICAL PROPHECY AND THE
BABYLONIAN EXILE

We should first review some recent discussions of the end of
prophecy. Inevitably, such discussions have started with the observation
that classical Israelite prophecy seems to have existed only during and
immediately after the period of the Israelite monarchy. If the prophetic
tradition continued at all thereafter, then it was only by virtue of its
transformation into something new. In particular, Frank Moore Cross's
elaboration of these ideas has had an important influence on the subsequent debate. Cross sees prophecy as coterminous with, and generally
functioning as a limitation upon, the monarchy, both "offices belong[ing] to the Israelite political structure which emerged from the
conflict between league and kingdom."[1] When the kingdom fell, classical prophecy, which for Cross is "prophecy *sensu stricto*," ceased, undergoing a transformation into apocalyptic.[2] Haggai and Zechariah "are
only apparent exceptions," a "last flicker of the old prophetic spirit" at
the time of a royal "pretender," Zerubbabel.[3]

Paul D. Hanson took up this theory about prophecy's transformation and developed it systematically. His thesis is that "the rise of
apocalyptic eschatology . . . follows the pattern of an unbroken develop-

---

    1. Frank Moore Cross, *Canaanite Myth and Hebrew Epic* (Cambridge, Mass.:
Harvard University Press, 1973), 223.
    2. Ibid., 343. Cross suggests that in Ezekiel's oracles, which coincide with the fall
of the monarchy, one can see "the transformation of classical prophecy into proto-apoc-
alyptic" (223 n. 15).
    3. Ibid., 343.

ment from pre-exilic and post-exilic prophecy," apocalyptic eschatology being "the mode assumed by the prophetic tradition once it had been transferred to a new and radically altered setting in the post-exilic community."[4] The crucial distinction here is between prophets, who affirmed history as a suitable context for Yahweh's activity and understood their task as translating their visions from the cosmic to the historical-political sphere, and "visionaries," who abandoned this "prophetic task of translation" as a result of pessimism over their social-historical circumstances.[5] The resulting "polarization" of vision and pragmatic program signaled "the demise of prophecy."[6] The social and historical "matrix" of this demise was "an inner-community struggle" that raged in postexilic Judah, especially during the years 520 to 420 B.C.E.[7] During this period, prophecy became "democratized," with the result that "the individual office of the prophet develop[ed] toward a collective office."[8]

What finally results is an evaluation of prophetic figures in terms of the content of their utterances. Visionaries are said to "stem in an unbroken succession from the prophets."[9] How is this so? Presumably, the continuity lies in their vision of Yahweh's sovereignty,[10] but the prophet differs from the visionary in how the vision is reported: the prophet translates "the activities of the divine council into the categories of the historico-political realm."[11] To speak in this way is the prophet's "mission."[12] Indeed, prophetic "activity" is recognizable in the early church, at the time of the Protestant Reformation, and even today in the struggle of individuals "to maintain the vital creative tension between vision and realism which is the heart of genuine ethical religion."[13] Let the reader be aware: no preacher of apocalyptic themes can be a "prophet." Probably, no one who is not a Jew, Christian, or Muslim can be one.

4. Paul D. Hanson, *The Dawn of Apocalyptic* (Philadelphia: Fortress Press, 1975), 7–8, 10.

5. Ibid., 12, 26; cf. 409.

6. Ibid., 210; cf. 219–20, 246–47, 354, 406.

7. Ibid., 29, 409.

8. Ibid., 69.

9. Ibid., 10 n. 8.   *prophets → Visionaries*

10. See, e.g., ibid., 12.

11. Ibid., 304.

12. Ibid., 406.

13. Ibid., 31.

Given this emphasis on their utterances, we should not be surprised that Hanson's concern with the social dynamics of prophecy is limited to a proposal about how the social status of the visionaries motivated them to adopt their peculiar theological or interpretive perspective on events. He then evaluates this perspective by the standard of preexilic prophecy, especially Isaiah. However, this approach leaves open other questions relating to the social dynamics of prophecy. For example, did people (support groups) within the Jewish community believe that these visionaries were actually prophets?

As a recent panel discussion of the topic shows, regardless of some disagreement with Hanson on specifics, the consensus tends to be that prophecy underwent a transformation in the postexilic period.[14] Eric M. Meyers, for example, sees a transformation in the direction of priestly activity and concerns. In a situation with "no realistic opportunity to reinstate the office of kingship," Haggai and Zechariah "presuppose[d] the hegemony of Persian authorities in all local affairs and never question[ed] the appropriateness of the office of governor or high priest." In Zechariah the high priest is the principal actor in the drama of the temple's refoundation (3; 6:9–15), "while the Davidic scion . . . is relegated to an eschatological status" (3:8; 4:6b–10a; 6:12). Haggai, who was closer to the rebellions and problems of succession occurring at the beginning of Darius's rule (522–486 B.C.E.), repeatedly mentions Zerubbabel and "reflects a more heightened eschatology" (2:20–23). However, his exhortation and use of a priestly ruling (2:10–14) "presages a new role for the post-exilic prophet, one that is drawn more and more closely to the priesthood."[15]

14. I refer to the "Social Roles of Prophecy in Israel Group" at the Society of Biblical Literature meeting in Anaheim, California (November 1985), which featured papers by Eric M. Meyers, "The Persian Period and the Judean Restoration: From Zerubbabel to Nehemiah," in *Ancient Israelite Religion: Essays in Honor of Frank Moore Cross*, ed. Patrick D. Miller, et al. (Philadelphia: Fortress Press, 1987); David L. Petersen, "The End of Prophecy: Perspectives from Deutero-Zechariah and Malachi"; Walter Harrelson, "Post-Exilic Prophetic Eschatology and the End of Prophecy"; and Stephen B. Reid, "The End of Prophecy in the Light of Contemporary Social Theory," *SBL 1985 Seminar Papers*, ed. Kent H. Richards (Atlanta: Scholars Press, 1985), 515–23. Robert Wilson responded to the papers.
15. Elsewhere Meyers has written that the "unique usage of *tora* in [Hag] 2:11 demonstrates . . . [that] post-exilic prophecy went hand-in-hand with priestly concerns and provided the critical linkage between two disparate loci of society which come together in the Restoration period for a little while but remain together forever in the history of Judaism, where the sage or rabbi is the true inheritor of the biblical prophet"; "The Use of *tora* in Haggai 2:11 and the Role of the Prophet in the Restoration Commu-

In Walter Harrelson's view,[16] the transformation of prophecy after the exile is to be seen mainly as an eschatological reinterpretation of prophetic traditions addressed to a believing community. This view allows him to propose the thesis that "prophecy in the period following the return from Babylonian Exile continues to exercise a highly significant function in the political, social, and religious life of the Israelite community." We can, therefore, speak of the end of prophecy only in the limited sense that we no longer encounter individual prophets like those of the preexilic and exilic periods and that the collections of material named for these earlier prophets are brought to completion. Harrelson suggests that "never is prophecy more alive . . . than when the collections entitled Isaiah . . . [etc.] . . . have definitely taken shape and begun to be the reference-points for a community that wishes to know what the prophets of Israel have said and taught, or what message God has to speak through God's servants the prophets." The collectors of the prophets' words "did not merely edit them," but "added to them striking prophecies of their own" (see Isa. 4:2–6; 19:23–25; 35:1–10).

Harrelson's proposition is that if "prophetic eschatological texts" added to the collections in the postexilic period "offer guidance in the here and now for a faithful community," then "prophecy is by no means at an end." I take him to be suggesting that until the arrival of the End (i.e., the consummation of God's work in the world), prophecy cannot be said to have come to an end, although by the standards of classical Israelite prophecy it underwent a change in form: "once the great prophetic collections are assembled, the prophetic office consists largely in the interpretation of these prophetic texts." A virtue of this position is that it does not tie the definition of prophecy to one specific manifestation of that phenomenon. The problem seems to me to be its ambiguity about the nature of prophetic activity. What separates this

---

nity," in *The Word of the Lord Shall Go Forth: Essays in Honor of David Noel Freedman*, ed. C. L. Meyers and M. O'Connor (Winona Lake, Ind.: Eisenbrauns, 1983), 70. Important to Meyers' view of the transformation of prophecy in the direction of priestly instruction is the assumption that "Darius' attempts to have the laws of conquered Persian territories codified" gave impetus to the canonical process which ultimately defined as authoritative the collections of the Pentateuch and Former Prophets. The law occupied center stage; the great period of prophecy was acknowledged to be in the past. See Carol L. Meyers and Eric M. Meyers, *Haggai, Zechariah One to Eight* (Garden City, N.Y.: Doubleday, 1988).

16. See n. 14.

type of ongoing interpretation from homiletics practiced by people making no claim to be prophets and not believed by their audience to be such? Would such people be performing actions recognizable by their contemporaries as those of a prophet?

The situation seems to be ambiguous. Israelite prophecy in its preexilic form apparently disappears, but not entirely! David Petersen reviews the evidence for this in a series of propositions about the end of prophecy. The first is that "there is a radical polemic against prophetic activity in the Persian period" (cf. Zech. 13:2–6 and Jer. 23:34–40), which seems to be a more "broad-based" and "generic" condemnation than had existed before the exile. Second, the various writers define as prophetic a variety of activities during the Persian period (e.g., the Levitical singers in Chronicles and the prophets and prophetess in Neh. 6:1–14), that seem somewhat different from the behavior of preexilic prophets. Third, evidence for literary connections between preexilic and postexilic prophets indicates both continuity and discontinuity.[17]

Like others, Petersen identifies the monarchy as "the political-religious locus of the prophet-as-mediator." To speak of "the end of classical Israelite prophecy" means that at some point "no one uttered oracles or wrote tracts in the way that Isaiah or Jeremiah had," or at least no such efforts were accepted by "the canonical process."[18] At the end of the monarchy, a "transition from classical prophecy to an organically connected but profoundly different enterprise" occurred.[19] Indeed, prophecy was conceived differently by different groups within the society.[20] In the deuteroprophetic literature, for example, identifiable individuals functioning as prophets can no longer be discerned,[21] and the oracles depend upon and interpret the classical prophetic traditions. In Chronicles, prophecy is conceived of as an activity that Levitical singers could perform. His conclusion is that "prophecy in the post-exilic period did not develop unilaterally into apocalyptic."[22]

An important caveat here is that our judgment that prophecy in the classical Israelite mode came to an end in the period after the fall of

17. See n. 14.
18. David L. Petersen, *Late Israelite Prophecy* (Missoula, Mont.: Scholars Press, 1977), 5.
19. Ibid., 6.
20. Ibid., 8; Petersen uses the notion of "theological streams" in this context.
21. E.g., Deutero- and Trito-Isaiah; Jer. 23:34–40; Zech. 13:2–6; Joel 3:1–5; Malachi.
22. Petersen, *Late Israelite Prophecy*, 102.

the monarchy is dependent upon knowledge preserved for us by the canonical process. Saying that such prophecy was no longer officially (canonically) recognized is one thing, saying it no longer existed is another, and yet another is to say that no one any longer performed the prophetic role. As long as classical prophecy is tied by definition to the monarchy, the first and second of these are plausible, although not without some ambiguity. (Haggai and Zechariah must be understood to be "a last gasp of classical prophecy."[23]). The third is very much open to question.

What we see in the Hebrew Bible is that one type of prophecy ("classical") has been transformed, sometimes in ways that (by the standard of preexilic forms) look somewhat strange. However, this transformation does not necessarily require us to believe that the phenomenon of prophecy itself came to an end. As Petersen notes, those postexilic groups who denied the existence of prophecy in their own times had strong motivations for doing so (e.g., the desire "to protect the past ideal of classical prophecy from spurious encroachment in the present" or in the case of the Chronicler the desire to appropriate the title and features of classical prophecy for Levitical singers).[24] Furthermore, he suggests that the deuteroprophetic critique in fact "established the formative pattern in which prophecy would be viewed in the future: the return of prophecy either in the form of an individual or as the spirit of prophecy given to the entire religious community."[25] Theoretically, for these people prophecy was still possible, only not in their present situation.

Robert Wilson has also noted the ambiguity involved in speaking about prophecy's end. After Haggai and Zechariah, no biblical book claims to be prophetic. Furthermore, late prophetic material is in some respects different from its preexilic and exilic counterparts (e.g., in its stronger connection with the priesthood). Yet in a later period one encounters Christian prophecy and rabbinic materials in which the teaching priesthood is considered to be spirit-inspired. Although we tend to understand certain texts from the Hebrew Bible to say that prophecy had ceased, the Essenes, Christians, and rabbis obviously did not read them that way.[26]

23. Ibid., 97.
24. Ibid., 98–100.
25. Ibid., 102.
26. See n. 14.

In an earlier study, Wilson criticized Hanson's distinction between visionaries and priests as being too sharply drawn and argued that a direct line cannot be drawn from a single tradition or movement in Israel to apocalyptic. Ultimately, the shape of apocalyptic religion and literature depended on the unique characteristics of each apocalyptic group.[27] I draw one implication from this criticism: when dealing with the problem of prophecy's end/transformation, difficulties are likely to arise when one focuses too much on the content of what the figures say.

Finally, we may note that Joseph Blenkinsopp shares this general view of the development of Israelite prophecy: it "did not come to an end during the Babylonian exile, though it did undergo rather profound transformations."[28] Among these he lists the Deuteronomists' making "prophecy serviceable to their contemporaries by reading a message of judgment as one of salvation through judgment," the prophetic subgroup that owed allegiance to Deutero-Isaiah and that by the time of Trito-Isaiah was on the way to becoming a sect, prophecy's "reabsorption into the cult" (Joel, Chronicles), and the "eschatological reinterpretation of prophecy" by people who did not consider themselves to be prophets (additions to Joel and Zechariah).[29]

PROPHECY BEYOND THE EXILE

One obvious feature of this discussion has been the emphasis on the transformation of prophecy into something else. Implicit in this notion is the identification of the phenomenon of prophecy with one of its possible manifestations, the "classical" prophecy of the Israelite monarchy. Having adopted "classical Israelite" as the norm by which prophecy is to be discussed, doubt is cast on the social and religious status of postexilic, biblical figures who seem to stand in some continuity with the prophetic traditions. In effect, instances of authentic prophecy in postbiblical times have been defined out of existence. At base, what we have is a tendency to define the end of prophecy as the last visible manifestations of a specific type of prophetic performance.

27. R. R. Wilson, "From Prophecy to Apocalyptic: Reflections on the Shape of Israelite Religion," *Semeia* 21 (1981):82–3, 93.
28. J. Blenkinsopp, *A History of Prophecy in Israel* (Philadelphia: Westminster Press, 1983), 178; cf. 188.
29. Ibid., 192, 249–51, 252, 263.

After Haggai and Zechariah (at the latest), the tradition shades off into other forms.

Petersen[30] points in the direction of another approach to this problem when he suggests that attention to social context may reveal "givens" that enable prophecy to occur, the absence of which "might allow us to speak about a time in which prophecy was not important." He proposes that we accept as these givens the four "social prerequisites of intermediation" outlined by Wilson: for intermediaries to be able to function in a society, the requirements are (1) "a belief in the reality of a supernatural power or powers"; (2) the further belief that these powers can influence affairs in this world and can in turn be influenced by humans; (3) a society that views intermediaries positively, encouraging, or at least tolerating, them; and (4) "social conditions" such that "the services of an intermediary" are required.[31]

Postexilic Judaism obviously qualifies on the first two counts. On the third count, Petersen notes that Zechariah 13 and Jeremiah 23 indicate the presence of at least one group that did not encourage or tolerate prophetic behavior. As to the fourth, the sixth and fifth centuries B.C.E. were "a period without significant international interference in Syria-Palestine," during which Yahwistic prophetic activity could be expected to decline in importance.[32] He concludes that "classical Israelite prophetic behavior" ended, but veneration of the words of the prophets continued; he agrees in substance with Wilson that prophetic support groups metamorphosed into apocalyptic groups.[33]

In short, prophecy came to an end when prophets lost their base of support within society. As Wilson has put it, "There can be no socially isolated intermediaries."[34] I believe this factor is the key that allows us to move the discussion onto different ground.

When thinking about the end of prophecy, we need to remember that prophets were purveyors of a particular message only by virtue of being performers of a certain recognized and accepted social role. Their

30. See n. 14.
31. R. R. Wilson, *Prophecy and Society in Ancient Israel* (Philadelphia: Fortress Press, 1980), 28–32.
32. Thus Wilson: "Even in societies which are supportive of intermediation in general, intermediaries tend to be forgotten or disappear when they have no social function"; ibid., 32.
33. Cf. Wilson, "Prophecy to Apocalyptic"; and *Prophecy and Society*, 308.
34. Ibid., 30.

speech was but one aspect of a larger pattern of social interactions, which has been examined in detail in the preceding chapters. Therefore, according to this model of the prophetic process, what would pass as the end of prophecy?

Theoretically, the absence of any element primary to social interaction (revelation, proclamation, feedback from the audience) would be sufficient to render prophecy nonexistent. However, both prophecy and its end are social phenomena, and the question needs to be rephrased to take that reality into account: of which element(s) of the prophetic process could we say that its (their) absence would necessarily be apparent and thereby sufficient to bring prophecy to an end?

If the problem is phrased in this way, clearly we cannot rely on the interactions along the revelation axis to signal prophecy's end. Because revelation is in essence a private matter not normally (or ever fully) observable by people other than those who are its recipients, its presence can be *claimed* even in its absence. Furthermore, its presence may be *attributed* even in the absence of such a claim, as in the case of Yali, a social reformer of sorts whose audiences interpreted his activity as that of an inspired cargo cult leader even though he made no claims along those lines. The prophet's feedback to God and additional revelations are not structurally necessary for an act of prophecy; the original revelation is the critical component on the prophet-God axis. On the prophet-audience axis, some "message" from the God to the people is theoretically necessary, and its absence would be easily noticed. However, mitigating factors can occur. The audience, for example, can understand as prophetic proclamation something not intended to be such (as in the case of Yali), leaving the primary God-prophet-audience-prophet sequence intact.[35] On this axis the original message is primary, so the absence of additional proclamations is not a reliable signal for the absence of prophecy. "Supernatural confirmations" enhance a prophet's authority but are not necessarily present.

Feedback from the audience to the prophet turns out to be the key. Although a speaker may claim to have received a revelation from the god and to be a prophet by virtue of proclaiming it, the failure of the audience to acknowledge, in effect to authorize, this activity means

---

35. An account of Yali's activities may be found in Thomas W. Overholt, *Prophecy in Cross-Cultural Perspective* (Atlanta: Scholars Press, 1986), 295–308.

that the God-prophet-audience-prophet chain is truncated, thus losing its final stage. Prophecy comes to an end, but for how long? To what does the end of prophecy refer? In my view it refers in the first instance to the absence of persons who are acknowledged by members of their society as performing the role of prophet. To say that in a given social context prophecy came to an end is not to deny the theoretical possibility of valid prophetic activity but rather to note the failure of members of that society, at least for the moment, to credit (authorize) specific instances of prophetic behavior. Within a given society, prophecy cannot be said to come to an absolute end until such time as the "social prerequisites" for this type of intermediation have ceased to exist. Until that happens, prophetic behavior itself will always (at least potentially) be with us; societal acknowledgment and toleration of such behavior, however, may wax and wane and even sometimes disappear altogether. In this respect we can note that although Zech. 13:2–6 polemicizes against prophetic behavior on the grounds that those currently indulging in it were speaking falsehood in Yahweh's name (v. 3), it does not claim that visions themselves had ceased (v. 4). Similarly, Jer. 23:34–40 seems to acknowledge the possibility of divine-human communication (vv. 35, 37) while disapproving of current instances of prophetic behavior (vv. 34, 36, 38–40).

In fact, numerous manifestations of prophecy took place within Judaism during the last centuries B.C.E. and the first century C.E.[36] In his discussion of Jewish prophecy, David Aune points out that although some rabbinic texts express the rather "theoretical" view that prophecy had ceased, according to "other rabbinic traditions, famous rabbis claimed the gift of prophecy and/or the possession of the Spirit of God." Sects like the Qumran Essenes "do not appear to have regarded either prophecy or the Holy Spirit as completely absent from Jewish religious experience."[37] As types of "early Jewish revelatory speech," Aune discusses eschatological (the "charismatic" leaders of millenarian movements), clerical (priests with the gift of prophecy; cf. John 11:49–52), and sapiential (connected with the faculty of wisdom)

36. See David E. Aune, *Prophecy in Early Christianity and the Ancient Mediterranean World* (Grand Rapids: Wm. B. Eerdmans, 1983), 103–52; Richard A. Horsley and John S. Hanson, *Bandits, Prophets, and Messiahs: Popular Movements in the Time of Jesus* (Minneapolis: Winston Press, 1985); R. A. Horsley, "'Like One of the Prophets of Old': Two Types of Popular Prophets at the Time of Jesus," *CBQ* 47 (1985):435–63.
37. Aune, *Prophecy*, 104.

prophecy. In addition, he believes that some of the writers of apocalyptic literature had "actual visionary experiences."[38]

The situation was similar in early Christianity. Not only was Jesus considered by some to be a prophet but also Christianity produced considerable prophetic activity from its beginnings down through the Montanist movement in the last half of the second century.[39] It must be assumed that within Judaism and Christianity, prophecy has remained a possibility virtually down to the present, even in contemporary America (cf. chapter 7). The conceptual structure of the faiths allows for its continued existence.

We could reasonably assume that if the role of prophet is possible (conceptually available) within a society, some will feel themselves drawn towards performing it. How, then, are we to account for the apparent absence of a continuing sequence of generally accepted performers of this role? The most obvious answer is society's (periodic) lack of interest in (or hostility toward) the role, resulting in its performers not being credited with an authentic performance. That is to say, they may be ignored or credited with performing other roles than what they intend (e.g., preacher, evangelist, crazy person, religious fanatic). The reticence of the actors themselves may also be part of the answer. Some may have been reluctant to announce themselves as prophets, although they have performed, or attempted to perform, that role. Some, of course, were no doubt unnoticed by those who have preserved the past for us.

The bias of the audience clearly comes into play. In scholarly and many religious circles, David Wilkerson's *The Vision* is probably either unknown or rejected out of hand as a record of prophetic activity (something like the canonical process is still at work), but this rejection is not the case in all circles.[40] In response to a question, some of my students suggested it immediately as an obvious example of contemporary prophetic literature. Established groups are unlikely to recognize marginal activities—Protestant or Catholic charismatics, for example, or channelers of spirits—as manifestations of true prophecy, although

---

38. Ibid., 114. On the rabbis' motivation for the claim that the holy spirit was no longer operative, cf. F. E. Greenspahn, "Why Prophecy Ceased," *JBL* 108 (1989): 37–49.

39. Aune, *Prophecy*, 153–346.

40. David Wilkerson, *The Vision* (Old Tappan, N.J.: Fleming H. Revell, 1974). See the discussion of this book in chapter 7.

we have abundant evidence that such persons are considered authoritative in their own groups. People's views are greatly influenced by the group to which they give allegiance.

In my view, then, we cannot correctly say that prophecy ended with the exile, either in the sense that it ceased or that it was transformed into something else. According to the understanding of the social dynamics of prophetic activity presented in this book, we ought to conceive of prophecy as a continuing potentiality in a given society, based on that society's particular religious beliefs and past experience. This view allows for the intermittent appearance of prophets within the society and defines the conditions under which prophecy can be said to end, as well as begin again. To return to our analogy, it provides a "program" that enables us to identify prophetic "performance" and, therefore, prophets.

7

By Their Fruits
You Will Know Them

I have just argued for the possibility that prophecy still exists within the Judeo-Christian context; at least some people are convinced that it does. Therefore, we can appropriately conclude our discussion of prophecy with some reflections on the problem of identifying and responding to prophetic claims in the present.

When and if such claims or claimants surface, the existential problem of the audiences who hear them will be exactly the same as that of ancient Israelite audiences: are they authentic prophecy or not? This question is by no means easy! For the biblical prophets, one has the benefit of hindsight. The compilers of the Hebrew Bible had already decided that Jeremiah and not Hananiah (Jeremiah 27—28) and Micaiah ben Imlah and not his rivals (1 Kings 22) were authentic prophets. In the prophets' own days this opinion was not unanimous; subsequent events eventually proved them correct. The compilers of the biblical stories knew this, and so do we!

Comparisons with intermediaries from other cultures have enabled us to enrich our understanding of the social dynamics of prophetic activity. The model I have used to make these comparisons describes an observable process. It is inclusive, and we have found that many people from a variety of times and cultures fit it well. Details of this process—how a person becomes an intermediary, how intermediaries behave, the social functions of intermediaries—can be isolated and discussed.[1] All of this can be done with relative objectivity by people who are outsiders with respect to the communities being studied.

1. See R. R. Wilson, *Prophecy and Society in Ancient Israel* (Philadelphia: Fortress Press, 1980), 42–88; T. W. Overholt, *Prophecy in Cross-Cultural Perspective* (Atlanta: Scholars Press, 1986) 10–22.

In making such comparisons, I have consistently bracketed the specific content of what the various intermediaries said. This bracketing was necessary because of the diverse times, places, and cultural situations represented by the intermediaries discussed. Bracketing was part of the scholarly enterprise of studying the social dynamics of prophetic activity.

However, the existential dilemma of prophecy differs from the scholarly quest to identify prophetic intermediaries and to understand their activities. The act of judging the authenticity of a prophetic claim necessarily takes place within a particular culture. At this point specific aspects of prophetic behavior can no longer be bracketed. They are of critical importance. Members of a particular religious community have to consider the whole range of the activity they witness in order to make a judgment about the validity of prophetic claims. This project is not interdisciplinary, although our cross-cultural study can give us some guidance.

Which elements of the intermediary's behavior become the focus of attention of course differs from culture to culture. Among the Tungus of Siberia, the perceived quality of the shaman's actions during trance and his or her ability to recite fixed lists of clan spirits carry great weight with the audience.[2] Among the Kwakiutl of the Pacific northwest coast of North America, the deftness with which the shaman works and effectiveness in curing are important.[3] In the Judeo-Christian tradition, the crucial aspect of prophetic behavior is speech.

Toward the end of the Sermon on the Mount, Matthew records a warning against false prophets:

> Beware of false prophets, who come to you in sheep's clothing but inwardly are ravenous wolves. You will know them by their fruits. . . . A sound tree cannot bear evil fruit, nor can a bad tree bear good fruit. Every tree that does not bear good fruit is cut down and thrown into the fire. (Matt. 7:15–21)

The warning assumes that false prophets will appear and that they will be recognized by their behavior (the fruit they bear). It is specific about the community's obligation to identify and pass judgment upon them,

2. Overholt, *Prophecy in Cross-Cultural Perspective*, 165–80.
3. Ibid., 23–58, esp. n. 8.

but vague about the criteria for doing so. How do we recognize "evil fruit"?

The question is not simply hypothetical. In contemporary North America, potential manifestations of prophetic activity are not difficult to discover. I now proceed to discuss some of them. From time to time I will raise questions useful in critical reflection on such prophetic claims, but such questions can never be more than tools for facilitating judgment. An unambiguous and foolproof set of criteria for separating true from false prophecy has never existed! Ultimately, judging is a risky business for which individuals and their communities must take full responsibility.

PROPHECY TODAY

For all the talk of its demise, the notion of prophecy is by no means absent from contemporary Christian discourse. Paul Hanson, who believes that prophecy as such came to an end in the early postexilic period, claims that prophetic "activity" is recognizable in the early church, at the time of the Protestant Reformation, and even today.[4] Gene Tucker speaks of the need to "take seriously a prophetic role for the church in our society."[5] He apparently does not look to individual prophets to perform this role, however. Rather, the people who constitute the church are to "maintain a continuous dialogue with the Old Testament prophetic words and allow them to shape [their] consciousness of the present and [their] visions of possible futures." In a word, they must do corporately what the biblical prophets did individually, namely, interpret present events in terms of the theological traditions in which they stand.[6] Some speak of the professional ministry as having both priestly (pastoral) and prophetic functions.[7]

To speak of a prophetic church or ministry is to make a distinction between prophetic activity undertaken by persons who are not as

4. P. D. Hanson, *The Dawn of Apocalyptic* (Philadelphia: Fortress Press, 1975), 30–31.

5. G. M. Tucker, "The Role of the Prophets and the Role of the Church," in *Prophecy in Israel*, ed. D. L. Petersen (Philadelphia: Fortress Press, 1987), 159.

6. Ibid., 170–71.

7. See P. J. Paris, "The Minister as Prophet," *Princeton Seminary Bulletin* 7 (1986):15–19. Note the title of H. E. Quinley's study: *The Prophetic Clergy: Social Activism among Protestant Ministers* (New York: John Wiley & Son, 1974).

individuals considered to be prophets and the actions of actual prophets. In this way one can envision the legacy of the prophets living on as a vital force in the contemporary church without having to reckon with the possibility of actual individuals performing the prophetic role.

Not everyone, however, is so reticent about identifying specific individuals as prophets. Claims have been made that persons like Martin Luther King, Jr., functioned as genuine prophets. Some go so far as to maintain that in the Christian context "anyone can prophesy," and, presumably, many do. Some people in contemporary Christian churches seem to have taken up the prophetic role, apparently consciously, but to have exercised it without explicitly claiming to be prophets. Moreover, on the fringes of the Judeo-Christian tradition is a veritable din of spirit voices, speaking through what have come to be known as *channelers*. They may serve as samples of the smorgasbord of prophetic manifestations on the contemporary scene. They may also serve as a challenge to anyone who would begin by attempting to limit severely the scope and content of prophetic activity.

Contemporary Prophets of
Social Reform

William Ramsay has undertaken a self-conscious and disciplined application of the term *prophet* to four twentieth-century Christians: Walter Rauschenbusch, Martin Luther King, Jr., Gustavo Gutiérrez, and Rosemary Radford Ruether.[8] His rationale for doing so can be fathomed quite nicely in terms of the four social prerequisites of intermediation discussed in chapter 6.[9]

Ramsay begins by assuming that a God exists and that this God is both able to influence human affairs and wishes to do so. The existence of a community of believers who are receptive to such influence is also assumed. Ramsay, who describes himself as "a southern, white, evangelical Protestant of Scottish descent and orthodox Presbyterian theology,"[10] is a member of that community, as are, by implication, at least some of his readers.[11] These assumptions cover the first three of the

8. W. M. Ramsay, *Four Modern Prophets* (Atlanta: John Knox Press, 1986).
9. See p. 157 above. This way of formulating the "prerequisites" depends upon R. R. Wilson, *Prophecy and Society*, 28–31.
10. Ramsay, *Four Modern Prophets*, 5.
11. His "hope and faith" is that "millions . . . will respond actively" to the message of contemporary prophets; ibid., 94.

social prerequisites of intermediation. Furthermore, in each case the conditions were right for the emergence of prophecy because the times during which these four leaders live(d) are (were) characterized by "stress and rapid social change." This factor is the fourth of the prerequisites.

For Ramsay, prophets are people who have a vision of a changing social order. King, he says, "was a prophet in the traditional sense of the term. He was a man with an inspired vision of the future."[12] The discussion of the four figures focuses on the situations of social crisis that each confronted: for Rauschenbusch the situation was the exploitation of immigrant factory workers in the period before World War I; for King the injustices of racial segregation; for Gutiérrez the poverty and oppression of Latin American peasants; and for Ruether primarily the struggle for justice and equality for women. Although much remains to be done, their work provides us, says Ramsay, with "clear indications that God is bringing the kingdom in."[13]

The designation of these people as prophets does not rest on claims they themselves have made but rather on acceptance by a receptive audience. Ramsay, in fact, makes little effort to discover or discuss call experiences or the way in which any of the four might have received revelation from God. Yet his characterization of them as prophets is carefully thought out.

In Ramsay's view a prophet is one who "speaks forth for God in the Spirit which animated the work of Amos, Isaiah, and Jeremiah" and also Jesus, who although he was "more than a prophet . . . was a prophet." Scripture, therefore, is our guide: "Since the Spirit is not going to contradict what the Spirit has already inspired in the Scripture, we have at least one helpful way of judging just how authentically inspired a preacher or writer may be."[14] To view the activity of such people as genuine prophecy involves the judgment that they were inspired by "the same Holy Spirit which inspired the biblical writers." Such a judgment is based on the content of what they have said, and Ramsay sees as a common element in the four that "they love the great biblical prophets and call for right relationships among people which we find in Jesus. They are united in their call for social justice in God's

12. Ibid., 46. For similar statements about the others, see 14, 22–24, 66, 84.
13. Ibid., 89.
14. Ibid., 2.

name," and like the biblical prophets "they made predictions. . . . spoke out of a hope, a dream, a vision of the coming of the kingdom of God."[15]

For Ramsay, then, consistency is the key. God exists and is consistent in his desires for human society. God therefore may be expected to speak when the situation is right for such intervention, and when he does God's past speech is definitive. Times may change, but God's goal for humans remains the same. We must expect prophets to emerge from time to time, but they will be prophets of a certain type. We have earlier seen that such stereotyping of expectations is normal in societies that reckon with the possibility of intermediaries.

Every Christian a Prophet

Although Ramsay suggests the possibility that many Christians may perform a prophetic function, Robert B. Hall widens the horizon of expectation with the claim that "anyone can prophesy."[16] Hall, who is an Episcopal priest,[17] bases his claim on the assumptions that God is good, cares about people, and acts to meet people's needs. In acting to meet people's needs, he frequently utilizes "the agency of another human being." Anyone who is "willing and informed and sensitive to the promptings of the Father" can be such an agent.[18] Prophecy is not limited to a few virtuosi.

Prophecy, as Hall understands it, is "letting God speak through us" to other persons.[19] It is to be distinguished from guidance—God speaking directly to and for a single individual[20]—and from preaching. Even though preachers may believe that their message has come from God through prayer, meditation, and study, the words are usually their own.[21]

That Hall deals specifically with the nature of revelation is appropriate to the how-to orientation of *Anyone Can Prophesy*.[22] He also

15. Ibid., 3–4. The case of Yali (see pp. 84–85 above) is an example outside the Judeo-Christian tradition of a person being recognized as a prophet on the basis of the content of what he said and in the absence of any specific claims on his part that he was performing that role.

16. R. B. Hall, *Anyone Can Prophesy* (New York: Seabury Press, 1977).

17. Ibid.; see 18, 64, 75, 78.

18. Ibid., 1–2.

19. Ibid., 11.

20. Ibid., 3.

21. Ibid., 21.

22. One of his criteria for judging revelation is that it must come from God and not from some other resident of the spirit world; see ibid., 41–46.

describes various "kinds of prophecy," using a typology based on the content of the prophet's message.[23] "Occasions for prophecy" may be either public (church groups and committees, preaching, Sunday School, Bible classes, prayer groups, nonchurch activities) or private (a time of grief, a family quarrel, a career decision, or the like).[24] Prophetic acts usually involve speech, but on occasion nonverbal acts like touching may be more appropriate.[25]

Because in this view prophecy is likely to be quite widespread, being able to judge the genuineness of particular manifestations of it is important. Indeed, Hall suggests that "prophecy must be tested, it never stands alone . . . we do not proceed on the basis of prophecy until we have checked it."[26] It may be evaluated by means of three principles:[27] The first is that prophecy "doesn't stand alone. Something either precedes or follows it that fits it, joins with it, completes it, and agrees with it." The second principle is conformity with past revelations ("God is consistent; He is true and does not contradict Himself");[28] and the third is "the law of love" (because God is loving, prophecy must be also). The second principle is of great importance because it allows us to sort out and reject certain ideas and practitioners which do not conform to "the lore and heritage of our faith."[29] Hall in fact assumes the kind of dual authorization of prophetic activity discussed earlier in this book:

> Anyone can prophesy, but not everyone who prophesies will be known as a prophet. . . . anyone who prophesies can be called a prophet when he is actually prophesying, but the office of prophet in the Church of God calls for more than this. One who is to be known and listened to regularly as a prophetic voice within the body of Christ must be called, must be sensitive to that call, must receive what God has to give, must transmit this accurately, *and must be recognized by the body itself for who he is*.[30]

23. Prophecy may build up, encourage, console, edify, take the form of speaking in tongues and its interpretation, offer guidance, or make predictions; ibid., 29–40.
24. Ibid., 68–74.
25. "When Jesus . . . wants another body to use in the particular place on earth where only we have entrée, He may want to speak to someone in words through our mouth. But He may also find that the touch of a hand, your hand borrowed temporarily by Jesus, may suffice"; ibid., 31; see 80–81.
26. Ibid., 13.
27. Ibid., 14–16.
28. When applying this criterion, Hall does not intend for one to be limited to an appeal to Scripture. He speaks also of the understanding of God's will "determined by our denomination" in conferences, conventions, and meetings and expressed by local clergy. "It is dangerous to bypass this system that devout men and women have built up under God's guidance over the centuries"; ibid., 27.
29. Reincarnation and Edgar Cayce are specifically mentioned; ibid., 47–51.
30. Ibid., 25; emphasis added.

The widening of the potential scope of prophecy from Ramsay's "many" to Hall's "all" is due in part to the latter's conviction that the crisis situations that evoke prophetic activity may include matters of personal as well as more broadly social concern (see pp. 112–15). In either case the identification of individual prophets may not be easy because the people engaging in prophetic activity may not conform to the main biblical stereotype of such action by standing before live audiences and speaking in God's name. To return to a previously cited example, they may write books instead.

A Doomsday Prophet

The cover of a current paperback edition of David Wilkerson's *The Vision* announces that it is "a terrifying prophecy of DOOMSDAY that is happening NOW!" Copyrighted in 1974, the book had its seventeenth printing in January 1981. That Wilkerson has had an audience is thus fairly clear, although sales alone do not reveal the disposition of its members toward him and his message.

At the front of the book are three separate pages containing biblical quotations on the theme "vision" (Acts 26:19; Hab. 2:2–3; Acts 11:5; Dan. 8:27; 10:14). In the Introduction that follows, Wilkerson is at pains to establish his credentials as a visionary. He does this in part by mentioning an earlier vision (1958) that took him "from a little town in Pennsylvania to New York City to work with teen gangs and drug addicts." The subsequent success and wide distribution of his youth centers is taken as proof that his "was not a false vision."[31] He does it also by the way he characterizes his second vision (summer 1973) and his reaction to it. This vision came to him while he was praying. He initially resisted its message as "too apocalyptic," but it recurred "night after night." Finally, despite "fears and apprehensions," he came to "a conviction that this vision must be *published*." The vision speaks of events that will occur in the interval between "the very near future" and the end of "this generation." Ultimately, the sanction for making it public and the reason why people should pay attention to it is that it "could be the actual warning from God" anticipated in Joel 2:28.[32]

---

31. D. Wilkerson, *The Vision* (Old Tappan, N.J.: Fleming H. Revell, 1974), 11.
32. Ibid., 11–14; emphasis added.

The book, then, is a record of this vision, although nowhere in it does Wilkerson make an explicit claim to be a prophet.[33] How are we to understand the role Wilkerson assumed when he published his vision? If we analyze *The Vision* in terms of our model of the prophetic process, we seem to have on our hands an instance of prophecy. On the revelation-feedback-revelation axis, we note Wilkerson's claim to have received two separate and distinct visions and to have responded to God with protests and questions.[34] As for the proclamation-feedback-proclamation axis, we have rich documentation. Like a biblical prophetic book (although better organized), *The Vision* is virtually all proclamation. It elaborates its message in sections devoted to major topics (worldwide economic confusion, natural disasters, pornography and perversion, and the like), announcing the conviction throughout that all of this comes from God.[35] We get some indication of feedback from the audience in Wilkerson's reference to advice from his "closest friends and associates" not to publish the vision.[36] In addition, he makes explicit appeals to people of like mind by employing phrases like "many praying people now share this very same vision," "others, like me, are fully convinced," "my message to true Jesus people is loud and clear," and "God gave me a very special message of hope for all true believers."[37] Such expressions are both a claim to speak with authority and an anticipation of assent by people who share his evangelical agenda.

We can also observe that the situation Wilkerson addressed was appropriate for such a message, because the present age (at least as he perceived it) is a time of social breakdown and crisis.

The impression that *The Vision* can be viewed as a prophetic utterance is confirmed by observing that it is replete with speech patterns appropriate to someone performing the role of an intermediary between God and humans. For example, in the process of setting out his message for our time, Wilkerson makes many references to his vision and the conviction it inspired in him, thereby making a claim about the divine origin of that message that is certainly the functional

33. At one point he does say, "I am prophesying," but the context makes clear that the term is here synonymous with "making a prediction"; ibid., 68.
34. Ibid., 12, 116.
35. Ibid., e.g., 12, 26, 40, 41.
36. Ibid., 12.
37. Ibid., 15, 41, 90, 115.

equivalent of the biblical prophets' "Thus says Yahweh."[38] Sometimes his words seem couched in biblical forms: page 43 begins with a "woe" oracle and pages 123 to 125 contain an admonition.

In a manner reminiscent of Jer. 28:5–9, Wilkerson consciously sets himself within the context of biblical prophecy as he understands it. As he narrates the contents of his vision, he makes frequent appeals to Scripture.[39] Indeed, sometimes he appropriates passages of the Bible into his own message,[40] and sometimes he appears to add to the contents of Scripture.[41] In chapters 6 and 7 he abandons the vision language altogether and speaks of the fulfillment of Bible prophecies.

Therefore, *The Vision* could be accurately said to present its readers with a claim that it is a genuine word of prophecy from the God of the Judeo-Christian tradition. We cannot deal with such a claim by inquiring into the genuineness of the author's visionary experiences, which were essentially private in nature. Nor can we simply write it off with the counterclaim that the age of prophecy has passed. We must look at the content of the message.

An evaluation of Wilkerson's message could begin with a critical analysis of his interpretations of present events and predictions about the future. By what objective measure, for example, could we corroborate the following statement: "The way tragedies and disasters are striking the earth with such frequency and intensity would suggest that the earth is suffering labor pains"?[42] To what extent do they simply name trends that would have been obvious to any reasonably alert observer in the early 1970s (e.g., the increasing availability of "pornographic" materials)[43] or escalate to apocalyptic proportions things that

---

38. Note, for example, the following phrases: "In my vision . . ." (ibid., 15, 31, 50, 55, 56); "this vision . . ." (20, 21); "I have had . . . a vision . . ." (53); "I have seen a vision of coming judgment and the Bible backs it up" (112); "I see . . ." (16, 18, 19, 24, and often); "what I have heard and seen is . . ." (54); "what I perceive . . ." (86); "I believe . . ." (12, 17, 22, 29, 31, and often); "I am convinced . . ." (26); "I predict . . ." (44, 64, 65, 68); "the message I receive for . . . is . . ." (85).

39. See ibid., 20, 28, 35, 39, 44, 49, 55, 61–62, 65, 70, 71, 73, 79.

40. Ibid., for example, 29, 55–56.

41. In a subsection entitled "a homosexual epidemic," Wilkerson says, "Believe me when I tell you the time is not far off that you will pick up your local newspaper and read sordid accounts of innocent children being attacked by wild homosexual mobs in parks and on city streets. The mass rapes will come just as surely as predicted in the Gospels. I see them coming in our generation"; ibid., 51. I am not familiar with any such prediction in the Gospels.

42. Ibid., 114.

43. Ibid., 47.

have long been a normal part of our society (e.g., tensions between teenagers and their parents that come to be expressed in disagreements over "hair styles, funky clothes, freaky music, and lazy attitudes about dress")?[44] To what extent do they mirror a particular group's agenda and its own particular appropriation of the Christian tradition (e.g., the tirades against homosexuality)?[45]

Several other features of this extended proclamation are relevant to such a critical evaluation. For one thing, Wilkerson implies that at least some biblical prophecies have their primary reference not to events in the time of their composition, but rather to events of our own day.[46] From a critical point of view, this assumption is dubious. For another, he frequently qualifies his predictions with words like "could"[47] and "may,"[48] which only heighten the impression that what we have in his book is a standard set of apocalyptic assertions about the unfolding of contemporary events. Finally, we may be offended by the apocalypticist's apparent joy in what he perceives as the deterioration of the social and moral order of the world we all share. "These are exciting days for true Christians," Wilkerson asserts,[49] and we understand that he anticipates the day when God will destroy the many and rescue and reward the few. The visionary clearly considers himself among the few.[50]

When we confront a body of proclamation like that contained in *The Vision*, we are in a situation reminiscent of the conflict between two prophetic opponents of the Hebrew Bible, Jeremiah and Hananiah (Jeremiah 27—28). The possibility always exists of disagreement among persons standing within a religious tradition, and ultimately the evaluation of all claims to speak for God requires a combination of historical awareness and theological understanding. The choice made has important social implications. To accept Wilkerson's vision leads to abandoning the world and absolutizing social and religious divisions. By contrast, to accept Ramsay's notion of prophecy leads to creative efforts to transform the world that are inclusive in their intensions. In

44. Ibid., 66.
45. Ibid., 50–51.
46. Ibid., 61–62.
47. Ibid., 19, 99, 105.
48. Ibid., 19, 87, 105, 108.
49. Ibid., 114.
50. For an extended critique of the "new apocalypticism," see Robert Jewett, *Jesus Against the Rapture* (Philadelphia: Westminster Press, 1979).

choosing who to believe, we are, in effect, choosing how to respond to the social turmoil of our time.

The evaluation of prophetic claims is in some sense easier when "strange" spirits speak. Yet even the case of channeled entities is not unambiguous, unless one is content to foreclose any possibility that God could, or would wish to, speak in new ways.

Channelers of Prophecy

The phenomenon of channeling is by no means new, but it has recently received extensive exposure in the electronic and print media. Shirley MacLaine's *Out on a Limb*,[51] its dramatization as a two-part miniseries on ABC-TV (January 1987), and her subsequent writings and TV talkshow appearances seem to have been an important stimulus. The number of people who claim to channel spirits ("entities") of one type or another is fairly large, but the movement has its stars in people like Kevin Ryerson (through whom MacLaine made her first contact with spirit entities, a contemporary of Jesus named John and an Irish pickpocket from the Elizabethan era named Tom McPherson), J. Z. Knight ("Ramtha"), and Jach Pursel ("Lazaris"). Fame has its rewards. J. Z. Knight employs a staff to help stage seminars (which masses of people pay $400 each to attend) and publish Ramtha materials. Her admitted earnings are in the millions of dollars.[52] Other channelers are engaged in similar activities.

Channeling has been defined as "the communication of information to or through a physically embodied human being from a source that is said to exist on some other level or dimension of reality than the physical as we know it, and that is not from the normal mind (or self) of the channel."[53] From this point of view, channelers are understood to be intermediaries and to share that function with a wide variety of religious practitioners in all times and ages. Under the rubric channeling Jon Klimo includes mediums, shamans, soothsayers, visionaries, saints, mystics, and the like. He counts as channelers people such as Moses, the Israelite prophets, Jesus, Paul, George Fox, H. P. Blavatsky, and Edgar Cayce.[54]

51. S. MacLaine, *Out on a Limb* (New York: Bantam Books, 1983).
52. J. Klimo, *Channeling: Investigations on Receiving Information From Paranormal Sources* (Los Angeles: Jeremy P. Tarcher, 1987), 44.
53. Ibid., 2.
54. Ibid., 76, 86–128.

Our model of the prophetic process describes the activity of channeling well. Along the revelation-feedback-revelation axis, we may place putative call experiences,[55] efforts by potential channelers to resist the incursions of the entity into their lives,[56] and the continued contacts with spirit entities that are the stock in trade of the activity. With respect to the proclamation-feedback-proclamation sequence, we may note that the central element in the activity of channelers is the verbal presentation of advice, predictions, and the like to individuals and to groups of people both large and small. Entities may even submit to interviews, a peculiarly modern kind of feedback situation, and may allow their channelers to be filmed during possession.[57] Like intermediaries in any culture, channelers depend for their support on groups of persons sympathetic to their claims.[58] The fees they collect for their services are one good indication of the extent to which they have been accepted. In many cases their messages seem to be quite consistent over time.

We do not have to witness very many televised channeling sessions to become aware of the pattern of stereotypical behavior charac-

55. Of her first encounter with "Seth," Jane Roberts says, "A fantastic avalanche of radical, new ideas burst into my head with tremendous force, as if my skull were some sort of receiving station, turned up to unbearable volume." Roberts insists that "Seth" is her "channel to revelational knowledge, and by this I mean knowledge that is revealed to the intuitive portions of the self rather than discovered by the reasoning faculties." James Hurtak reports that while praying he "found himself bathed in light . . . [and] . . . felt himself taken out of body and into regions from which he could receive information for years to come." There she was presented by his guide, Enoch, to "Metatron, the Creator of Light in the outer universe," who took him "into the presence of the Divine Father." See ibid., 29–31, 66.

56. For example, Helen Shucman's "inner debate with her own 'Voice': 'Why me? . . . I'm not religious . . .'" and Jach Pursel's early alarm at hearing tape recordings of his speech while in trance. See ibid., 40, 47. Shucman channeled the book, *A Course in Miracles*; Pursel channels "Lazaris."

57. Klimo records an interview with Pursel ("Lazaris") during which, among other things, the entity (Lazaris) answers technical questions about how he communicates with his channel (Pursel); ibid., 67–74. An interview between this same entity and Barbara Marx Hubbard is commercially available on videotape; P. Price, *The Complete Guide to Channeling* (Los Angeles: Penny Price Productions, 1986). The video production of MacLaine's *Out on a Limb* contains a channeling session with Kevin Ryerson. In that production, Ryerson played himself, and he and MacLaine subsequently claimed in televised interviews that, although the sequence reenacts a past event, Ryerson actually went into trance during the filming.

58. Klimo notes that channelers depend on "a subculture" for psychological and financial support, and "may suffer" if this is not present. Channelers may, in fact, choose to regulate their overall behavior in such a way as to increase their acceptability and to live in places where they are more likely to find acceptance (for example, Jose Stevens ("Michael"), who resides in Berkeley, California); *Channeling*, 135, 138–39.

teristic of that activity. First the channeler sits down and, with eyes closed, relaxes, perhaps with the aid of deep breathing. Shuddering, slumping, moaning, and the like occur as the spirit enters the channeler's body, which then becomes more alert and animated. When the spirits speak, they typically employ accents, vocabularies, and rhetorical patterns appropriate to their personalities but different from those of their human channelers. When the spirit leaves, the channeler may seem to deflate visibly and then wake up and resume normal conversation. Channelers usually claim not to remember what the spirits said through them while they were in trance.[59]

For those whose contact with intermediaries—biblical prophets, shamans, spirit mediums, and the like—has by necessity been limited to written accounts, seeing a televised trance-channeling session is a new and interesting experience. The channelers look and sound so normal. Even with the changes in speech that the trance effects, we hear a human being, not a god. The same would of course be true for the rhetoric of Martin Luther King, Jr., and the others considered by Ramsay to be prophets, as well as, we suppose, for the biblical prophets. What this ordinariness points out is the absolute necessity for stereotypical behavior that can indicate to an audience that a person is playing the role of intermediary. The behavior I have outlined serves the audience as a marker, setting off the period of trance from what precedes and follows it and in the process undergirding the claim that the words uttered during trances are not the channelers' own.[60]

The activities of intermediaries are always subject to scrutiny by members of their audiences, and the channelers are sensitive to this scrutiny. Pursel ("Lazaris") has even tackled the problem head-on by suggesting criteria for evaluating the messages of channeled entities.[61] Although Pursel may seem to have addressed only "easy" questions to

59. See ibid., 187–89. The Pursel ("Lazaris") and Ryerson ("John-Tom") sessions mentioned in n. 57 are good examples of this behavior.
60. Of course, like everything else, such behavior is subject to critical evaluation. We might ask, for example, what level of theatrical display is acceptable and whether actions during trance must be purely spontaneous (and thus presumably from the entity itself). On the possibility of "fraud," see below.
61. The criteria he gave during the interview with Barbara Marx Hubbard included: the consistency of the message over time, the consistency of the entity's personality, the helpfulness of the message to individual persons, and the tone of the message (was it uplifting, allowing persons to become all that they are capable of being?); Price, *Complete Guide to Channeling*. Klimo quotes from another interview in which a similar, but not identical, list of criteria is given; *Channeling*, 323.

the practice of channeling, his comments suggest that even the community of those who accept channelers as genuine intermediaries has a need for critical evaluation of and judgments about individual practitioners.

Within the Christian community, the evaluation of channelers has been more difficult than we might have suspected. Indeed, I first learned of channeling in a newspaper account of an Episcopal priest, the Rev. Laura Cameron Fraser, whose belief in a channeled spirit named Jonah had caused her to be accused by her bishop of heresy. Unwilling to recant, she resigned from her Issaquah, Washington, church.[62] As we have seen, Hall would exclude from Christian prophecy the utterances of any spirits strange to the biblical tradition,[63] a strategy for evaluating this type of intermediation that assumes a rather narrow delimitation of God's ability to communicate with humans. We might in fact ask whether someone like Hall who believes in the continuing reality of prophecy is guilty of inconsistency if he is not open to the possibility of new and different words for new times. Those sympathetic to channeling are, predictably, opposed to such an exclusive claim.[64] This point was not lost on Fraser, who clearly takes channeling seriously as a Christian phenomenon. She told an interviewer from the *Seattle Post-Intelligencer* that her experiences with channeling had changed her life. Arguing that it is "unreasonable to believe that God spoke to humans only in the past and cannot be heard today," she concluded, "I have every reason to believe that Jesus Christ's voice is being heard today through channeling."

How, then, might an evaluation of channelers proceed? The startling financial success of some is perhaps not as hot an issue as it might at first seem. Affluence may breed skepticism and suspicions of fraud (although to my knowledge none is as financially successful as Christian televangelists), but surely some form of maintenance is reasonable. In our society religious professionals are commonly paid a living wage for their activities, and at least some channelers seem to fit that category. The question is the extent to which considerations of the amount of remuneration are critical in judging an intermediary's authenticity.[65]

---

62. Caroline Young, "Woman priest quits in dispute with bishop over talking spirit," *Seattle Post-Intelligencer,* July 28, 1986.
63. See nn. 22 and 29.
64. See Klimo, *Channeling,* 297.
65. On the matter of fees for services, see pp. 128, 132.

We might also scrutinize the trance activity of channelers. If a channeler were known to rehearse the entity's actions and speech while not in trance, or if one channeler were suspected of consciously or unconsciously imitating the behavior of another, would a charge of fraud be warranted? Examples are available of both. J. Z. Knight ("Ramtha") is given to posturing and pontifical actions during trance.[66] Steven Bakker, a former advance man for Knight, told an interviewer for ABC television's *20/20* "how devastated he became when during a desert hike he observed Mrs. Knight smoking and practicing the Ram's gestures, slipping in and out of her Ramtha personality without bothering to have trances."[67] Penny Torres, who channels "Mafu" and has been seen on NBC's *Today* show, is accused by her critics "of consciously or unconsciously trying to emulate . . . [Knight/"Ramtha"] . . . 'Mafu's' channeling is peppered with the same repeated phrases—'indeed,' 'so be it,' 'that which is termed'—and the same stylized ways of talking to and touching those who come to her group sessions, as those displayed by 'Ramtha.' "[68] However, such a charge against all channelers would be unfair.

If we turn to the messages of the channeled entities, several things are fairly obvious. First, the basic concern of many of the entities seems to be with the development of human potential. We have already noticed that Pursel ("Lazaris") wants us to become all that we are, and indeed the theme "we are all gods" (or like gods) seems to run through this material.[69] This theme is in stark contrast with Ramsay's modern prophets, who display(ed) a passion for social justice.

Second, some of the assumptions underlying the messages have close affinities with the religious traditions of the East, particularly Hinduism and Buddhism: reincarnation, the underlying oneness of all things, and that ultimate reality is to be discovered not outside but within ourselves.[70] That ideas have their origin or most systematic

66. See Klimo, *Channeling*, 43.
67. M. Gardner, "Isness Is Her Business," *New York Review*, April 19, 1987, 19.
68. Klimo, *Channeling*, 65.
69. See Barbara Marx Hubbard's interviews with Terry Cole-Wittaker and Ken Carey (Price, *Complete Guide to Channeling*) and Klimo, *Channeling*, 43. One thinks of the scene in *Out on a Limb* where Shirley and David stand on the beach and chant, "I am God."
70. For a systematic statement of the second of these, see Klimo's "concluding metaphor"; *Channeling*, 293–99. As an example of the last, consider Shirley MacLaine's observation that channeled entities all over the world had advised people to "look into yourselves, explore yourselves, *you* are the Universe"; *Out on a Limb*, 166; see also 87, 187, 208.

expression in religious traditions outside the Judeo-Christian orbit implies nothing about their validity. Insofar as such underlying assumptions are at odds with a person's understanding of the nature of physical reality and of human life, however, they become a focal point of the evaluation, an occasion for reflection and for acceptance or rejection.

Third, what the entities say or do can be measured against what we know about the world. For example, channelers frequently talk of extraterrestrial beings and of the vanished civilizations of Lemuria (a now-sunken continent) and Atlantis,[71] and we hear of "Akashic Records," "vibrations," and "astral projection." Notions of causality are strange. The television version of *Out on a Limb*, for instance, contains a scene set in an occult bookshop in Hong Kong. As MacLaine stands browsing, a book that will prove important for her spiritual development literally hops off the shelf and into her hands. She is startled, but the proprietor is unperplexed. "Those kinds of things," she says, "happen to me quite often." The accuracy of the historical information presented can be judged, for example, the statement in *Out on a Limb* that in 553 the Council of Nicaea "voted to strike the teaching of reincarnation from the Bible."[72] We recognize that all religious belief requires the acceptance of assertions that cannot, strictly speaking, be proven. However, individual assertions that seem farfetched (Atlantis; jumping books) and facts that are patently wrong certainly affect our judgment about the credibility of the system as a whole.

We can recognize quite easily in an account like MacLaine's the motivation for openness to belief in channeled entities. As she tells the story, she was moved by a certain configuration of events in her life to ask the question "What's it all about?"[73] and she was comforted by the growing conviction that there are "no accidents in life," that the events of our lives do constitute an intelligible "pattern," that we do things because we are "compelled" to or "supposed" to, in short, that "there is

71. See Klimo, *Channeling*, 161–62.
72. MacLaine, *Out on a Limb*, 181. There was no council at Nicaea in 553; the television adaptation corrects this error. Some further observations: Kevin Ryerson's "Tom," the Elizabethan Irish pickpocket, speaks of "karma," something difficult, if not impossible, to imagine; perhaps the reader is meant to understand that he acquired this vocabulary after his death as "Tom" and his acquisition of some higher knowledge (191). One also wonders about MacLaine's failure to entertain seriously the possibility that the "grapevine" was the source of the information about her life that the channeled entities seemed to have somehow miraculously acquired.
73. Ibid., 86.

a higher purpose going on."[74] In MacLaine's case and many others, this pattern and purpose is explained by channeled entities, who see the exigencies of our present lives as the result of characteristics and relationships we had during previous incarnations, sometimes in fantastic times and places.

Besides the need to detect pattern and meaning in our lives, we have the desire to actualize our own highest potential as individuals. This theme is important in *Out on a Limb* and in MacLaine's television interviews. It is expressed as well by Barbara Marx Hubbard at the conclusion of her interviews with channelers. Getting in touch with higher wisdom is becoming popular, she says, and rightly so, because our purpose ought to be to become the highest persons we can.[75] Whatever our final appraisal of the claims made by channelers may be, sympathizing with these motivations is relatively easy.

That differences of opinion exist about the validity of individual intermediaries is not surprising. Fundamental to the ambiguity inherent in judging prophetic claims is the fact that persons and communities differ in their assessments of a given individual's activity. Yet none of the intermediaries discussed in this book—or hundreds of others like them—could have been accepted if they had not been perceived as filling a real need, if the activity of the intermediary had not borne "good fruit," for anyone. The contemporary figures discussed in this chapter speak to different needs: the need for social justice (Ramsay), the need to resolve the everyday crises of the community and of individuals (Hall), the need to understand the "apparent" moral collapse of modern society (Wilkerson), the needs to explain the accidents of one's life and to develop one's own potential (channelers). Note that the items on this list are not mutually exclusive.

These instances do not exhaust the examples of contemporary prophecy, even if we limit ourselves to North America, but they should adequately demonstrate that for some, at least, prophecy still lives. Furthermore, our discussion should have made apparent both the necessity for and the difficulty of making reasoned judgments about such claims.

74. Ibid., 20, 201; 117; 17, 147; 95.
75. Price, *Complete Guide to Channeling*.

JUDGING THE FRUITS

In the first six chapters of this book, I have demonstrated some important things about prophecy: (1) Prophetic intermediation is a widespread, cross-cultural phenomenon. We have seen that *prophet* is an ambiguous term. Various roles, including diviner, fit within the larger category *intermediary*. (2) Prophecy is a social phenomenon. Whatever authority they may get from on high, prophets are dependent upon audiences for their effective authorization. (3) We have every reason to believe that, for some persons, prophecy continues to exist. Some audiences remain willing to recognize intermediaries as authoritative.

In this chapter, the focus narrowed to the hard question: How do we test prophetic claims in the present North American cultural context? In shifting focus, however, we have not forgotten the results of the cross-cultural analysis: Intermediation *is* a social process that is not confined to a single culture or religion. Acceptance by a group *is* the basis of the authority of intermediaries, for we have direct access to the prophets' behavior but not to the putative revelations that in their eyes are its ground. In practice, this is the way William Ramsay (who does not concern himself with isolating specific revelatory experiences) conducts his search for contemporary Christian prophets.

Our model demonstrates the continued existence of prophecy but guarantees its validity in only a generic sense: *it exists as a socially valid phenomenon in those specific instances in which a group acknowledges it.* A group accepts a given individual as an intermediary. This acceptance is based on the group's evaluation of the intermediary's behavior.

Given their own assumptions about God and his relationship to humans, religious persons can hardly take claims about the occurrence of prophecy lightly, although they may ultimately reject all or most of them. Writing at the end of the 1960s in a climate of social upheaval and change in America, a climate in which many persons both religious and secular were being referred to as prophets, W. Sibley Towner made this point quite clearly. What is at stake for Jews and Christians, he said, is to determine "the locus of authoritative moral and religious utterance in our time." Therefore, testing such claims is "part of our serious effort to discover who is speaking to us with authority, whose words faithfully represent God's words in our time, who is prophetically laying valid claims upon our own words and deeds."[76] Towner ultimately, and rightly, I think, focuses on the content of the prophetic message as the key to judging the authenticity of prophetic claims within the Judeo-Christian context. In this tradition, the most significant behavior of prophets is that they talk.

According to Towner, the challenge is to discover who in our time speaks God's words to us "with authority," but what are the criteria by which we may judge among claims? We are able to state general principles that might be employed: to be judged authoritative, the message must be sufficiently grounded in the audience's cultural and religious traditions and relevant to its current sociopolitical situation. In a Judeo-Christian context we frequently appeal to Scripture, but this appeal does not eliminate ambiguity. Ramsay and Wilkerson come to Scripture with quite different concerns, and imagining them agreeing on a list of contemporary candidates for the title *prophet* is difficult. A further complication arises from the need not to limit God's freedom of speech. Messages may change with time, so exact conformity with old content is no guarantee of present validity.

In fact, all such criteria are inherently ambiguous. The examples cited earlier in this chapter display what everyone already knows: *we have no one definitive interpretation of the tradition against which all claims can be easily and objectively measured.* Furthermore, a fact of life in the late-twentieth century is that even if we limit ourselves to people in the Judeo-Christian tradition, no common understanding of the nature and intentions of God can be assumed. This fact guarantees we will find no unanimity of judgment about individual claimants. Evaluations will be subjective with respect to the religious inclinations of both individuals and subgroups of the larger community.

I have now given several examples of possible contemporary manifestations of prophecy and have made some suggestions about strategies for evaluating such claims. Yet in the last analysis, we have no easy way to resolve the problems inherent in judging the fruits of prophetic activity. Those who stand within the Judeo-Christian religious tradition, could conveniently say that prophecy ended with the exile of Judah in the sixth century B.C.E., but I have argued against this

76. W. S. Towner, "On Calling People 'Prophets' in 1970," *Int* 24 (1970):496, 509.

conclusion. Whatever the reader thinks of that argument, the examples cited earlier in this chapter certainly indicate that many assume its continued existence. One lesson of our cross-cultural investigation is surely that we cannot give privileged status to any single instance of intermediation. Jews and Christians have no proprietary claim on prophecy. We have to confront individual claims and make judgments.

My intention in this chapter was not to offer either a comprehensive catalogue of modern prophets or a definitive critique of any of them. Rather, it was to suggest that today, no less than in biblical times, religious people must give attention and careful, critical thought to such claims. Like those earlier times, individuals and the groups to which they belong finally bear the responsibility for identifying the truth and authorizing prophets.

Prophets can exist only in a dynamic interaction with an audience. The audience has to judge whether the visible behavior—the fruits—of a particular actor merits the acknowledgment (or suggests the denial) that this is an occurrence of genuine intermediation. In their efforts to make such judgments, members of an audience ought to avoid easy answers and take responsibility for their decisions. They will not be without resources for this task (broadly speaking, their religious tradition), but in the end their decisions will rest on nothing more or less firm than critical intelligence and commitment. Their judgments will not be universally shared. No guarantees can be made that such prophets and prophecies as they accept will in the long run prove fruitful to the ongoing life of the communities and individuals who believe. There are, finally, no risk-free communications about how we should live, even from God.

Subject Index

185

Modern Authors Index

189

Made in the USA
Monee, IL
03 September 2020